STUDY AND EXA... ....

AP® ART HISTORY

The Official Genius Exam Coaches™ Edition

- Designed for crammers
- Strategic and concise study guide
- Genius Exam Coaches™ Check-ups

DR. VINCE MIKAEL POWERS

CONTENTS

CHAPTER 5: LATER EUROPE AND THE AMERICAS 155

GENIUS EXAM COACHES™ (GEC™) INTRODUCTION

Welcome to the *Genius Exam Coaches*™ (GEC™) Study Guide program! The approach is based on the learning program designed by Dr. Artyom Zinchenko (Ph.D. in Cognitive and Neuroscience) and Dr. Wallace Panlilio II (Ph.D. in Educational Psychology). Their program is based on thousands of hours of combined research on optimal learning and helps you achieve the best possible test results. What sets GEC apart from other test preparation programs is that it is designed for crammers or people who have very limited time to review for an exam. The book's structure and design incorporate the most recent and most promising techniques from the area of educational experimental psychology and neuroscience, which should speed up and solidify learning experience. So how can you get the most out of the GEC program?

First, we encourage you to answer the GEC Learning Questionnaire found on the next page—our questionnaire highlights various learning factors, such as motivation, attitude, and strategies. Answering the questionnaire will help you prepare for your test more holistically.

You will be able to establish a solid foundation as you prepare for your exam.

Second, as you go over the books, you will find that there will be questions at the top section of each page. The questions will prompt you to recall or reflect on the subject matter. The goal is to reinforce your knowledge and develop critical thinking skills. Instead of rereading, you must try to remember and reflect on what you have learned first, even if you have to struggle at first. The effort is an essential part of the learning process. You interrupt the learning process if you immediately reread whenever you struggle to remember. Do your best to delay finding the answer. Doing so will be well worth it.

Third, you will also find questions asking you to reflect on your learning approach, including your motivation, attitude, and strategies. Being mindful of one's learning process is essential to ensuring that how you learn continues to be optimal.

Do not be surprised when the questions are about the previous chapters' concepts. This approach is intentional because this will dramatically reinforce a deeper knowledge about the topic and make you familiar with uncertainties when you encounter complex and confusing questions in the exam.

Finally, there will be a checklist at the end of each chapter. We encourage you to take the time to mentally recall each item, then elaborate on what you have learned by writing or talking about your insights or even discussing what you have learned with your peers. The more you write or talk about it, the more connections your brain cells can establish about such a topic. As a result, you will have a stronger foundation for better results in your exam.

GENIUS EXAM COACHES™ (GEC™) QUESTIONNAIRE

1. Why are you studying for this exam?
2. How will passing this exam impact your life?
3. How can you motivate yourself to study even if you do not feel like studying?
4. How can you reduce, if not eliminate, the different distractions like phones, emails, social media, internet, among others?
5. What are your daily, weekly, or monthly learning objectives?
6. How can you manage your time to help you achieve your objectives?
7. How can you organize your study environment to help you achieve your objectives?
8. How often can you mentally recall and elaborate on what you have learned?
9. How often can you write test items for you to answer as part of your mock test simulation?

10. Can you take a step back before, during, and after your study period to assess how you are learning in order to ensure that you are learning effectively?

> Are you ready to make the necessary sacrifice to achieve your exam preparation objectives?

CHAPTER 1

ABOUT THE TEST

1.1. Introduction to the AP® Exam in Art History

Unlike other Advanced Placement® (AP) art programs, where you are instructed to create art, AP® Art History teaches you about the various art forms that have been created around the world since the prehistoric era. The material covered in AP® Art History is designed to provide a broad understanding of the different art styles applied throughout human existence, going back roughly 30,000 years. A set list of 250 artworks have been selected by The Advanced Placement College Board, which will enable you to critically evaluate the diversity and connection between different art forms, their creation, and how each fit into a wider artistic style.

The AP® Art History program is not designed to encourage the memorization of facts about art pieces, artists, or cultures. Rather, the course material aims to allow students to develop their understanding of art-making and artistic developments over time. The essential components of the course framework include art historical thinking skills, and the content is organized into 10 units each focusing on a specific timeline and location. This provides a conceptual understanding of what colleges and universities commonly expect students to master in order to receive course credit and advanced placement qualifications.

The 10 units include:

1. Global Prehistory, which took place from 30,000 years ago– 500 BCE
2. Ancient Mediterranean, spanning from 3500 BCE to 300 CE
3. Early Europe and Colonial Americas, which took place from 200–17500 CE
4. Later Europe and the Americas, which took place from 1750–1980 CE
5. Indigenous Americas, characterized by art from 1000 BCE until 1980 CE.
6. Africa, spanning from 1100–1980 CE.
7. West and Central Asia, characterized by art from 500 BCE to 1980 CE.
8. South, East, and Southeast Asia, which existed from 300 BCE until 1980 CE

9. The Pacific, which took place from 700–1980 CE.
10. Global Contemporary, including works from 1980 CE to present-day art.

The foundation of the course consists of five main elements that enable students to develop a deeper contextual understanding of the influences on art. These elements include: the cultural practices and belief systems that often affect art; interactions between cultures' effects on artistic patterns; the theory and interpretation of art across continents and time; the access to and use of materials and techniques; and, the viewer's effect on art-making.

1.2. Test Scoring

The formal AP® Art History exam is divided into two sections comprising 80 multiple-choice questions, two long essays, and four short essays. When completing your exam, you will have one hour to complete the first section. This section presents you with color images of selected artworks, asking you to analyze any of their visual and contextual properties. It also asks you to classify artworks according to historic patterns, compare different pieces, credit additional artworks not presented in the questions, and provide historical interpretations. These multiple-choice questions can be asked in sets of two to three related or individual questions. The weighting of each unit in the multiple-choice section is as follows:

- Unit 1: 4%
- Unit 2: 15%
- Unit 3: 21%
- Unit 4: 21%
- Unit 5: 6%
- Unit 6: 6%
- Unit 7: 4%
- Unit 8: 8%
- Unit 9: 4%
- Unit 10: 11%

The second section needs to be completed in two hours, during which you will get six essay questions. (Questions three to six are each worth five points.)

- Question one—with a total of eight points—asks you to compare a designated work of art with another of your choice, highlighting the differences and similarities between them with supporting evidence in a long essay format.
- Question two—answered in a long essay format of six points—requires you to select and identify an art piece and use evidence to explain various claims about its characteristics and historical context.
- Question three is a short essay format question that asks you to describe the features of a work of art beyond the prompts provided through images and to link it with an art style or period.

- Question four requires you to briefly describe the contextual influences of a designated art piece in addition to explaining how context can affect the meaning of a work of art.
- With a focus on an artist, style, or culture, question five asks you to use evidence to attribute an artwork beyond the provided images.
- Lastly, question six requires an analysis of the relationship between a specified work of art and a relative art style or practice.

The multiple-choice section of your test will be scored by a machine, whereas your essay questions and course performance assessments will be marked by college faculty and AP® teachers.

An annual AP® Reading is held where highly trained and supervised staff score thousands of tests. Free-response and performance scores are combined with those of section one—which had been marked online—and the total is converted into a scale ranging from one to five. This scale is interpreted as follows:

- 5: Extremely well qualified with a college grade equivalent of A.
- 4: Well qualified with a college grade equivalent of A-, B+, or B.
- 3: Qualified with a college grade equivalent of B-, C+, or C.
- 2: Possibly qualified.
- 1: No recommendation.

Considering the above, most universities and private colleges award advanced placement to students with a score of three, four, or five. Keep in mind that all tertiary institutions have their own credit and AP® policies.

1.3. What's New About the Redesigned Exam

The program had been redesigned to more accurately prepare students for college-level classes, with changes aimed to simplify the understanding of the global scope of art themes throughout history.

This was accomplished by refining the number of artworks from over 500 to only 250. This enables students to dive deeper into each piece of art. Whereas the former curriculum placed a focus on becoming an expert on each work of art, the redesigned course teaches students to develop analytic and contextualizing skills to better understand art styles and periods.

The new exam tests a student's general knowledge of artistic themes, traditions, and art skills. The format of the test was also altered and where you used to get 115 multiple-choice questions, you will now only answer 80. The six, 10-minute short answer questions—accompanied by the two, 30-minute long essay questions in section 2—were replaced by four, 15-minute short essay questions to test analytic and critical thinking skills instead of factual knowledge.

Throughout this AP® course, students will develop a series of thinking skills specific to art history that will aid in taking the exam. These skills include: visual analysis, contextual analysis, comparison of art, artistic traditions, visual analysis of unknown works, attribution of unknown works, historical interpretations, and argumentation.

These skills will be explored as follows:

1. Visual analysis—Identify a work of art by providing the title, artist, date of creation, and culture of origin. Describe the visual elements like the style, form, technique, content, materials, and the decision-making in the creation of the piece.
2. Contextual analysis—Describe the function, siting, physical context, subject matter, and reception of the piece. Explain how the intended purpose shaped the meaning and creation of the artwork. Explain how contextual elements as mentioned influence works of art. Lastly, explain how decision-making affects the work's reception.
3. Comparison of art—Use relevant points of comparison to describe the similarities and differences between multiple works of art and how they weigh up in meaning.
4. Artistic traditions—Explain the significance, meaning, how, and why specific art pieces present continuity or change within an art style or tradition. Explain the influences on art within and across cultures.
5. Visual analysis of unknown works—Analyze a work of art beyond what is provided and explain the influences of decision-making on form, style, materials, technique, and content.

6. Attribution of unknown works—Attribute an art piece to a specific artist, style, era, or culture, and justify the attribution through similarities.

7. Historical interpretations—Describe historically relevant interpretations, receptions, or meanings of artworks. Explain how these interpretations are derived from visual and contextual analysis.

8. Argumentation—Communicate defensible claims, use relevant evidence in support of these claims, and explain the justification of claims on different works of art. Confirm or modify a claim on artwork to form a complex argument that might explain the expression of an issue, insightful connections, how, or why a claim is ineffective, or considering alternative evidence.

The main skill of focus within each unit will be highlighted at the start of each chapter.

1.4. Test-Taking Strategies and Tips

Looking at some data from the AP® scores for 2021, the exam difficulty can be determined as follows: an average of 12% of students scored a 5 on the exam, 19.6% scored 4, 23.8% scored 3, 30.1% scored 2, and 14.6% scored 1 (Sarikas, 2022). Given the passing rate of the exam was 55%—which is below average—and there are only 12 AP exams out of 44 with a lower passing rate than AP® Art History, it is considered more difficult than the average AP® course.

Therefore, it is important to take note of these test-taking tips:

- Complete the easy questions first. There is no set rule for answering the questions in a specific order, so when you see a question that seems time-consuming, leave it for when the majority of questions are done instead of wasting time while pondering the answer.
- It is best to answer every question. Do not leave answers blank. When you are unsure of the correct answer, particularly in the multiple-choice section, use the process of elimination to find the best possible answer and increase your chances of choosing the correct one. Partial points are better than zero.
- Aside from starting to study long before the exam, it is best to do some practice tests and plan out your essay questions. This way, you will be able to jot down your thesis and outline before writing the final, which will result in a better-organized and more coherent essay.
- While it seems trivial, remember to drink a lot of water and bring a snack to eat during the break to help you stay energized.
- Additionally, motivate yourself through positive self-talk. It is important to keep calm when you hit a mental block during the exam and tell yourself that you are doing great.

Key Concepts

- The **aim** of the AP® Art History program is not the memorization of facts about art pieces, artists, or cultures but allowing students to develop their understanding of art-making and artistic developments.

- The content of the course framework is organized into **10 units**: *Global Prehistory; Ancient Mediterranean; Early Europe and Colonial Americas; Later Europe and the Americas; Indigenous Americas; Africa; West and Central Asia; South, East, and Southeast Asia; The Pacific; and Global Contemporary.*

- The **structure** of the modified AP® Art History exam is as follows: it is divided into two sections with 80 multiple-choice questions, two long essays, and four short essays.

- These are the following **thinking skills** that will be helpful for students as they take the exam: *visual analysis, contextual analysis, comparison of art, artistic traditions, visual analysis of unknown works, attribution of unknown works, historical interpretations, and argumentation.*

- Here are some **test-taking tips** to take note of: *complete easy questions first; answer every question; work on some practice tests before the exam and plan out your essay questions; bring water and snacks for the break; and motivate yourself through positive self-talk.*

CHAPTER 2

GLOBAL PREHISTORY

Learning objectives:

- Analyze the relationships between works of art based on similarities and differences.
- Analyze how contextual variables lead to different interpretations of artworks.

2.1. Prehistoric

Recent studies have concluded that art has been created since the Neanderthals decided to produce non-representational ornamentation found all across Africa.

The Prehistoric Era is defined as the period before written records existed. The first pieces of representational art had been created since 30,000 BCE, yet the earliest writing was found in ancient Mesopotamia, near 3,500 BCE. The timeline consists of major shifts in climate and environments resulting in the Stone, Bronze, and Iron Ages.

2.2. Paleolithic

The First Age—also known as the Old Stone Age—between 30,000–10,000 BCE is known as the Paleolithic Era. This was the earliest presentation of the extensive use of tools made from stone.

Apollo 11 Cave Stones

During his research from 1969 to 1972, the German archeologist W.E. Wendt came across seven painted brown-gray quartzite stone slabs in the Middle Stone Age—approximately

25,500–25,300 BCE—deposited in a cave. Wendt named this cave after the rocket used for the successful American moon landing, Apollo 11. The location was in the Huns Mountains in the Namibian area, known by the locals as Goachanas. The seven slabs of Apollo 11 became known as the oldest scientifically-dated art in the world. The slabs presented animal figures that had been painted with charcoal, ochre, and white pigment. The animals are not identifiable as exact species, but some appear to be cats, cattle, giraffes, zebras, and/or ostriches.

A significant find was that of two pieces that appeared to have originally been one completed slab that broke into two. These slabs depict a somewhat unidentifiable feline that seems to have the hind legs of a human and two slightly-curved horns like an antelope that can be faintly seen on its head. Furthermore, the therianthrope's underbelly presents the sexual organs of a bovid, suggestive of a complex system of shamanistic ritual.

Although Apollo 11 is the oldest dated work of representational art in human history, it has been proven by genetic and fossil evidence that *Homo sapiens*—modern humans—developed and migrated around and beyond Africa from approximately 80,000 BCE. The discovery of additional art pieces like patterned stones and perforated shells adds to our ideas regarding early creative expression as a means of communication before the invention of writing.

While it remains an assumption that art originated in the southern part of Africa, archeologists have discovered evidence of roughly

100,000 years of ongoing human settlement within African caves alongside *art mobilier*—moveable art—which highlights that much like mobile art, rock art is not unique to Africa, and has, in fact, been found all across the Americas, Asia, Australia, and Europe.

Great Hall of The Bulls

Nearly 350 caves exist in the regions south of France and north of Spain, all similarly representing the coexistence of Neanderthals and *Homo sapiens* since 30,000 BCE. Among these is the cave of Lascaux near Dordogne, France, where humans observed the migratory patterns of wildlife.

In 1940, explorers found roughly 1,500 drawings and paintings of a series of animals in calcite-walled rooms with nonporous rock roofs beyond the smaller crawl spaces of the cave entrance. This presented the perfect conditions for a canvas to prehistoric artists, as they used charcoal and ochre to portray the encyclopedia of the area's wildlife during the Middle Stone Age—including bear, bison, deer, elk, horses, lions, and rhinoceros. Accompanying the animal figures are abstract drawings of dot and line configurations.

What became known as the Great Hall of The Bulls is a room big enough to hold 50 people, with art on the walls that incorporated "twisted perspectives" animals, meaning their bodies were drawn as side profiles, but their horns were presented from a frontal perspective. Some illustrations were line art defining the animal's contour, while others showed solid animal figures in blended colors that had been blown onto the walls with mouths. Additionally, softer calcite areas were engraved with animal figures, and some grooves were filled with color pigment. This implies that each drawing was carefully plotted out before it was lined and filled with color. The overlapping drawings in some areas of the cave highlight the serious, or perhaps ritual, significance of the process of repetitive drawing. Although the true function of the artworks is unclear, interpreters have theorized that it was created for either storytelling purposes or as part of hunting rituals; for example, when a priest named Henri Breuil used ethnography to support his theory of "hunting magic." (This is the theory that the people of the ancient civilizations who inhabited those caves believed that creating visual representations of their prey would result in a successful hunt.)

Art historians estimate that these paintings, covering a width of 11 feet and 6 inches, are between 16,000 and 14,000 years old.

Archeologists also discovered stone tools, fossilized pollen, and holes in the Lascaux caves that suggested the support of tree-limb scaffolding that elevated the artists toward the upper surfaces of the rooms.

The cave of Lascaux is now closed to the public for preservation purposes and is a designated UNESCO world heritage site.

2.3. Mesolithic

The Mesolithic Era is defined as the brief period between the Paleolithic Era, with its chipped stone tools, and the Neolithic Era, with its polished stone tools.

While very few firm dates exist around prehistoric art, researchers have tried to provide detailed descriptions of all artworks and place them into chronological order according to their content and style.

Camelid Sacrum (Canine)

In 1870, a sculpture of a canine was accidentally discovered by an engineer approximately 40 feet deep in a drainage site in Tequixquiac, Mexico. Art historians argue that the piece is indicative of being created around 14,000–7,000 BCE. The dog-like animal's eyes and nostrils were carved into the now-fossilized piece of the sacrum—a large triangular bone at the base of the spine—of an extinct camelid (a member of the Camelidae family, such as an alpaca, camel, or llama).

Although the exact date of the sculpture's creation is indeterminable because no stratigraphic analysis was done before its removal from the layers of soil, it had been in the possession of the Mexican botanist and geologist, Mariano de la Bárcena, in 1882. As Bárcena wrote the first scholarly article on the Camelid Sacrum, he included (Anda, 1965):

What types of animals are thought to be
depicted on the Apollo 11 Cave Stones?

[T]he fossil bone contains cuts or carvings that unquestionably were made by the hand of man…the cuts seem to have been made with a sharp instrument and some polish on the edges of the cuts may still be seen…the articular extremity of the last vertebra was utilized perfectly to represent the nose and mouth of the animal. (p. 264)

While the true meaning behind the sculpture will never be known, historians have theorized that since the sacrum was considered a sacred bone in Mesoamerican cultures—some indigenous languages associated words like 'divine' and 'resurrection' with it—the sculptor was likely inspired by the importance attached to the bone.

2.4. Neolithic

Following what was known as the "Neolithic Revolution," when individuals progressed from hunting and gathering to farming and animal domesticating, the Neolithic Era made up the timeline from 9,000–2,000 BCE, otherwise known as the New Stone Age. The change in the way people lived during this time also influenced the artistic styles of the advanced era. People did not have to move around constantly and carry their belongings with them anymore. The creation and use of pottery for storage became widespread, architecture and interior decoration developed, and alcohol was first produced as people began to settle in one place.

Running Horned Woman

Lieutenant Brenans of the Camel Corps French Foreign Legion wrote multiple detailed descriptions, with sketches, of his rock art findings between 1933 and 1940. Among these was a series of sites hidden within the canyons of the Tassili n'Ajjer, located in the Algerian section of the Sahara Desert near the border connecting Niger and Libya, Northern Africa.

Brenans shared his findings with the Bardo Museum in Algiers and it was confirmed to be one of the richest rock art concentrations in history. French archeologist Henri Lhote frequently visited the site, and in 1958 he published the best-seller *A la Découverte des Fresques du Tassili,* which highlighted the importance of the work, and is one of the most popular texts in archeological studies today.

During one of his observations, Lhote inspected a curious figure with a sponge and a can of water in hand. Many researchers at that time moistened art for reproduction, which altered the physical, chemical, and biological balance on the rock surfaces, ultimately damaging them. The figure—dubbed the "Horned Goddess" by Lhote's team—was located in the highest of all the "rock cities" of the Tassili, Aouanrhet massif. The work of art is described as a silhouette of a woman with horizontal horns next to her head, running with one leg touching the ground and slightly flexed while another is lifted to the back. Around her head is a heavily dotted area that represents "a cloud of grain falling from a wheat field" (Lhote & Brodrick, 1959). The art piece is most commonly known today as *Running Horned Woman*.

Given that the figure was discovered in such a secluded area, it is assumed that she was a goddess of an agricultural religion—much like Isis, the Egyptian goddess of agriculture. Lhote claimed that the series of artworks around this massif showed Egyptian influence. However, his claims were later disputed when it became public knowledge that Lhote's French team members copied Egyptian-like figures and passed them off as authentic Tasilli art reproductions.

Bushel with Ibex Motifs

Found near a fertile river valley in ancient Susa—modern-day Iran—dating back to 6,000–4,000 BCE, the *Bushel with Ibex Motifs* include a series of terracotta clay vessels with painted animal and geometric patterns buried in prehistoric cemeteries.

The works of art were excavated by Jacques de Morgan between 1906–1908 and were later taken to be held in the Musée du Louvre, Paris.

While some historians theorize that these pots could have been made on a slow-turning wheel, it is evident that they were handmade and hand-painted.

It remains unclear why the dead were buried with these decorative pots, but each piece was created with a balance between circular forms and forms that are hard-edged and linear. Each piece also has stylized animal figures that are most likely symbolic in nature, much like works from the later era of ancient Mesopotamia.

Anthropomorphic Stelae

A three-foot-tall human-like stele—an inscribed vertical stone marker or monument—dating back to 4,000–3,000 BCE was located near Ha'il in northwest Saudi Arabia along with two other similar figures. Despite being discovered more than 1,429 miles apart, these stelae share stylistic characteristics.

The stone marker was carved on both sides, with the front presenting an abstract anthropomorphic representation with a trapezoidal head and a face on squared shoulders, a chest that shows a necklace and awl attached to two cords crossing its body diagonally, and a double-bladed dagger hanging from a belt around its waist.

How did archeologists deduce that scaffolding might have been used by the prehistoric artists in the Lascaux caves?

During the Neolithic period, Saudi Arabia was more like a savannah than a desert. People were able to live in fertile and lush areas while hunting ostriches—that have not been able to survive there for thousands of years—and domesticating goats, sheep, and cattle. Although people settled in areas of this region for years, objects and ideas traveled. A rock wall at Tabuk, Jordan, depicted images of figures carrying the same awl and double-bladed dagger seen in the stele of Ha'il. In Riqseh, Southern Jordan, a broken anthropomorphic stele again displayed the same awl and dagger, and examples from Rawk, Yemen, showed a similarly abstract style and exogenous materials, suggesting that cultural exchanges were made during the Neolithic Era. However, it is important to consider that the function of the stelae differed across regions, whether it be as a grave marker, dedication, commemoration, or distinction.

Jade Cong

The Liangzhu people that lived in the region now called Shanghai became expert rice field growers and allowed themselves to develop these crops in sophisticated ways. This culture became popular for using jade—translated from the Chinese "yu," meaning transparent or semitransparent stone—to create objects such as square hollow tubes known as cong. The cong was decorated with lines and circular shapes to form faces, suggesting that there was some meaning allocated to each piece when the Liangzhu people created it.

Given that jadeite—or nephrite—is a tough material that cannot be cut into, it almost seems impossible that these artists used rubbing sand and water to engrave the stone with precise shapes, including extremely thin lines parallel to each other. The pieces were created with careful effort, and show much similarity in form, uniformity, and intentionality. Jade work is one of the world's oldest artistic traditions and is still one of great importance. As the Chinese proverb says, "Gold is valuable, but jade is invaluable" (Shan, 2018).

The cong pieces were found in graves and some were short in shape while others appeared stacked on top of each other. Some art historians have theorized that the rectilinear vertical structures represent earth, whereas the rounded inner symbolizes heaven and sky.

Stonehenge

One of the most popular artworks associated with the Neolithic period is Stonehenge, located on Salisbury Plain in Wiltshire, England. The monument receives roughly a million visitors a year.

Although the exact timeline of the construction of Stonehenge remains unclear among archeologists, it has been suggested that it existed in three phases that lasted for about 1,000 years. It is believed that the first phase of construction started around 3,000 BCE with the use of wooden beams and blue stone erected in pits roughly three feet in diameter. The second phase occurred 100–200 years later, during which time the site was mostly used for burials.

The last phase took place some 400–500 years thereafter when the former blue stones and wooden beams were replaced with much harder sarsen and lintel stones. The vertical stones are about 13 feet in height, 7 feet wide, and weighed around 25 tons each. When the weight of the horizontal lintel stones is considered, each trilithon—two upright stones with a lintel stone spanning their tops—equals more than 50 tons.

This monument, presenting extensive organization and labor, has led scholars of the 18th century to believe that Stonehenge shared a connection to the lunar and solar calendar. It was perceived that the midsummer solstice sunrise was precisely framed by one end of trilithons, whereas on the exact opposite end, the midwinter sunset aligns in the center of the stones. These two days were known as the turning point of the two major seasons. Therefore, many believe that Stonehenge was built as an ancient astronomical center or as a ritual temple for those who worshiped the sun.

Not far from Stonehenge is Woodhenge, which theoretically acted as the settlement for the living—as life was prehistorically symbolized by wood—and when people passed, they were buried at Stonehenge, as stone was commonly associated with the dead.

Ambum Stone

Around 1,500 BCE, the *Ambum Stone* was created in the highlands of an area we now call Papua New Guinea. However, it is unclear who carved the stone and what its original purpose might have been. Many art historians theorized that the carving had been part of a set of ancient stone mortar and pestles. The *Ambum Stone* has a smoothly carved head and neck of about eight inches that fits comfortably into someone's hand. The fat base could have been used to crush herbs and food.

The detailed sculpture resembles a series of 12 similar creations excavated from the mountains in New Guinea. Most other ancient pestle carvings commonly depict the heads of humans or birds, while mortars hold geometric images beside avian—bird—and anthropomorphic narratives. The *Ambum Stone* particularly resembles an anteater, or echidna, which was valued for its fat during the time before the presence of pigs.

It is one of the oldest sculptures made in Oceania and presents only a slightly shiny patina on its raised surfaces of smoothened greywacke stone, suggesting it was handled with care over the years. Greywacke stone is a hard-sedimentary stone that reveals its age through fracture lines, making it a marvel that ancient stone tools were used to carve such a symmetrical and visually pleasing design.

In the 1960s, it became public knowledge that *Ambum Stone* mortars and pestles were commonly used by the Enga people in the western highlands of Papua New Guinea. However, the Enga refer to these pieces as *simting bilong tumbuna*, which translates to "bones of the ancestors" (Egloff, 2008).

Tlatilco Female Figurine

In the small settlement of Tlatilco near central Mexico, archeologists found more than 340 burial sites, each containing small ceramic figurines known as Tlatilco—given the Nahuatl meaning "place of hidden things"—Female Figurines. These figurines date back to 1,500–900 BCE.

The Tlatilco figurines portrayed mostly females with detailed and elaborate hairstyles doing daily activities, which indicated the already remarkable and sophisticated artistic style of the time. The female figurines were shaped with wide hips and spherical upper thighs, whereas their waists were pinched. No particular emphasis was given to hands or feet. An interesting series within the *Tlatilco Female Figurines* involved some bicephalic (double-headed) faces attached to singular bodies. One, in particular, involves a female with a bifurcated face with two mouths and two noses, yet only three eyes on one head. The exact meaning behind this artistic tradition is unknown; however, many scholars argue that the artists were expressing a sense of duality.

While male figurines were very rare, artists created some male figures who were depicted with masks or costumes. However, the female figures showed detailed expression in their hairstyles and body paint, whereas the male figures were more simply presented as males in this culture were valued more for their religious roles rather than aesthetic aspects.

Tlatilco figurines were handmade without the use of molds. Artists shaped their bodies by pinching wet clay and adding linear motifs with a sharp object. The majority of the sculptures included traces of red, yellow, or black paint and were no bigger than six inches.

Lapita Pottery

The Lapita people are known for using red-slip—tiny clay particles dispersed in water and colored with iron oxide or other minerals—in their pottery artworks. These artworks were discovered thousands of miles across the regions of the Pacific during the 1950s.

Archeologists confirmed that the Lapita people traveled from Southeast Asia and arrived at the Bismarck Archipelago nearly 4,000 years ago. The Lapita people were different from the local cultures they encountered in modern-day New Guinea, as they had seafaring and navigation capabilities. They were also considered more sophisticated for creating and decorating pottery in particular ways.

The creations were done by hand. No evidence suggests they had access to a pottery wheel. Yet, perhaps they had the assistance of a paddle-and-anvil technique to thin the walls and baked the works over an open, low fire, a traditional technique some Lapita people still use today.

Their artworks mostly consisted of terracotta bowls, where some had flat bottoms and others were placed on pedestals. These vessels were either used for serving or storing food, but not cooking.

To produce the pottery pieces, the Lapita people mixed clay with
sand to reduce the elasticity of clay and to avoid cracking once
baked. Archeologists found that both materials are only available in
certain regions of the Pacific, whereas potsherds—fragments—were
discovered in areas that would have suggested the Lapita people had
the means to travel and transport either raw materials or the pots
themselves between significant stretches of ocean.

Although the potsherds were discovered miles apart, the designs
remained consistent, incorporating incised and stamped motifs presented in very structured and repeated patterns, clearly following
the rules of a defined design system. These linear and curved motifs
were applied by the use of a small dentate—tooth-like—stamp or a
sharp-edged tool. A paste of white coral lime was then applied to the
pattern, enhancing its appearance in contrast with the red slip.

Key Concepts

- According to recent studies, art has been created since the
  Neanderthals decided to produce *non-representational ornamentation* during the **Prehistoric Era**.
- The **first pieces of representational art** had been created
  since 30,000 BCE.
- The **earliest presentation of the extensive use of tools** made
  from stone was during the **Paleolithic Era**, also known as
  the Old Stone Age or the First Age. Two notable works of art
  during this era were the *Apollo 11 Cave Stones* and the *Great
  Hall of The Bulls*.

- The **Mesolithic Era** is the brief period between the Paleolithic Era and the Neolithic Era. The *Camelid Sacrum (Canine)* sculpture was one of the notable works of art during this era.
- During the **Neolithic Era**, also known as the New Stone Age, the creation and use of pottery for storage became widespread, and architecture and interior decoration developed. Examples of art during this era are the *Running Horned Woman*, the *Bushel with Ibex Motifs,* the *Anthropomorphic Stelae*, the *Jade Cong*, the *Stonehenge*, the *Ambum Stone*, the *Tlatilco Female Figurine*, and *Lapita Pottery*.

CHAPTER 3

ANCIENT MEDITERRANEAN

Learning objectives:

- Analyze the relationships between works of art based on similarities and differences.
- Describe how context influences the artistic decisions in creating an artwork.
- Analyze the form, function, content, and context to explain the intentions for creating the artwork.

3.1. Ancient Near East

The ancient Near East was where modern-day Iraq is. The Near—or Middle—East consists of Egypt, the Gulf states, Iran, Israel, Jordan, Lebanon, Syria, and Turkey. The "East" part of the naming is named so due to their proximity to Western countries.

The ancient Near East has often been referred to as the "cradle of civilization" because it was the first destination where complex urban centers grew.

More than 5,000 years ago, life began to emerge in ancient Uruk—present-day Warka, Iraq—which was also the birthplace of the writing form. The importance of this place was even further emphasized when a white temple was built on the monument Anu Ziggurat, a raised platform with four sloping sides made of mud bricks, between 3,500–3,300 BCE in honor of the sky god Anu, towering nearly 40 feet above the city.

The only access to the temple was by a steep stairway running up the north side of the ziggurat. The four slope sides were decorated with recessed stripes. The top surface was covered in bitumen (or asphalt) and brick to ensure a firm waterproof foundation for the temple.

Appropriately named, the White Temple was a rectangular construction of 17.5 x 22.3 meters (roughly 57 x 73 feet), whitewashed from the inside out. The temple has a tripartite plan with a rectangular central hall, rooms on the adjacent sides, and three entrances that can only be accessed by walking around the building from the ziggurat stairway. This allowed people to fully appreciate the bright façade, and once inside, the fire-stained altar sat at a 90-degree angle. This was a typical layout for ancient Near Eastern temples.

Furthermore, 19 gypsum tablets with cylinder seal impressions were uncovered on the temple floor. Archeologists also discovered

What is the focus of the "argumentation"
skill in examining a work of art?

fragments of a lion and leopard in the foundation deposits—objects and bones buried during a ritual—in the eastern corner.

Statues of Votive Figures

Roughly 5,000 years ago, a series of alabaster figures were produced and buried on the floor of a temple in Eshnunna, ancient northern Mesopotamia—present-day Tell Asmar. The series consisted of 12 mostly male figures. These figures ranged from standing nearly three feet tall to under one foot. Art historians believe that the figures were produced as part of the Sumerian culture in honor of the god Abu.

The most prominent figure was called the *Male Worshiper*. The figure shows a long-haired Sumerian man with clasped hands, broad shoulders, and wide eyes. Initially, he was meant to be looking attentively at a sculpture of a god. It was believed that the god was embodied in the sculpture, similar to the belief that the Sumerian was embodied in the alabaster figure. Taking a closer look, the figure's eyes and eyebrows are inlaid shells, and the pupils are black limestone. The lower part of the body is cylindrical, with incising at the bottom of the skirt, contradicting the flattened torso.

Around 3200 BCE, writing emerged from the cities in this area around the Tigris and Euphrates rivers. These cities were the first to incorporate administrative buildings, temples, and palaces.

Standard of Ur

The *Standard of Ur* was created in the city-state of Ur—present-day Iraq—around 2,600–2,400 BCE. Excavations during the 1920s and early 1930s found the standard, along with other ritually-buried artifacts, in some of the largest graves at the Royal Cemetery.

While a standard is usually a flag brought into battle, the original excavator, Leonard Woolley, said that this beautifully-detailed object was perhaps placed on a pole and carried into battle; yet, there is no supporting evidence of this hypothesis.

The art piece presents one side with a peaceful narrative divided into three registers, showing the involvement of long-distance trade by the materials that were used. It incorporates blue lapis lazuli from Afghanistan, red limestone from India, and shells from the gulf of the south of the Mesopotamian region now called Iraq. The work of art reminds the viewer how success in agriculture allowed these cities to prosper at the time. It also presents how people started to have different roles within a society because of the surplus of food and the fact that there was no need for everyone to farm.

The three registers present the cultural roles of those who had more influence at the top and the common laborers at the bottom.

On the other side, three registers show scenes of warfare. If you look closer, you can see that some detailed elements are included, such as the fallen enemies who have wounds and blood running from them,

Why was the ancient Near East often referred
to as the "cradle of civilization?"

captured soldiers being taken into slavery by the king, the particular engineering presented in the chariot wheels, and the way the bottom register shows the movement of the chariot from a walk into a gallop. This side is commonly known as "War," which is very contradictory to the side known as "Peace," showing a celebratory scene between the king's men.

The Code of Hammurabi

The *Law Code of Stele* of King Hammurabi is housed at the Louvre Museum in Paris. It dates back to 1792–1750 BCE Babylon.

This stele was carved from basalt—a hard volcanic rock—and shows a relief at the top and inscribed cuneiform on all of the sides. The script was written in the court language of the Babylonians— Akkadian. The cuneiform is divided into three sections: the first speaks about the scene between King Hammurabi and the sun god of justice, Shammash, at the top. The rest of the inscriptions present the divine laws that King Hammurabi received from Shamash, represented through the scepter and ring being handed over.

More than 300 laws are structured as an action and the consequence thereof, which are listed from judgments that had already taken place before the stele's creation.

While such law stelae are not uncommon, this piece was found only broken into three, which conservators were able to put together.

What is the significance of ancient Uruk in the history of writing?

Lamassu from The Citadel of Sargon II

The Ancient Near East was under the rule of the Assyrians from 1000–500 BCE. It was around 800 BCE that sculptures were created for the kings in different cities. Some of these statues include guardian figures placed at palace gates for protection. These were winged bulls with the heads of humans and were referred to as "Lamassu."

Although these figures stood between huge arches, each figure was a monolithic stone at a height of about 13 feet and 9 inches. This means the figures were constructed of one massive piece of stone with no cuts.

These sculptures also have exquisite detail and elaborate decoration, such as delicate rosettes on their crowns and circular patterns representing hair. This is interesting, given the fierce size of each figure. The Lamassu figures were designed to be viewed from the side and the front. Interestingly, they have five legs, which assists in showing it walking from the profile view but standing still when viewed from the front.

Audience Hall (Apanada) of Darius I and Xerxes

Present-day Southwest Iran used to be Ancient Persia, where an enormous multi-ethnic empire ruled from the Indus Valley to Northern Greece and from Egypt to Central Asia. The Persians were the first to acknowledge the different beliefs, languages, religions, and political structures of the indigenous people of each area they conquered.

How could one access the White Temple from the Anu Ziggurat?

Around 600 BCE, Darius the Great founded a city called Persepolis. Here, a great hypostyle hall with impressive columns was constructed for the king's receptions. The hall, known as "Apanada," incorporated 72 columns and 2 stairways that were decorated with hundreds of carvings of the 23 different ethnicities bringing gifts to the Persian king as the figures lead to the hall entrance.

King Darius I also built a reception hall in the ancient city of Susa, where 36 columns were erected during the period when Ancient Greece started to produce its most famous architecture, around 500 BCE. The wooden roofs were between 40 and 60 feet high. The capitals of the columns in the Achaemenid Empire were more extravagant in form and included animals that represented royal authority, such as lions, eagles, and bulls. One prominent capital design is of two bulls' heads, chests, and kneeling frontal legs connecting to a singular body cradling the beams of the palace in the notches of their backs. It was popular to have a great capital at the top of a slender column during that period, making artwork appear to tower above the viewer on a greater scale. The columns and capitals were carved from stone from the nearby mountains, whereas the rest of the palace was built from mud bricks. Taking a closer look at the bulls' column, it seems as if it was made of two different-colored stones. This is due to the archeological restoration, where they made a composite from different pieces of capitals.

The main aim of the capitals and other Persian art pieces was to reinforce Persian rule and the king's claim to power. The city of Persepolis was excavated by the German archeologists Ernst Herzfeld, Friedrich

What objects and discoveries were found on
the floor of the White Temple?

Krefter, and Erich Schmidt between 1931 and 1939 and was registered as a World Heritage Site in 1979.

3.2. Ancient Egypt

Other cultures were immensely influenced by Egypt, as Egyptian trade took place in regions as far as the Indus Valley. Because of this, evidence of Egyptian imagery, architecture, and concepts can be seen everywhere. Contrary to the Ancient Near East, Egypt was a stable empire for over 3,000 years. For example, the earlier representations of royalty in the Narmer Palette, c. 3100 BCE, show the same clothing and poses as those in later artwork from other regions as late as 1100 BCE. Egyptian art had stayed impressively consistent on purpose because, to them, consistency symbolized stability and divine balance.

How was the *Male Worshiper* figure crafted
and what materials were used?

Although Egyptian art has always seemed strangely static, formal, abstract, or blocky compared to the more naturalistic Greek art, these artworks served a vastly different purpose to that of other cultures. Egyptian statues and reliefs were never meant to be observed by others at all; rather, they were dedicated to the divine or deceased. Royal statues acted as intermediaries between human rulers and the gods. Historians have preserved letters from these burial sites appealing for assistance from the deceased in this world and the afterlife.

Palette of King Narmer

The *Palette of King Narmer* is so valuable that it has never been permitted to go beyond Egyptian borders. The palette has a height of more than two feet, is carved from smooth grayish-green siltstone, and is decorated on both sides with detailed reliefs. Although historians know the vital importance of the piece, it has always been more challenging to decipher the messages within the scenes.

The palette was uncovered in 1898 by James Quibell and Frederick Green, among other sacred implements and votive objects that were ritually buried in a temple of Horus in Hierakonpolis. The piece shows a high quality of workmanship, and the complex imagery indicates its significance as a tribute to a god. However, a satisfactory interpretation thereof has been difficult to find and has thus resulted in many different theories.

Palettes were commonly used during the Predynastic period to grind and mix minerals for cosmetics. All Egyptians used dark eyeliner to

> How did the Liangzhu people engrave the tough jadeite
> or nephrite stone to create the cong pieces?

reduce the sun's glare. However, these palettes were small and not as elaborately decorated. Other larger palettes also served as grinding surfaces, but they were carefully carved with relief and are believed to have been used purely for temple ceremonies.

The *Narmer Palette* shows conventional two-dimensional characteristics, such as the position in which the figures are presented, the scenes being divided in horizontal registers, and the indication of relative importance through the use of a hierarchical scale. King Narmer is depicted on the palette twice in human form, and perhaps also in the form of a bull—in later texts, a pharaoh is referred to as a "strong bull"—destroying the walls of a city. The piece includes two serpopards—mythical leopards with long serpent necks—with intertwined necks leaving a circular recess in between where cosmetic mixing took place. On both sides, the lowest register shows his defeated enemies and the top registers show Narmer's name and hybrid human-bull heads connected to the sky goddess Bat.

Some theories regarding the imagery include the record of a historical narrative of the unification of Egypt under one ruler. Besides the supportive timing being close to the unification, each side of the palette shows King Narmer wearing the crowns of Upper and Lower Egypt. An alternative theory includes the fundamental elements of the Egyptian belief in the cosmos; the careful balance between order (*ma'at*) and chaos (*isfet*). In early Egyptian history, the pharaoh's main role was to be the champion of *ma'at* and help protect the cosmic order from the *isfet* surrounding their people.

How do the defining characteristics of the *Male Worshiper* relate to the Sumerian culture's beliefs about gods and sculptures?

Seated Scribe

Although this statue is almost 4,500 years old, it continues to draw the interest of viewers because it is very lifelike. The amount of pigment that survived in this sculpture is unique and enhances the lifelike qualities of the artwork. While most of the statue is painted limestone, the nipples are wooden dowels, and the eyes are made from polished crystal, with indented pupils and irises colored with an organic adhesive.

While the figure seems more relaxed—having human qualities that contradict the Egyptian presentation of pharaohs that were seen as god-like—it remains formal and frontal. The *Seated Scribe* is meant to be viewed solely from the front, and the symmetry of the piece enhances this; that is, except for the asymmetry of one of his hands holding a rolled-up piece of papyrus and the other intended to hold a brush.

In Ancient Egypt, scribes were highly valued for their ability to read and write. Again, this sculpture was made for a tomb. Although it was discovered in an Old Kingdom necropolis southwest of Cairo, the uniquely momentary representation was never meant to be viewed by the living.

The Great Pyramids and The Great Sphinx

Being the last of the Seven Wonders of the ancient world, the Great Pyramids are undoubtedly the most famous structures in history.

For thousands of years after their construction, humans could not build anything that exceeded their height and perfection.

The Great Pyramids include three primary pyramids built during the rule of three generations: Khufu, Khafre, and Menkaure. Each structure was intended as a mortuary complex with a funerary temple at the base and a long stone causeway from the Giza plateau to a valley temple. Surrounding the primary pyramids are smaller pyramids that belonged to the queens. Spaced in a grid to the east and west of the pyramid of Khufu were the mastabas—flat-roofed rectangular constructions with sloping sides—where prominent members of the court were buried near the pharaoh's tomb.

Art historians believe that the shape of a pyramid is a reference to the sun and acts as a solid imitation of sun rays. Texts also speak of sun rays being a pharaoh's ramp to climb to the sky. Additionally, a pyramid symbolizes the sacred *ben-ben* stone that is the icon for the place of initial creation, connecting to the belief that a pyramid provides regeneration for the deceased.

People are still enthralled with the construction of the pyramids and the methods used by the large workforce necessary to build them; they are still a topic of discussion more than 4,500 years after their creation. Evidence from worker towns in the area suggests that there were skilled builders involved who had conscripted multiple groups of up to 2,000 workers to assist with the labor. These workers physically moved stones from the quarries to the pyramids by use of wet silt as a lubricated surface. Nearly 340 stones were moved daily.

The Pyramid of Khufu is the largest of the three primary pyramids, tipping at 481 feet high. Hence its name, it was constructed under the rule of King Khufu between 2551–2528 BCE. The first structure to surpass this pyramid's height was the 489-foot-high steeple of Old St. Paul's Cathedral in London, and that was not until 1221 CE. (The steeple collapsed roughly 350 years later.)

This particular pyramid consists of about 2,300,000 blocks—some exceeding 50 tons in weight—including inner rough-hewn stones that are visible today and white Tura limestone as an outer casing. The smooth casing has since been removed but initially provided a bright, reflective surface. At the top of the pyramid, craftsmen placed a gold-covered pyramidion that would have been seen from a great distance. Inside, the king's red-granite sarcophagus lay centrally aligned with the capstone above.

Not only is the structure's scale magnificent, but the precision with which it was built is nearly impossible to replicate, even with modern engineering and construction methods.

Khufu's second son, Khafre, ruled after him between 2520–2494 BCE. This was when the pyramid of Khafre was built. This pyramid still has small amounts of the white Tura limestone casing visible at its top. The funerary temple at the base of the Khafre pyramid was filled with over 52 life-size and larger statues of the king. Next to the causeway spanning from Khafre's pyramid to the valley temple sits one of the first colossal sculptures of Egypt: The Great Sphinx.

How does the *Code of Hammurabi* visually depict the interaction between King Hammurabi and the sun god of justice, Shammash?

The Great Sphinx incorporated the body of a lion and the head of a king, carved from the bedrock of the Giza plateau, especially for Khafre, who took the royal symbol of a lion in association with the connection between the sun and the horizon.

The smallest of the three Great Pyramids of Giza, at only 213 feet, belonged to Menkaure. However, the chambers of this pyramid were more complex, being carved with decorated panels. The king's black stone sarcophagus was decorated with recessed panels. Neither the funerary temple nor the valley temple was completed before King Menkaura's death.

King Menkaura and Queen

Although his pyramid complex remained incomplete, archeologists uncovered numerous statues of King Menkaura in the valley temple in 1908, including a series of triad statues depicting the king, the goddess Hathor, and a personified nome—as well as the dyad of *King Menkaura and Queen.*

The meticulously smooth surface of the dark stone sculpture captures the physical ideals at the time King Mekaura ruled, from 2490–2472 BCE. The greywacke—or schist—stone presented a sense of eternal youth, as there are no signs of age. It shows the king with an artificial royal beard, in a traditional short-pleated kilt—a *shendjet*—and the iconic striped *nemes* headdress, standing beside his queen. Menkaura holds ritual cloth rolls in his clenched fists hanging down his sides, while the queen presents ideal mature feminine beauty, neither she nor the king is depicted as idealized, like artists commonly did at the time. Contrary to other Egyptian sculptures where female feet are presented together, the queen's left foot strides forward with Menkaura's.

Although the statue shows signs of incompleteness, there are traces of red paint around Menkaura's ears and mouth, and yellow pigment on the queen's face, suggesting it was erected in the temple and painted anyway.

Temple of Amun-Re and The Hypostyle Hall

When the New Kingdom flourished in 1550 BCE, one of the largest religious complexes in the world developed in Thebes. This was the Karnak temple complex, the cult image of the god Amun-Re. However, Karnak also held the precincts in dedication to the gods Mut and Montu and was considered "The Most Select of Places" (*Ipet-isut*); the largest precinct incorporated nearly 20 temples and working grounds for the priestly community, including a kitchen, a sacred lake, and workshops.

Unfortunately, the site's preservation is at a low state, as the temple was looted. However, some unique architectural features survived. This includes a one-piece red-granite obelisk dedicated by the female pharaoh Hatshepsut during the New Kingdom in 1478 BCE, also known as the tallest ancient obelisk in Egypt.

During the Ramesside period—when 11 pharaohs named Ramses
ruled over Egypt—the hypostyle hall at Karnak was built with 134
sandstone columns; the 12 in the center were 69 feet tall. Some
remaining pigment of the formerly brightly-painted hall is found on
the columns and the ceiling. Due to the taller center, the walls on the
sides allowed for clerestory lighting—windows placed just below the
roof—making it the earliest evidence of clerestory lighting ever found.

Mortuary Temple of Hatshepsut

The pharaoh Hatshepsut was interested in how art portrayed the
power of authority. A structure that speaks of immense authority
was her mortuary temple. Hatshepsut commissioned the erection
of numerous stone sculptures within the mortuary temple, including kneeling figures and Hatshepsut in Sphinx form. As the second
confirmed female pharaoh after Sobekneferu—with a reign of only
three years and ten months—Hatshepsut adopted the male visual
language, such as the royal beard and the cobra head cloth, of the
previous two millennia. She did this to show herself as a true king
in art form. Although her figure was represented as masculine, with
broad shoulders and deemphasized breasts, the hieroglyphs inscribed
on the artworks identified her as female.

Hatshepsut ruled for 21 years, and after her death, her co-ruler at
the time, Thutmose III, systematically destroyed all of her imagery.
As someone with enormous influence at the time, Hatshepsut was
seen as out of place and was negatively viewed as a usurper. During

How does the *Standard of Ur* present the hierarchy
within society through its registers?

the excavations, Hatshepsut's sculptures were found in large fragments—especially the hard-stone mediums such as granite—and
were pieced together for museum display. In the 21st century, she is
seen more sympathetically.

Akhenaten, Nefertiti, and Three Daughters

Before the reign of Akhenaten, art had stayed consistent for more
than 3,000 years. However, around 1350 CE, a radical shift occurred
when Akhenaten changed the state religion from worshiping the god
Amun to a new sun god called Aten. It was at that time that pharaoh's
name changed to Akhenaten, meaning "Aten is pleased," and he made
himself and his wife, Nefertiti, the only representatives of the earthly
embodiment of the god Aten. This brief period upset many Egyptian
priests, as Akhenaten claimed that only he and Nefertiti had access
to the god. When he died, Egypt returned to its traditional religious
beliefs, again worshiping the god Amun.

One prominent art piece of this period is a stone plaque that shows
Akhenaten and Nefertiti's relationship to the god Aten. The indented
relief work is very informal in comparison to former Egyptian sculptures. The image also includes their three daughters, with the eldest
being tenderly held in Akhenaten's arms as he appears to kiss her, a second daughter on Nefertiti's lap pointing at the king, and the youngest
daughter sitting on Nefertiti's shoulder as she plays with her earring.

Their anatomy is presented strangely—swollen bellies, elongated
heads, and thin arms—which made many historians wonder

Why does the *Standard of Ur* emphasize the roles of
agriculture and long-distance trade in ancient society?

whether there was something medically wrong with Akhenaten and
his family. However, it is believed that this was merely a stylistic
break to represent a new age and religion. Whereas previous works
were based on purely rectilinear forms, Akhenaten incorporated
contrasting soft curvilinear forms, yet, we still see a composite view
of the body: a profile view of the face but a frontal view of the eye.

The presence of the god Aten is emphasized by the sun disk with
a small cobra—signifying that this is the only deity—making
Akhenaten a monotheist, as opposed to the pantheon of gods present in traditional Egyptian art. Taking a closer look at the sun's rays,
there are ankhs—the Egyptian symbol of life—close to the king's
and queen's faces, as if to show that Aten is giving life to them.

Tutankhamun's Tomb

Between 1332–1323 BCE, at nine years old, Tutankhamun became
King of Egypt. The discovery of his tomb was made by the archeologist
Howard Carter in 1922, and soon afterward, his story and the unique
insights of this ancient Egyptian period became public knowledge.

After the reign of Akhenaten, Tutankhamun changed Egypt's religious beliefs back to worship the god Amun. Sadly, Tutankhamun
only lived to the age of 18, resulting in many theories around his
death including murder, a chariot accident, and a hippo attack. His
much older advisor married Tutankhamun's widow, Ankhesenamun,
and became the pharaoh Ay.

> Why did many believe that the Stonehenge was built as an ancient astronomical center or ritual temple for those who worshiped the sun?

Egyptologist Howard Carter discovered a royal burial ground west of the religious center, Thebes. Carter, along with his financial backer Lord Carnarvon, entered the tomb together on November 26, 1922. The earl of Carnarvon noted (1933):

> At first, I could see nothing, the hot air escaping from the chamber causing the candle flame to flicker, but presently, as my eyes grew accustomed to the lights, details of the room within emerged slowly from the mist, strange animals, statues, and gold–everywhere the glint of gold. (p. 95-96)

Tutankhamun's sarcophagus consisted of a solid gold coffin inside two wooden coffins layered with gold, lapis lazuli, and other semi-precious stones. The gold coffin in the center was initially doused in an anointing liquid during the burial ceremony, leaving a black pitch-like layer over the gold surface.

Similar to how gods were believed to have golden skin, silver bones, and hair of lapis lazuli, Tutankhamun's image presented him as such a god entering the afterlife. A crook and flail—kingship symbols—are held in his hands, and he is accompanied by the goddesses Nekhbet, Wadjet, Isis, and Nephthys.

Inside the innermost coffin, Carter discovered a death mask covering Tutankhamun's mummified face. The mask, weighing 22.5 pounds, was constructed of two layered sheets of gold. Considered a masterpiece of Egyptian art, the mask shows Tutankhamun wearing the striped *nemes* headcloth, and the goddesses Nekhbet and Wadjet presented again for protection. Furthermore, he had an artificial royal beard, and a broad collar, and the back of the mask is inscribed with Spell 151b from the *Book of the Dead*. This spell was used by the Egyptians to guide the limbs of the deceased into the afterlife.

Last Judgment of Hunefer

Dating back to the Old Kingdom, Egyptians used a set of text—first on pyramids, then on coffins, and in the New Kingdom on paper made from papyrus reeds from the Nile Delta—that was called many names but was most commonly known as the *Book of the Dead*. Papyrus scrolls contained written spells, prayers, and incantations used during burial ceremonies as a type of instruction for successfully entering the afterlife. These writings were initially only placed in the tombs of the royal family, but they later became common among other people of high ranks, such as that in the tomb of the scribe Hunefer. At that time, scribes had priestly status and were valued for their writing and reading skills.

Around 1310 BCE, Hunefer held multiple prominent administrative titles, including Royal Scribe, Scribe of Divine Offerings, Overseer of Royal Cattle, and Steward of King Sety I.

The papyrus scroll, *Last Judgment of Hunefer*, shows imagery of this man sitting in front of a row of deities above a scene where he is being judged on whether he had lived a good or bad life. The deities seem to be supervising the judgment. On the far left, we see Anubis—a god associated with the afterlife—leading Hunefer into the area where he is presented with a scale. Anubis has an ankh in his hand, symbolic of eternal life, which is what Hunefer wants. Hunefer's heart, shown as a pot, is placed on the judgment scale to be weighed against the symbol of ma'at, a feather. Ma'at is also presented at the top of the scale. According to Egyptian beliefs, a human heart holds emotion, intellect, and character. Only those who had lived an ethical life, according to ma'at, can continue to the afterlife. Thus, if the heart was heavier than the feather, the human was condemned to non-existence and was devoured by Ammit, the hybrid crocodile-lion-hippopotamus beast. The god Thoth is recording the results of the test on the right of the scale. Hunefer's papyrus ensured his continued existence, as it is seen that he is shown to the right as Horus—again with an ankh in hand—takes him to Osiris. Osiris is sitting behind a lotus blossom—an additional symbol of eternal life—that holds the four children of Horus who will carry Hunefer's internal organs—placed in canopic jars—where preservation is of importance again.

This is known as *Hunefer's Book of the Dead*, produced in a fine quality especially for him, reflecting his high status. The papyrus is well preserved and contains clearly painted illustrations. In addition to *Hunefer's Book of the Dead*, a Ptah-Sokar-Osiris figure was also found in his tomb.

3.3. Ancient Greece

Most architects consider the classical order of ancient Greece architecture as the building blocks for Western design. This includes the Doric (c. seventh century), Ionic, and Corinthian styles that had been invented mostly for use in temples but have since been used for more than 2,500 years. The ancient Greeks used a fundamental architectural system that can be seen in the creation of Stonehenge, called post and lintel architecture. This incorporates vertical elements (posts) that support a horizontal element (lintel). They went on to evolve this basic system into a decorative one by using the classical order.

When looking at a Doric temple design, what comes below the pediment—the triangular piece at the top—is part of the order. This

includes the entablature and frieze that incorporated triglyphs, meaning "three marks," and metopes, which were the spaces between the
triglyphs that often-held sculptures. When looking at the columns, the
Doric capital consisted of a flair running up to a simple square slab on
top. The shaft, or column itself, used fluting as a decorative pattern of
vertical lines. Furthermore, the Doric order did not add a decorative
base to the shaft; instead, it went straight into the temple floor.

Athenian Agora

Perhaps the most important public space in Athens during 500
BCE was the Agora. Originally, the space was used for markets
and trade. It was then used as the starting point for the Athenian
experiment of democracy during the archaic and classical eras,
where the citizens of Athens were able to participate in government. However, this participation did not realize itself in the use
of votes. It meant that if you were wealthy or an excellent speaker,
you could become politically powerful.

Only a small number of positions that required specific skills were
democratically elected. The ideas of democracy at the time were limited to public decision-making, and governmental involvement was
allowed only if you were a male, Athenian-born (both parents) citizen.

Similar to how individuals were elected, voting took place by inscrib-
ing small pieces of pottery with the names of individuals thought to
be corrupt and dangerous to the state. Those public leaders were then

ostracized and forced to leave Athens. These ideas of equality before
the law are the fundamentals of modern Western democracy.

Anavysos Kouros

Produced in 530 BCE, the Anavysos Kouros *Youth* is a life-size
sculpture of what the ancient Greeks believed was the ideal male
youth. This became a very powerful subject in Greek art, and thousands of kouros sculptures were created for grave markers, ritualistic
offerings, and sometimes to represent a god.

Some art historians have argued that these monumental sculptures
were inspired by ancient Egypt. Earlier kouros shared many similarities with ancient Egyptian sculptures in that the male body was presented as an abstraction that gave a sense of stiffness. The body somewhat corresponded to a block of stone, and forms were symbol-like
instead of a true likeness of what you would see on the human body.
With the progression of the archaic period, the sculptures developed
into more rounded, natural, and integrated representations.

Many art historians believe that this particular figure was erected by
an aristocratic family in honor of their son, Kroisos, who had died in
war. An inscribed base found near the location of the sculpture's origin
read, "Stay and mourn at the monument of dead Kroisos who raging
Ares slew as he fought in the front ranks" (Smarthistory, 2014).

While the statue is a reference to an individual, it is not based specifically on the individual as it represents the ideal man.

What is the significance of the scepter and ring being
handed over in on the Code of Hammurabi?

Peplos Kore

Whereas kouros represents a male figure, kore is representative of the ideal female.

The *Peplos Kore* received its name from appearing to wear a peplos, a piece of ancient Greek clothing consisting of a rectangular linen cloth pinned at a figure's shoulders and falling down the body. Thus, a kore is the clothed female counterpart of the nude male kouros.

Kore figures were usually small offerings to the goddess Athena. The identity of the *Peplos Kore* is undetermined. However, historians believe that instead of a female figure offered to the goddesses, she might have been a reference to the goddess Artemis. While the reconstruction is incomplete, it is believed that if she held a bow and arrow, she would clearly be a representation of the goddess of the hunt. While most paint pigments had faded, traces of red paint can still be seen in the hair and eyes. Under special lighting, historians have discovered numerous patterns and animal images on her dress, perhaps symbolic of fertility.

Although her legs cannot be seen, there is a sense of movement in the Archaic piece. Her smile is also characterized as Archaic, not intended to show happiness but as a symbol of well-being.

Niobid Krater

A krater is a large punchbowl-like vase used by the ancient Greeks for mixing wine with water. Ancient Greek vases were created from terracotta and clay. Before production, pebbles and large chunks had to be removed, then the raw clay was mixed in large outdoor water pools. As the purified liquid ran into another pool, it was left to dry in the sun, resulting in refined clay. Greek vases were assembled using this clay on potter's wheels.

The Niobid painter, a well-known artist during 460–450 BCE, was famous for painting one of these vases with a scene of the children of a mortal woman named Niobe—who had bragged about her seven daughters and seven sons being more in number and beauty than the children of the goddess Leto—being murdered by Leto's children, Apollo and Artemis.

The figures presented on the vase are characterized by the stiffness of the early Classical period. Whereas prior painted vases had the figures on one ground line, this vase shows different levels, suggestive of an attempt at the illusion of space without the use of a diminishing sense of scale.

Polykleitos, Doryphoros

Polykleitos was an artist famous for creating representations of the perfect human figure, using mathematical relationships between the different parts of the body and the body as a whole.

Doryphoros—meaning spear bearer—is one of Polykleitos' famous sculptures that had originally held a bronze spear. Polykleitos initially referred to the piece as canon, a rule for a standard of beauty. As said by Galen (Harris & Zucker, 2015):

> Beauty consists in the proportions, not of the elements, but of the parts, that is to say, of finger to finger, and of all fingers to the palm and the wrist, and of these to the forearm, and of the forearm to the upper arm, and all the other parts to each other. (par. 9)

The artwork was found in a palestra in Pompeii, where athletes worked out and were perhaps inspired by the artwork. It presents the idea of creating the perfect human figure based on mathematics. Like most Greek statues, Doryphoros was presented naked to celebrate the ideal body.

The ancient Romans often copied the bronze Greek sculptures in marble, such as in this case, because its signified luxury, leisure, and learning. Few original Greek sculptures survived because they were melted into weapons by the ancient Romans who conquered the Greek cities.

Doryphoros was created during the classical period after the archaic period. Artists moved away from the sense of stiffness in designs and focused more on understanding physiognomy. The statue is in a contrapposto pose, showing the figure bearing his weight on his right leg. The left leg is relaxed, and the left hand originally bore the spear. This creates a sense of counterbalancing and harmony, contradicting the symmetry of archaic—kouros—figures.

The Parthenon

Created for the goddess of wisdom, Athena, the Parthenon is a marble temple on the Acropolis of Athens. Around 500 BCE, what was known as the High Classical period, Athens was the most powerful city-state. The Parthenon was created by the architects Iktinos and Kallikrates and was decreed to be a sacred precinct by the Athenian statesman, Perikles.

A large gold and ivory statue of Athena, created by Phidias, originally stood inside the Parthenon. Furthermore, three types of architectural sculpture of Athenian culture and mythology decorated the building itself. This included a colorful *frieze*—low relief—that ran across all four sides inside the colonnades, *metopes*—high relief—that covered the outside of the temple in between the triglyphs, and the *pediment* sculptures on the triangular spaces on the east and west ends. As all sculptures were overseen by Phidias, it is referred to as Phidian sculpture.

The Parthenon is considered a Doric temple, with columns that have simple capitals, also referred to as the abacus, accompanied by Ionic elements such as the frieze and four Ionic columns inside the west end of the temple. Similar to other Greek artworks, the architects used mathematics to produce perfect proportions and harmony at an enormous scale.

The building uses entasis, which describes the subtle adjustments—such as columns that bulge in the center—to create the illusion that the construction is perfectly proportioned.

What does "simting bilong tumbuna" mean, and
how is it related to the *Ambum Stone*?

In total, the building had 524 feet of decorated frieze, 92 metopes, and more than 17 pediment sculptures that showed scenes of mythical battles between the Greeks and Trojans, the Greeks and Amazons, the Lapiths and Centaurs, and the gods and titans; all of which symbolize the Athenian civilization's triumph against barbarism.

The Parthenon was originally used as a treasury by the Athenians. It was later used as a church by the early Christians, a mosque by the Ottoman Turks, and in 1687, it was used to store gunpowder that exploded and destroyed the roof, colonnades, and most of its walls during the Venetian siege. After surviving 2,000 years, the Parthenon became a ruin in the 17th century. The sculptures that had been destroyed were only identified through sketches from 1674.

Any sculptures that survived the blast of 1687 were removed from the Parthenon by Lord Elgin, the British representative for the Ottomans, after the French revolution, and are currently hosted in the British Museum in London. They include frieze panels, metopes, and pediments that express naturalism and anatomy in great detail. A competition for classical antiquity emerged between those in power across Europe, and Napoleon even brought scholars with him to identify artworks as he conquered cities. This is why today, sculptures that originally belonged to the Parthenon can be found in Paris and Athens.

Western buildings—especially like those seen in Washington, D.C.—were largely inspired by the Parthenon's architecture. This is because this architectural style became symbolic of democracy.

The frieze originally found inside the first colonnade of the west end of the Parthenon showed the *Panathenaic Procession*. This included scenes of women bringing peplos to dress the olivewood sculpture of Athena—which unfortunately did not survive—and other scenes depicting ancient ceremonies that required acts, including animal sacrifice and libation.

The Parthenon also held a smaller temple known as the temple of Athena Nike, representative of Athena's victory. As the temple was located close to the edge of the Acropolis, the Greeks added a four-foot-high parapet—railing—that had sculptures facing the walkway up to the temple. A prominent sculpture on the parapet shows a winged Athena (Nike) adjusting her sandal. Presumably, her wings are helping her maintain her balance as she is in the awkward position of removing her sandal. This is a significant addition because the High Classical period emphasized balance and harmony in all artworks.

Grave Stele of Hegeso

Nearing the end of the High Classical moment, funerary sculptures—similar to modern tombstones—resurfaced in ancient Greece. Like the korai and kouroi figures were used during Archaic times, stelae were used by wealthy families to commemorate their deceased members.

These sculptural stelae started to appear near the outer gates of Athens. One prominent piece, known as the *Grave Stele of Hegeso*, shows a seated woman—Hegeso—being presented with a jewelry box by one of her servants to examine a necklace. The image includes all of the elements that signified the High Classical period, such as the intricate folds of the drapery around her body and the incorporation of her whole body in a shallow space.

Winged Victory (Nike) of Samothrace

Discovered in the sanctuary of the gods on Samothrace, an island in the northeastern Aegean Sea, the *Winged Nike* currently stands at 18 feet tall on the grand staircase at the entrance of the Louvre Museum, Paris.

This sculpture dates back to the expressive Hellenistic period after the death of Alexander the Great. This period was known for the creation of energetic pieces showing drama and power. The sculpture shows a great balance between Nike's lower body standing firmly on the ship, and her upper body still somewhat in flight as the wind approaches her from the ocean.

Great Altar of Zeus and Athena (Pergamon)

Another prominent art piece of the Hellenistic period is the fragment of the frieze from the Pergamon—present-day Turkey—called the *Great Altar of Zeus and Athena*. The image shows dramatic scenes of Zeus and Athena, along with the other gods of Mount Olympus, in a battle with giants.

The scene of Athena shows how she is centrally in control between fearful figures—specifically Alcyoneus and his mother—as they are defeated. Simultaneously, Athena is crowned by a winged Nike on the right. The eye is led in a counterclockwise motion through a drama-filled scene around Athena's shield. It includes many diagonal lines that give a further sense of contrast between the highlighted events and the shadows in the background.

Like Athena, the fragment of Zeus shows him being in complete control as he takes on three giants simultaneously. As king of the gods, he is assisted by thunderbolts and eagles. This story of heroism between the gods and the giants was very important to the ancient Greeks as a reminder that they can overcome chaos.

The high-relief sculptures beside the stairs appear to allow the figures to enter our world as they move out of the walls, and some rest parts of their bodies on the stairs.

It is important to remember that these scenes were originally painted in bright colors, contrary to the white marble we see today.

Alexander Mosaic (House of the Faun)

The detailed mosaic of the battle between Persia and the Greeks shows a significant event in time in tiny fragments of colored stone and glass. It presents the turning point in the battle where the Persian ruler Darius III has decided to retreat, as we see his chariot hastily turning away from the Greeks while soldiers still face their spears toward their enemies, and others have fallen to the ground.

One impactful detail includes a Persian soldier seeing himself—presumably about to die—in the reflection of his shield. Additionally, the drama is captured by a horse with all four of its hooves airborne as it is pulled to the right after facing the left.

Alexander's face shows confidence, whereas Darius seems fearful. Art historians suggest that Darius looks as if he is seeking mercy from Alexander for the lives of his soldiers, and Alexander was known for his compassion towards Darius's family.

Many believe this piece is linked to a literary description of a Greek wall painting—of which none survived—by an artist named Philoxenos.

The mosaic was found under the layer of ash that preserved the city of Pompei after the eruption of Mt. Vesuvius in 79 CE. It was on the floor of an extravagant mansion known as the House of the Faun.

Seated Boxer

Although most examples of Greek sculpture are Roman copies in marble, there are rare occasions where ancient Greek originals of bronze were discovered. The *Seated Boxer* is one of them.

Dating back to around 100 BCE, during the last phase of Greek art—the Hellenistic period—this sculpture contradicts the beauty of traditional Greek art. Whereas previous athletes were presented as young and attractive, the *Seated Boxer* is not young, shows inlaid copper scars over his face, and gives a sense of defeat or exhaustion. The artist intended for the viewer to feel sympathy toward the figure.

Usually, Greek figures are nobly standing and represented heroically, but this one is seated and shows a collapsed torso, a broken nose, and a swollen ear, all indicative of humility and humanity.

This aligns with the fact that the Hellenistic period moved away from artistic expression of the ideal to more naturalistic expression in art.

3.4. Ancient Etruria

Before the Romans claimed the area in 509 BCE, the Etruscan civilization controlled the northern peninsula of present-day Italy. This culture formed the foundation of ancient Roman art and the later Italian Renaissance movement. The Etruscans were responsible for establishing important cities like Florence, Pisa, Siena, and others in Tuscany. Unfortunately, the culture is rarely mentioned, as none of their histories survived.

However, ancient Rome inherited many of its artistic and cultural systems from the Etruscans, including the alphabet, engineering, gladiatorial combat, and temple design. Unfortunately, Etruscan cities were inhabited by those who hid their traditional works under the guise of Roman, Medieval, and Renaissance styles. Most of what art historians know of the Etruscan culture comes from their burial grounds, as they were considerate in providing their dead with everything necessary for

Why do historians believe that the *Narmer Palette* might depict the unification of Egypt under one ruler?

the afterlife. Etruscans cremated their dead and provided a "new home" in a hut urn made from impasto—unrefined clay—that indicates what Iron Age Etruria (900–750 BCE) homes looked like. As the Etruscans began to trade their natural resources with the rest of the Mediterranean, their wealth grew, and the homes for their dead became more extravagant.

Sarcophagus of The Spouses

An important piece found in one of the Etruscan tombs was a terracotta sarcophagus with two figures—*the Spouses*—depicted on the lid of the tomb. Differing from the Greek art of the same time, such as the stiff kouroi and korai that stand alone, the Etruscan sarcophagus shows two very life-like figures embracing each other at what appears to be a banquet. In Greek and Roman cultures, mixed-gender banquets where males and females dined together were frowned upon. However, Etruscan women held a higher status than those in other cultures, so an image of them attending events with men was not unusual for their people.

As offering perfume was a funerary ritual, many art historians theorized that the female figure was initially holding a bottle of perfume.

The sculpture that shows archaic elements, such as the archaic smile and stylized features, was discovered in a necropolis at Cerveteri, shattered into 400 pieces, and reassembled for display at the Etruscan Museum in Rome. A similar sarcophagus is housed at the Louvre Museum in Paris.

Terracotta sculptures were considered an elite commission requiring high technical achievement levels.

Temple of Minerva

Early Etruscans did not worship their gods and goddesses in temples; rather, they chose to worship in nature. It was only after Greek influence, around 600 BCE, that Etruscans built sacred structures. However, their temples differed greatly in style from ancient Greek and Roman temples. Etruscan temples were built with transitory materials, like wood, mud-brick, and terracotta. Only the stone foundations survived centuries of elemental damage.

While short-lived, the Etruscan temple style influenced Renaissance architecture. For example, the Tuscan columns that were Doric columns with bases were fashioned after the Roman architect Vitruvius wrote about the elements of Etruscan temples.

Archeological evidence from Etruscan temples, such as the Temple of Minerva in Veii, the Roman version of the Greek goddess Athena, confirms Vitruvius' descriptions. The evidence consists of the limestone foundation of the Portonaccio temple that reflects the described floorplan.

The temple includes a wide front porch with Tuscan columns and three rooms in the back. The three separate rooms, called a triple cella, are symbolic of a divine triad, presumably Menrva, Tinia (Zeus),

How were palettes, like the *Palette of King Narmer*,
used during the Predynastic period?

and Uni (Hera). Contrary to Greek architecture, Etruscan temples included high podiums and frontal entrances.

A series of life-size and larger terracotta sculptures associated with the temple have been found. These show Etruscan interpretations of Greek gods that were initially placed on the peak of the temple roof. A well-preserved and famous representation is that of the god Apollo, named *Aplu (Apollo of Veii)*. The sculpture shows Apollo confronting another—according to mythology, this was Hercules—for a Golden Hind (deer) sacred to his sister Artemis. Etruscan sculptures presented a sense of liveliness and movement, as seen in Apollo's forward stride, in a highly stylized manner.

Tomb of Triclinium

The elite members of Etruria participated in extravagant funerary rituals that changed according to time and place. One of the most powerful Etruscan centers, Tarquinia—formerly known as Tarquinii or Tarch(u)na—was famous for painted chamber tombs, such as the Tomb of Triclinium discovered in 1830 CE. Dating c. 470 BCE— referred to as the Advanced Iron Age—the tomb is located in the Monterozzi necropolis at Tarquinia, Italy. Chamber tombs held both the remains of the deceased as well as the grave goods that were offered along with the dead.

Frescoes decorate the Tomb of Triclinium with the rear wall showing the main scene of banqueters reclined on dining couches (*klinai*).

While only a fragment of the original fresco is preserved, it is suggested that the painting included three couches hosting a dining couple. Two attendants are caring for the banqueters who are dressed in sumptuous robes that emphasize their elite status. Also included are a large cat, a rooster, and other birds.

On the left wall, three female dancers are accompanied by one male dancer and a male musician playing an ancient instrument called a barbiton, which resembles a lyre. The right wall shows two more dancers, whereas the walls flanking the entrance present scenes of the ancient funeral games such as equestrian combat sports and the Dioscuri (mythological twins associated with the overall convivial tone of Etruscan funerals). Lastly, the ceiling is covered in a checkered pattern in a variety of colors that perhaps resembled the fabric tents used for the actual ceremony near the tomb.

It is important to note that Etruscan funerals were not somber. Rather, they were festive and were seen as an honored opportunity to share a last meal with the deceased. The funeral banquet acted as the transition from the living world into the dead, as the appropriate dishes and utensils were later transferred to the tomb. This tradition was also to reinforce the position of the deceased and to remind the living of their importance and standing in contemporary society.

What details are depicted on the Palette of King Narmer?

3.5. Ancient Rome

House of the Vettii, Pompeii

Although the eruption of Mt. Vesuvius silenced the ancient city, the remains of houses and decorations provide an idea of the daily lives of those who once inhabited Pompeii.

Located in the Roman city is the House of the Vettii (*Casa de Vettii*), a townhouse that acts as a prominent source of *domus* architecture. The form and function of ancient Roman houses had been debated for a long time before the 18th-century discovery of the preserved sites of the destruction of Vesuvius.

During the Roman Republic, aristocratic families used their homes
to display their ranking, reinforce social hierarchy, and advance their
fortunes within their communities.

The first century BCE author Vitruvius wrote about the key elements and aesthetics of Roman houses, resulting in a canonical
recommendation for *domus* architecture of that period. The canon
included several standard elements, including an entrance through
a narrow doorway (*fauces*) from the street, a central reception hall
(*atrium*) that was flanked by *alae* spaces, and bedrooms (*cubiculi*).
The head of the household's office (*tablinum*) divided the public
portion (*pars urbana*) and private portion (*pars rustica*) of the house.
The private area included the center of family living (*peristylium*)
that incorporated an open colonnaded courtyard, a kitchen (*culina*),
a dining room (*triclinium* or *oecus*), and a garden (*hortus*).

The House of the Vettii—roughly 1,100 square meters—was excavated from 1894–1896 and interior artifacts provided the identifi-
cation of its former inhabitants as Aulus Vettius Conviva and his
brother, Aulus Vettius Restitutus. The men decorated their home
with elements common among the newly rich, such as two lockable
strongboxes (*arca*) to store valuables, and signs of wealth that were
placed in its two large atria for public notice. However, the house
lacks a tablinum. The larger atrium held a stone-lined basin (*implu-
vium*) that was used for collecting rainwater and linked to the open
courtyard surrounded by fluted Doric columns (*peristyle*) through
folding doors. The space was used for entertainment, whereas the
smaller atrium acted as the service portion of the house.

What is the difference between the small palettes and the larger palettes like the *Narmer Palette* in terms of usage and purpose?

Art historians believe the decorative pieces in the house are representative of the transition between the Third and Fourth styles of Pompeian wall paintings—or the 'Ornate' and 'Intricate' styles—that became popular during the Imperial period. These images mostly incorporated mythological figures such as erotes or putti—a winged god associated with love—and landscapes.

Head of a Roman Patrician

During the reign of the Roman Republic, some powerful figures included older men from elite families who became aristocrats. Thus, some important artworks were the veristic—derived from the Latin word *verus* meaning 'truth'—portraits that portrayed the age, experience, pain, and wisdom of these figures. The artwork of this time showed serious facial expressions and thinly-pressed lips that evoked a sense of authority and stood out against other Roman busts, as they recall the ideals of the Roman Republic instead of ancient Greek traditions.

The *Head of a Roman Patrician* shows the deeply-wrinkled face of a seemingly toothless man with sunken and sagging skin that highlights how the seriousness of mind (*gravitas*) and virtues (*virtus*) of a public career of the Late Roman Republic is demonstrated through the physical effects of this aristocrat's endeavors. This piece is carved from marble.

Dating back to the mid-first century BCE, the portrait does not portray any emotion or dynamism seen in its near contemporaries.

Veristic portraiture—or verism—is described as hyperrealism used in sculpture to exaggerate natural features to an absurd extent. This stylistic tendency is symbolic of respect for ancestry, family, and tradition.

Augustus of Primaporta

As Roman art was connected to political propaganda, the emperors cared a lot about their image, especially the first emperor of the Roman Empire, Augustus.

Augustus used imagery as a powerful communicator of his ideology. One of his most famous portraits, *Augustus of Primaporta*, was created in 20 BCE and was named after the town of its discovery in 1863. This artwork shows the emperor as a great military victor, his support of Roman religion, and the 200 years of peace known as the Pax Romana (indicated through the figures on his breastplate).

The sculpture shows him in military regalia as he addresses his troops. Sharing a resemblance with the Greek sculpture *Doryphoros* we sense Augustus' leadership and the connection he is making with the youthful idealization of the previous Golden Age.

The Cupid and dolphin symbolize his connection to the god Venus, whom his adoptive father, Julius Caesar, claimed to have been a descendant of, as well as Augustus' naval victory at the battle of Actium. Furthermore, his breastplate (*cuirass*) highlights how Augustus is favored by numerous deities and acts as an allusion to the Pax Romana.

This piece is one of many examples of how the Romans used art for propagandistic purposes.

> How were the Great Pyramids constructed, considering
> the methods and the workforce involved?

Colosseum

Modern society sees the Colosseum as a remembrance of ancient Roman culture and attributes a sense of nostalgia to it; however, history reveals its horrific connections with the then-called Flavian Amphitheater. Moreover, the Colosseum is an important Roman structure, to be sure, but we often forget its function as a place of hundreds of thousands of deaths, as it was mainly used for spectated exotic animal hunts, prisoner executions, and gladiatorial combats.

The structure itself was only referred to as the Colosseum in the middle ages because of the colossal statue—roughly 100 feet tall—of the sun god that had been erected next to it.

The architecture of the Colosseum shows how the Romans combined the three Greek styles: the top stories present the Corinthian style, the second story is in the Ionic style, and the lower story has Tuscan and Doric style elements.

This is an excellent representation of the arches the Romans were famous for producing. Additionally, the Colosseum remains a symbol of Rome's power, brilliance, and despotism.

Later, this 'abattoir' was sanctified by the Christians and became a pilgrimage site.

Forum (Column) of Trajan

During the rule of Emperor Trajan, followed by two victorious wars against Dacia (Romania), the Romans were introduced to the Forum and the Column of Trajan (c. 112–113 CE). The Forum allowed the

Romans to participate in business and legal affairs, and at its center is the Column that depicts the two before-mentioned wars. The final of five Imperial *fora*—public spaces commissioned by the emperors—the Forum of Trajan reinforced their ideological messages.

The Forum of Trajan, built by the architect Apollodorus of Damascus, was the largest and most lavish of the fora, measuring 200 x 120 meters. Initially, the forum square was paved with marble and had trees and statues running parallel to the *porticoes*, the extended roofed colonnades. Individuals entered the forum from the south through an arch decorated with a statue of Trajan riding a triumphal chariot.

On the western end of the square stood the Column of Trajan at roughly 124 feet tall, which is considered a masterwork of Roman art. It has a helical frieze of roughly 623 feet which wraps around the shaft 23 times, portraying a pictorial narrative of Trajan's wars against Decebalus.

The ancient author Aulus Gellius describes the forum's decor: "All along the roof of the colonnades of the forum of Trajan gilded statues of horses and representations of military standards are placed, and underneath is written *Ex manubiis*" (Becker, 2013). In the center of the square, there stood a bronze equestrian statue of Trajan (*Equus Traiani*) that no longer exists, apart from its mention by Constantius II in 357 CE.

At the northern edge of the courtyard stood the Basilica Ulpia, named accordingly after Trajan's family. The structure included 96 Corinthian columns of white and yellow marble, a raised central floor, and gilded bronze roof tiles.

What purpose did the smaller pyramids
surrounding the Great Pyramids serve?

Pantheon

Referred to as the "sphinx of the Campus Martius," the Pantheon is considered a Roman architectural wonder. While it surprisingly does not fall on the list of the most popular structures in the world, many modern buildings are imitations thereof.

Although it is uncertain, the conventional understanding of the Pantheon's construction believes that the original structure was built by Marcus Agrippa in honor of Augustus' military victory at the Battle of Actium (c. 31 BCE). Written sources suggest that the original Pantheon was destroyed by fire in 80 CE and that it was later somewhat restored under the rule of Emperor Domitian. The building was damaged by fire again in 110 CE, and Emperor Trajan commissioned for it to be rebuilt. However, only partial groundwork was done before Trajan's death, and it is believed that his predecessor, Hadrian, designed the modern-day Pantheon. While Emperor Hadrian aimed to create a more impressive version of the Pantheon, he wanted the favor of the gods and, in pious humility, installed the false inscription that Agrippa was responsible for the new Pantheon.

At 141 feet tall, the building incorporates marble Corinthian order columns, a rectilinear porch that opens up to a curvilinear radial interior through large bronze doors that is based on eight arches where statues of deities and emperors initially stood. The structural system is made of concrete that was built on wooden beams that were removed once the concrete dried. It is suggested that the structure was initially used as a temple to the gods and later a catholic church, but Emperor Hadrian held court events inside the building as a symbol of his wealth and power. The oculus functioned similarly to a sundial. Again, the construction is mathematically proportioned and uses various geometric representations.

Ludovisi Battle Sarcophagus

Expressive sarcophagi started to appear more during the second century CE when Rome was filled with instability and war after a time of peace and stability. The chaotic piece known as the *Ludovisi Battle Sarcophagus*—named after its first modern owner—shows the historical shift to Late Imperial Rome.

The piece was inspired by the Hellenistic period and removed the focus from the beauty of the human body as it favored showing emotional interactions between people. The image shows a battle scene between the 'good' Roman and the 'bad' Celtic tribes, with the center focus on a splayed-out Roman soldier in heavy armor that signifies the invincible hero, presumably the initial owner of the artwork.

Although the main figure's identity is undetermined, the piece was used to mark the grave of a rich Roman, as it required a large payment for the marble and a highly-skilled sculptor's hire.

How does the depiction of the queen in the statue of King
Menkaura and Queen differ from other Egyptian sculptures?

Key Concepts

- The **ancient Near East**, also known as the "cradle of civilization," was the first destination where complex urban centers grew. Among being the home of other significant statues, structures, and early forms of writing, the ancient Near East—specifically ancient Uruk (present-day Warka, Iraq)—is also known as the birthplace of **the writing form** and where the **Anu Ziggurat** and the **White Temple** were built. Notable works of art from the ancient Near East are the *Statues of Votive Figures, the Standard of Ur, The Code of Hammurabi, Lamassu from The Citadel of Sargon II, and the Audience Hall (Apanada) of Darius I and Xerxes.*

- **Egyptian art** stayed consistent because consistency symbolized stability and divine balance for the Egyptians. Their art was also dedicated to the divine or deceased and were very much tied to their spirituality and beliefs about death and the afterlife. Some examples of these are the *Palette of King Narmer*, the *Seated Scribe*, the *Great Pyramids*, the *Great Sphinx*, the dyad of *King Menkaura and Queen*, the *Temple of Amun-Re* and the *Hypostyle Hall*, the *Mortuary Temple of Hatshepsut, Akhenaten, Nefertiti, and Three Daughters, Tutankhamun's Tomb*, and the *Last Judgment of Hunefer*.

- The classic order of the **architecture of ancient Greece** is considered by most architects as the building blocks for Western design. This includes the Doric (c. seventh century), Ionic, and Corinthian styles invented mostly for use in temples.

Noteworthy structures and works of art during this time
include the Athenian Agora, Anavysos Kouros, Peplos Kore,
Niobid Krater, the Doryphoros by Polykleitos, the Parthenon,
the Grave Stele of Hegeso, the Winged Victory (Nike) of
Samothrace, the Great Altar of Zeus and Athena (Pergamon),
the Alexander Mosaic (House of the Faun), and the Seated
Boxer.

- **Etruscan civilization** and culture influenced and formed
the foundation of **ancient Roman art** and the Italian
Renaissance movement. Etruscan culture is also known for
their burial grounds, as they provided their dead with everything they might need for the afterlife. Examples of art from
Ancient Etruria are Sarcophagus of The Spouses, Temple of
Minerva, and the Tomb of Triclinium.

- Some examples of **art from ancient Rome** are the House
of the Vettii, the Head of a Roman Patrician, Augustus of
Primaporta, the Colosseum, the Forum (Column) of Trajan,
the Pantheon, and the Ludovisi Battle Sarcophagus.

CHAPTER 4

EARLY EUROPE AND COLONIAL AMERICAS

Learning objectives:

- Identify a specific work of art.
- Explain why and how traditions and changes are depicted.
- Analyze how qualities and context elicit a response.
- Analyze how contextual variables result in various interpretations.
- Describe features of tradition or change in an artwork.

4.1. Late Antique Art

As described in the *Bible*, Jesus was a Jew who rebelled against the
Roman government in Palestine and was then crucified for under-
mining Roman authority and upsetting the social order. Thereafter,
Jesus' followers—known as disciples or apostles—spread the word
that Jesus rose from the grave three days after his sacrifice for
humans. His life story was written in the *New Testament* in the
Gospels of Matthew, Mark, Luke, and John. These stories became
common subjects of Medieval and Renaissance art.

According to the *Torah* and *Old Testament*, traditional Jewish theology—the religion known as Judaism—started around 1813 BCE,
when God chose Abraham to be a father to Isaac, who founded
the Jewish people. However, the foundation of the Jewish reli-
gion developed during the time Moses led the enslaved Jews from
Egypt to Canaan (Exodus), and presented the Israelites with the
Ten Commandments after forming a new covenant with God on Mt.
Sinai. Although the first Christians were Jews who read from the *Old
Testament* or the *Hebrew Bible*, it was only in the second century that
Christianity was seen as a religion separate from Judaism. As Christians
saw the predictions from the *Old Testament* fulfilled in the life of Jesus
Christ, the *New Testament* was added to make the Christian *Bible*.

Christians were mistreated and ridiculed until 313 CE when the
Roman emperor Constantine made it legal to be a Christian. Almost
a century later, the Roman emperor Theodosius made it the official
state religion.

> What design system is evident in the consistent patterns
> found on the potsherds of the Lapita pottery?

Christian art originally evolved from classic art and its illusionary qualities. However, artists moved away from naturalistic representation and started to create abstract art as Christian theologians argued it could be seen as idolatry (Exodus, 20:4). Artists no longer paid attention to details, modeling, perspective, or shading conventions.

Catacombs of Priscilla

The Catacombs of Priscilla include more than five miles of burial sites located directly underneath the grounds of Rome. The land was donated by a wealthy Roman woman named Priscilla and is located in the northern region where her family would first be buried, and later the Christian community. Around 40,000 tombs have already been discovered.

As you walk through the narrow dark passageways, you see a low ceiling, and on either side, horizontal niches are carved into the wall—just long enough to hold a body. The niches were commonly stacked on top of each other. Wealthy individuals were able to excavate larger spaces, named cubiculum, for a sarcophagus, but most of these shelf-like slots referred to as loculi, were for the poor, who were buried in shrouds and covered with a slab of marble or tiles of terracotta and plaster.

Some of the earliest Christian art that historians could locate—only from the third century onward—was discovered in the Catacombs of Priscilla. The works of art were both carved and painted, including inscriptions of those who were buried, Christian symbolism, and some general imagery. One prominent piece appears to be the earliest representation of *Madonna and Child,* where a mother is nursing, and another figure is pointing to the mother and child while holding a book.

Known as the Greek chapel—although it was not a chapel and only incorporated Greek letters—a small cubiculum shows a particular decoration style referred to as Roman First Style wall painting. This method involves building up plaster and painting over it to resemble marble panels. It was often used as an attempt to make a space appear rich. This is one of the oldest parts of the catacombs, adjacent to the basement of Priscilla's house, and held multiple sarcophagi of her family members. Furthermore, the Greek chapel presented imagery from both the *Old and New Testaments,* including scenes of Divine Intervention, the three youths in the fiery furnace, the Adoration of the Magi, and the Resurrection of Lazarus, all showing that early Christians valued the miracles of Christ.

Another significant space in the catacombs of Priscilla is called the "Cubiculum of the Veil." It was named under painted imagery on the ceiling in memory of a veiled woman's life. The three images reference her marriage, her motherhood, and a center image showing her in an orant pose—a pose of prayer to represent her resurrection in the afterlife. As her eyes are looking upward to heaven, the painting represents the woman's salvation.

The same room holds frescoes of Christ depicted as the Good Shepherd in the center of the shallow dome of the ceiling.

Accompanied by three goats—one over his shoulder—Jesus is in a contrapposto-like stance. The artist was familiar with Roman figure art conventions. In addition, there are two trees on either side, with doves at the top, signifying that Christ will care for people like a shepherd cares for a flock. Surrounding this painting are numerous images of peacocks—symbolic of heaven—and quail—symbolic of earth—suggesting that Christ exists between both the earthly and heavenly realms.

Santa Sabina

After Christianity was legalized, the Santa Sabina was constructed at the top of the Aventine Hill in Rome. Similar to how other important Roman temples were built on nearby hills, the Santa Sabina was placed there to signify the importance of the new religion in the Roman Empire.

Early Christians were influenced by the great architecture of ancient Rome, such as the basilica. A traditional Greek or Roman temple is seen as a house in honor of the god or goddess, without a lot of interior space other than that for the cult figure. The Christians found that the basilica had a sense of governmental authority, could hold a lot of people, and had a longitudinal axis directing viewers' attention to the opposite side of the entrance, the apse (place of the altar). The central space where people would come together is called the nave, which is flanked by side aisles.

Why is the Karnak temple complex, particularly
the precinct for Amun-Re, significant in the history
of ancient Egyptian religious architecture?

This inspired the design of the Santa Sabina. Enormous arches create a sense of rhythm that leads the eye to the apse and provides
an idea of what the original St. Peter's Basilica—commissioned
by Constantine after the legalization of Christianity—looked like
before its recreation during the Renaissance.

Upon entering the Santa Sabina, there is a wooden door carved with
scenes from the *Old and New Testaments* (c. fifth century). Although
it had been heavily restored, the survival of such organic materials
for so long is remarkable. The door includes a particularly interesting rendition of The Crucifixion in the upper left corner, which is
not a common theme in early Christian art.

Originally, the walls of the nave were decorated with mosaics; however, those have since been removed. As light was seen as a symbol
of divinity and Christ, the architect incorporated clerestory windows
that provided soft but direct light into the nave, creating a shimmer-
ing effect as it bounced off the mosaic walls.

Perhaps the most distinctive characteristic of the church is the spolia
columns inside, which had been reused from a former Pagan building and set in a Christian context. Above the columns, artists created
imagery of inlaid stones that depict chalices and bread plates, a reference to the eucharist—holy communion—a religious ritual that is
repeated down the aisles.

This church acts as the source of reference for Christian churches
built throughout the rest of history, except with the addition of a
transept to represent the cross.

How did Jesus' life story influence Medieval and Renaissance art?

4.2. Byzantine Art

While the Roman Empire fragmented in Western Europe at the start of the Middle Ages, it remained a strong political organization in the Byzantine East. Seen as New Rome, emperors ruled from Constantinople, where one of the world's largest churches, Hagia Sophia, was built.

Whereas Western Europe Middle Age art was broken into five smaller periods depending on time and place, Byzantine art is categorized into Early Byzantine—or Early Christian—art, Middle, and Late Byzantine art. The earliest existence of Christian art from 250 CE kicked in the Early Byzantine period. This also included Iconoclasm, which left a visible legacy, as artistic representation was limited. At the end of Iconoclasm in 842 CE, the Middle Byzantine period started and ended in 1204 CE when Constantinople was sacked by Latin Crusaders. This led to Late Byzantine art that extended to the fall of Constantinople to the Ottoman Turks (c. 1453 CE).

Vienna Genesis: Jacob Wrestling the Angel & Rebecca and Eliezer at the Well

One of the most significant manuscripts from the early sixth century, the Byzantine Era, is the *Vienna Genesis*. It presents the first book of the *Bible* with text at the top and illustrations at the bottom of each page. The 24 surviving folios—of what was considered to be an original 96—of the *Vienna Genesis* show the earliest illustrations of *Bible* stories, making it a rare find, as books were easily destroyed in fires and floods at that time in history. During the sixth century, the production of books was not common, as it was a time-consuming task, making this a truly unique representation. Although the text is now tarnished, it was initially written in silver to create a gleaming surface on purple-dyed paper, indicative of a royal commission.

The first page to look at shows Jacob in a brown and red tunic leading his servants, his wives, and his sons across a river. After they cross the river over a bridge, Jacob is separated from his family as he wrestles with a man who is also interpreted as an angel. Jacob is blessed by the angel, who renames him Israel, and his family continues their journey (Genesis, 31:22–28).

This artwork is an essential example of how classical elements, such as the ancient Greek columns and Roman arches of the bridge, are at odds with the Byzantine style, like intentionally ignoring rational perspective and warping the bridge so the viewer can see its front and back as Jacob's family moves over it.

Looking at the story of Rebecca and Eliezer at the well (Genesis 24), the illustration shows Abraham's servant, Eliezer, stopping at a well to give 10 camels water. Eliezer was tasked with finding a wife for Abraham's son, Isaac. When Rebecca arrives and assists Eliezer with the water, he knows that Rebecca is the perfect wife for Isaac. This story highlights how God intervened to ensure a sound marriage between Isaac and a suitable wife.

Common in Medieval art, the story shows two depictions of Rebecca. The first is where she is shown leaving town to fetch water, and later when she assists Eliezer with the camels. Again, some classical elements appear, such as the columns representative of ancient Greek and Roman architecture, shading that is used to show the spatial relationship between the camels, and the reclining nude figure acting as a classical personification of the source for the river's water. The sensuality of this classical figure strongly juxtaposes Rebecca's fully-covered body, which was standard in Christian art. Additionally, other Medieval elements include the spatial inconsistencies of the walled city and the colonnade and the figures appearing cartoon-like and simplified.

Typical of the early sixth century, *Vienna Genesis* portrays an artist caught in a time of cultural transition between those who loved realistic details and accuracy and those that preferred abstract representation and symbolism.

San Vitale, Justinian Mosaic

Between 526 and 547 CE, under Ostrogothic rule, the San Vitale was built in Ravenna, Italy.

The church holds an excellent example of Byzantine-style art: the mosaic of Emperor Justinian. The mosaic signifies Justinian's significant role in Christianity's history. In addition, it shows Justinian's ambitions during his reign, including restoring the territorial boundaries of the empire and establishing religious uniformity (Orthodoxy).

Within the San Vitale, Emperor Justinian is presented centrally in a frontal position; he is wearing a purple imperial robe and a crown and is haloed. Members of the clergy, such as Bishop Maximiannus of Ravenna, stand to his left, with members of the imperial administration—identified by the purple stripe—and a group of soldiers standing to his right. This shows the emperor's authority in the church and the imperial administration, as well as with the military.

The Byzantine liturgy of the Eucharist is presented by a censer, the gospel book, the cross, and a bread bowl that is passed along to the left.

An additional apse shows a seated Christ presenting the crown to Saint Vitale—the crown worn by Justinian—signifying that Emperor Justinian is Christ's vice-regent on Earth. Across from Justinian's mosaic is an image that shows his wife, Empress Theodora. This is the only image of the empress that survived, apart from written descriptions.

> What were some of the primary components and structures found within the largest precinct of the Karnak temple complex?

Hagia Sophia

In addition to the San Vitale, the Hagia Sophia is one of the Byzantine Era's greatest churches, built in 537 CE in Constantinople (modern-day Istanbul). It was believed that Emperor Justinian first saw the completed Hagia Sophia in a dream.

Taking a closer look at the church's dome, the columns present classic Ionic-style capitals. However, differing greatly from the spiraled columns of the Greeks, these capitals show intricate detail with deeply-drilled shadows behind a vegetative pattern, seeming visually incapable of holding the weight of the building above it. The deep drilling appears throughout the structures' capitals, entablatures, and spandrels.

Procopius, Emperor Justinian's biographer, describes the dome: "The huge spherical dome [makes] the structure exceptionally beautiful. Yet it seems not to rest upon solid masonry, but to cover the space with its golden dome suspended from Heaven" (Allen, 2015). The closely-spaced windows, lined in gold at the bottom, visually make the base float above the building. The faithful people of Constantinople believed that this floating effect resulted from divine intervention.

The church became a mosque in 1453 CE when the Ottoman Turks conquered Constantinople. In 1934, the structure was turned into a museum.

What architectural and design elements can be seen in Santa Sabina that provide insights into the original design of St. Peter's Basilica?

Virgin (Theotokos) and Child between Saints Theodore and George

Among those works preserved at Saint Catherine's Monastery (Mt. Sinai, Egypt) is the encaustic painting—a technique using wax to carry the color—of the *Virgin (Theotokos) and Child between Saints Theodore and George* (the two soldier saints). Above them, we see two angels looking up at the heavens, and in between them, an architectural structure creates a sense of symmetry in the piece.

The artist used a classic style and modeled the faces. Although the image appears flat, there is a sense of depth when looking at the throne's shadow, the footrest, and the slightly-twisted bodies.

A "hierarchy of bodies" is presented as the saints stand erect, looking directly at the viewer as if they are expecting something, whereas the Virgin's eyes are averted, and she does not make eye contact with anyone. The angels are focused on God's hand above and seem otherworldly as their rendering is almost transparent in contrast to the other figures. This creates visual movement: first inwards from the saints to the Virgin, then upwards toward the most sacred element in the scene. The viewer almost partakes in the scene, completing the journey from Earth to Heaven.

4.3. Early Medieval Art

Merovingian Looped Fibulae

A *fibula* is a brooch Roman soldiers wore to hold their cloaks in place. It consists of a body, pin, and catch.

During the early middle ages (c. 500–800 CE), ornate fibulae became some of the most common objects found during the Migration Period, when Europe was Christianized and the Roman Empire split as the Romans' existence evaporated in the West and others became part of the Byzantine Empire.

The Merovingian (Frankish) fibulae present the cloisonné—meaning 'partitioned' in French—a technique characterized by inlaid semi-precious stones. Wires are soldered onto a metal base, and the areas created are then filled with polished stones.

This particular piece is decorated with eagles, which was a popular motif during the Middle Ages. As a symbol of the Roman Empire, it was adopted due to its connotations of status and power. The top edges are shaped like eagle heads, and similarly, stylized eagle heads are used to create the loops on the other end of each pin. The main body presents a small fish. The eyes of the eagles use garnets in addition to multiple gems used in the rest of the fibulae.

Lindisfarne Gospels

It is believed that in the scriptorium of Lindisfarne, England, a medieval monk copied the codex of the Gospels of Matthew, Mark, Luke, and John created in Italy. It took this monk six years to copy the Latin script and add the images—curvaceous forms that overlap into an illusion of a third dimension—of snakes and birds.

Produced in the British Isles from 500–900 CE, the piece is an example of Insular and Hiberno-Saxon artwork. During this time of political conflict and invasions, the monks often read from the Gospels as part of rituals on Holy Island, where a Christian community held the shrine of the bishop St. Cuthbert.

The piece consists of 259 recorded Gospels with full-page illustrations of each evangelist. These pages are highly-ornamental, with large crosses in the background and the Gospels introduced by a historiated initial. In addition, the codex holds 16 pages of canon tables with correlating passages, side-by-side, to compare the narrations from each evangelist.

An inscription by Aldred, a priest from a priory at Durham, states that Eadfrith—a bishop of Lindisfarne (c. 698 CE)—produced the codex in honor of God and St. Cuthbert. Similarly, Aldred created the earliest known English Gospels after he inscribed a vernacular translation between the Latin lines.

The series of repetitive knots and spirals around a centered cross, seemingly mesmerizing, allows the viewer to imagine the devout monks entering a trance-like state while creating the swirls during meditative contemplation of the patterns in the book of Matthew. Eadfrith placed wine-glass shapes horizontally and vertically beside the intricate weave of the knots. Taking a closer look, the knots reveal themselves as snakes, curling in and around tubular forms while their mouths clamp down on their bodies. The bodies change color from blue to green and gold in between. The cross—outlined in red and outstretched arms that press against the page edges—transforms the repetitive patterns into a meditative force.

The book of Luke's first page presents spiraling forms and vortexes while also teeming with animal life. Similar to Matthew's incipit, the pages are characterized by knots that reveal themselves as snakes stealthily moving around each letter's edges. Blue shapes rotate in a repetitive vortex of a large 'Q' leading to the opening sentence. The page includes birds and a knot that encloses a rectangle on the far right and unravels into a heron's chest in the shape of a comma. This shape is repeated vertically down the column, transforming the comma into a cat's paw at the bottom. The cat's body is acrobatically twisted at 90 degrees as it stares at the written words on the page.

In contrast to his incipit page is Luke's portrait page, where the curly-haired evangelist is seated on a red-cushioned stool in front of a plain background. He is holding a quill, poised to write on the scroll on his lap, his feet hanging above a red-legged tray. His purple robe is streaked with red, and a golden halo is behind his head, signifying his divinity. A blue-winged calf—symbolic of Christ's crucifixion—is flying above his head; the bovine is holding a green parallelogram between his forelegs.

Art historians argue that Eadfrith included symbols in each evangelist's portrait. Whereas Matthew is a man, portraying the human aspect of Christ, Mark is a lion, symbolic of Christ of the Resurrection's divinity and triumph. John is the eagle that signifies Christ's second coming.

John's Gospel opens with a page decorated with stacked birds underneath the crosses. A prominent bird is shown with blue and pink stripes, contrasting the others that sport registers of feathers. Interestingly, in Medieval times, stripes had negative associations, as they appeared disordered and chaotic. Therefore, the mentally disturbed, prostitutes, criminals, sorcerers, and hangmen were often portrayed in stripes.

4.4. Romanesque Art

Church of Sainte-Foy

The Church of Sainte-Foy—Saint Faith—is an important church on the route to Santiago de Compostela in Northern Spain. Its importance took form as a pilgrimage, and it is also an abbey because the church forms part of a monastery where monks lived, prayed, and worked. While the monastery did not survive, the church remained intact. The construction of the church began around 1100 CE and was completed around 1150 CE. Featuring a barrel-vaulted nave lined with arches in the interior, the overall style is defined as Romanesque.

The main feature of the Church of Sainte-Foy is the cruciform plan, which is symbolic of the cross, and also regulates the flow of the crowds of pilgrims. (Pilgrims enter at the west and then circulate towards the apse on the east.)

A prominent message is carved into the tympanum above the central entrance. *The Last Judgment* shows Christ as judge, enthroned in the center with his right hand pointing upwards—signifying the saved—while his left-hand points down—signifying the damned. The scene acts as a reminder of Heaven and Hell. Christ is accompanied by Mary, Peter, some saints, and presumably the founder of the monastery.

Another important element is the reliquary of Saint Foy. This container—one of the most famous in Europe—holds the remains of a saint. Originally, the reliquary was located in a monastery in Agen, but to attract more wealth and visitors to Conques, monks plotted to steal the famous artifact. At the age of 12, Sainte Foy was sentenced to death for refusing to sacrifice to Pagan gods, becoming a martyr whose remains are held in the reliquary in Southern France.

The church and its artifacts remind us of the pilgrims' rituals of Medieval faith. Many still travel to the church to pay their respects to Saint Foy, and a celebration is held every October.

Bayeux Tapestry

The *Bayeux Tapestry* was embroidered on linen in Romanesque Europe from 1066–1080 CE. The tapestry was created from images described in manuscripts found in Canterbury in 1070 CE.

This tapestry depicts the battle of Hastings in 1066 CE, and the events that led up to it. The scenes show the conqueror of England, William, the Duke of Normandy, and his battle with Harold, the Earl of Wessex. William became the first Norman king of England, presumably shown in the last piece of the tapestry that is missing.

Being an important piece within the generation of the war, the tapestry was the first to be created so close to the event. Historians believe the patron who ordered its creation was the Bishop of Bayeux, Odo, the half-brother of William. They believe this because in the piece the Normans are presented in a good light, and Odo appears in scenes with the words "ODO EPISCOPUS (EPS)."

Originally, the artwork was produced to commemorate the victories and spoils of the Norman kings. Presently, it is used as a depiction of the war in 1066 CE.

However, unlike true tapestry, the image was not woven into the cloth. Instead, the scenes and text were embroidered—a method of sewing wool yarn—into the linen sheet. It is believed that Anglo-Saxon embroiderers were responsible for the high-quality needlework.

The scenes are described as "A continuous narrative presents multiple scenes of a narrative within a single frame and draws from manuscript traditions such as the scroll form" (Tanton, 2015).

While the unrealistic figures' skin has been left the color of the tapestry, eight additional colors can be seen: blue-green, buff, dark blue, dark green, gray-blue, light green, terracotta, and yellow.

There is no sense of depth in the piece, but the one-dimensional image is split into three sections—a thin stroke at the top and bottom and a broader middle—to portray space perception. Additionally, the top and bottom sections act as borders.

The artwork incorporates 75 scenes with the Latin *tituli* (names) inscribed. Including "First Meal," which shows the battle preparations. In this depiction, Bishop Odo is blessing the meal, dining practices are shown, there are examples of armor and food preparation, there are images of servants serving food, and there is also William, shown enjoying the banquet.

"Cavalry" portrays William's use of cavalry that can advance quickly and retreat easily, scatter the opponents' defenses, wear mail shirts and conical steel helmets with a protective plate over their noses, and carry shields and spears. These scenes also show foot soldiers who carry spears and axes, armorless horses, and mortally-wounded men that lie in the mid-bottom section of the tapestry. It is further described: "... air fills with arrows and lances, men lie dying. The English soldiers, who are all on foot, protect themselves with a wall of shields. The Normans attack from both sides. The lower border of the tapestry is filled with dead and injured soldiers" (Tanton, 2015).

What are the main elements present in the Byzantine liturgy of the Eucharist as portrayed in the San Vitale?

4.5. Gothic Art

Chartres Cathedral

Built on the site of a Roman temple—which itself was allegedly built on the site of a Druidic temple—the Chartres Cathedral has been used for Christian worship since 200 CE, and has an everlasting association with the Virgin Mary.

In the ninth century, this church received the tunic of Mary—known as the "Sancta Camisia"—that greatly advanced their popularity among pilgrims, thus making them quite rich.

The original cathedral burned down in 1194 CE, but the tunic was discovered unharmed three days later. The town's people saw this as a divine message and requested that the church be rebuilt as grandly as possible to become the worship place of Mary. The reconstruction started around 1220 CE.

The floorplan of the building shows a Latin cross, with an ambulatory, a short transept, and three aisles. The nave is supported by double flying buttresses and includes a three-part elevation of a nave arcade, clerestory, and triforium; instead of a four-part elevation that consists of a gallery, the architect wanted to create more space for stained glass windows.

Overall, the structure shows typical Gothic elements, incorporating pointed arches and ribbed vaults, intended to move the viewer's eyes upward. The structure is based on a cruciform basilica with a transept intersecting the nave—the largest in France at 121 feet high—and a total of nine doors. The focus in this building was on creating open spaces with thinner walls and geometry and, using perfect proportions to simulate harmony and balance.

The architects aimed to create a "Heaven on Earth" design (Harris & Zucker, 2015d), making the Chartres Cathedral one of the best Gothic examples in the world.

On the west-facing facade, part of the Roman cathedral still stands with its thick walls, small windows, and Golden Ratio proportions.

The doorways are decorated with reliefs of kings and queens of the *Old Testament* attached to columns. All of this resembles Gothic ornamentation, incorporating non-naturalistic spiritual beings that seem to levitate, their drapery obscuring their vertically stretched-out bodies. These figures act as 'gatekeepers,' keeping a kind eye on people who enter the church.

Being the first cathedral with exposed flying buttresses that determined the exterior aesthetic—instead of concealing them, the typical style in previous structures—the Chartres Cathedral was a breakthrough for Gothic architecture. The extensive flying buttresses allowed for large stained-glass windows that made people feel surrounded by light. This was seen as a divine symbol and spiritual presence because its immaterial beauty was the closest thing to a divine realm; and as the light entered the windows, it cast colorful patterns inside the church through the vibrantly colored stained panels. A large rose stained-glass window decorates the north transept specifically, depicting the Virgin Mary with her son, Jesus, and four thrones with the Kings of Judea and angels above and several prophets surrounding them below.

Intricate figures—including both Romanesque and Gothic styles—decorate the north portal. The pre-fire Romanesque sculptures show God speaking the Word, which then turns into written material that tells of the time before Jesus was born. It also depicts Mary's life, including her infancy, Mary holding baby Jesus, her crowning in the tympanum, and her ascension to Heaven. The post-fire Gothic-style sculptures present elongated, intricately draped figures of *Old Testament* prophets who foresaw the birth of Jesus. These figures show greater emotional expressions and interact with each other, depicting their didactic purposes.

However, the main purpose of Chartres Cathedral was to act as a pilgrimage site and was built with the effective flow of large crowds in mind. The aisles allowed pilgrims to walk around the church, view the relic (Sancta Camisia), and exit without walking in front of the altar. Pilgrimages were embarked upon in the Middle Ages by those seeking to attain good health, get divine goodwill, and ensure their place in Heaven. The figures and stories depicted on the stained-glass windows of the cathedral were intended to aid in the pilgrims' journey, whereas the figures (specifically 'gatekeepers') reminded them of the ever-present eyes of God. The didactic stories from the *Old and New Testaments* were helpful with conveying meaning to the illiterate majority.

Bible Moralisée, Dedication Page: Blanche of Castile and King Louis IX of France

The *Bible Moralisée* is filled with thousands of illustrated images, each representing a few sentences of biblical text, in addition to illustrations speaking of an interpreted paragraph of each story, called a "gloss" or "commentary text." Commentary authors often compared biblical events with events that took place in the Middle Ages, so that the text could be understood better by Medieval individuals. The illustrations of the biblical scenes and commentary scenes are depicted in eight circles—called roundels—divided between short snippets of either biblical or commentary text on each page.

The three-volume series of bibles, called moralized bibles, were created in France and Spain during the 13th century.

The unusually large number of illustrations allowed this to be among the most expensive manuscripts of the Middle Ages. As no one else would have been able to afford it, these works were mainly commissioned by members of royal families, including Balance of Castile and King Louis IX of France.

A dedication page inside the *Bible Moralisée* shows Blanche of Castile and her son, the youthful crowned King Louis IX of France at the top, and below them, a cleric and a scribe. Each figure sits under a trefoil arch with stylized and colorful buildings and has a background of burnished gold. This page symbolized a sophisticated city, such as Paris, which was, at that time, the capital of the Capetian kingdom. (The Capetians were one of the oldest royal French families.)

How does Procopius describe the dome of Hagia
Sophia in relation to its visual effect?

On this page, the king and his queen-mother wear traditional Medieval crowns decorated with stylized lilies and irises, signifying the French monarch's dynastic, political, and religious right to rule, called "fleur-de-lis." The queen is gesturing to her son on the right, with her hand raised in his direction, suggesting that she is dedicating the manuscript to the young king. The king, looking back at his mother, is holding a fleur-de-lis topped scepter in his right hand, symbolizing his kingship. In his left hand, he is holding a small golden coin, referencing the king's coronation in 1226 CE, as French royals often gave the presiding bishop of Reims 13 golden coins at the mass after their coronation ceremony.

This scene is similar to that of the Virgin Mary and Jesus sitting side-by-side on their thrones as celestial rulers of Heaven, especially prevalent in tympana carved from ivory, wood, or stone. When seeing the illustration in the moralized bible, a connection is made between the earthly queen and son, and the heavenly Queen Mary and Jesus.

4.6. Gothic Art in Italy

Arena (Scrovegni) Chapel

The Arena (Scrovegni) Chapel's walls and ceiling are covered with frescoes. Each scene uses flat figures and trompe l'oeil—using verisimilitude to deceive the viewer of the object's reality—to tell a narrative. Fake marble panels are used to separate the narratives, but it is a continuing fresco. The chapel is called "Arena" because it was built

How did the artist of the *Virgin (Theotokos) and Child between Saints Theodore and George* create a sense of depth in the painting?

on the grounds of an ancient Roman amphitheater (arena), and the Scrovegni family claimed ownership of the chapel as their palace had been built next to it.

The frescoes were commissioned by Enrico Scrovegni and were painted by Giotto around 1305 CE. As the son of a banker and being a banker himself, Scrovegni presumably requested the frescoes to atone for usury—charging interest for a loan—as it was seen as a sin. He worried about the afterlife because his father appeared in Dante's inferno and spent a great amount of money on the artwork. Part of his motivation was to "buy" a spot in Heaven. Additionally, the paintings were private devotional art.

Expensive materials were used, including lapis lazuli for the bright blue eyes. However, secco—or dry—fresco was used, as Enrico Scrovegni did not want the lapis lazuli to diminish. However, this method caused the artwork to fade from the walls.

The three narratives are divided into registers. This includes a top register that depicts Christ's maternal grandparents—Yoakim and Anna—and the life of Mary. The central section shows the life and miracles of Jesus's life and created a rhythm as he moved forward through the scenes. The bottom register depicts the Passion and Lamentation, whereas the lowest section of the chapel shows virtues and vices, with the wall opposite the altar depicting the Last Judgment.

The Last Judgment includes Enrico Scrovegni on the side of the blessed, handing over the chapel to the three Marys. The artificial paneling and illusionism create an earthly setting that breaks the overwhelming gold background typical in the Medieval Era. There is also a sense of humanism as the figures interact with one another and connect (crying, holding each other, kissing, etc.).

The Lamentation presents the time when Jesus was mourned by Mary and all Christian followers. The artwork portrays their grief realistically, unlike former Medieval representations that placed a focus on divinity and not dread. This image clearly depicts a mother holding her son, believing she will never see him again. Giotto accurately depicted her grief and humanistic emotions, having Mary hold Jesus as she supported him on her knee. Other figures are also seen acting out their grief; some with their hands thrown up in the air, sobbing and pitying Mary, and angels that are tearing at their hair and clothes in despair. The artist used lines—for instance, the hills—to direct the viewer's eyes to Jesus. Giotto included two figures with their backs to the viewer—which was very unusual for the Medieval style—and creates an illusion of space as they are joining us to look at Christ. This particular scene also incorporates symbolism. We see a dead tree—assuming it will grow again—that represents the rising of Christ. Additionally, the mountain continues into the next scene, showing the Resurrection.

The artwork is considered transitional because it is one of the first to present divine characters in humanist ways through the presence of intimacy in their depictions. Traditionally, Medieval art showed no realism, focused on simplicity, and removed all emotion. This piece

Why are Akhenaten and his family perceived to have
unusual anatomy in the art pieces depicting them?

uses foreshortening, a sense of depth, figures almost appear 3D-like, earthly settings, and architectural elements. The chapel leads us into the start of the Renaissance movement.

4.7. Late Medieval Art

Röttgen Pietà

Intended to create an emotional response, the *Röttgen Pietà* is a 34.5-inch-high painted wood sculpture created between 1300–1325 CE. This was a time known for its dramatism.

This sculpture portrays a scene of the Virgin Mary holding the crucified body of Christ on her lap. The artwork contains intense emotion, mysticism, and spirituality. The crown of sharp thorns and well-executed bloody wounds enhance the piece's violent and gruesome theme.

The sculpture has suffered damage, showing faded patches of paint and holes in Mary's head. However, the fact that it was made from wood is what makes it most unique, as many Pieta sculptures from Germany were made of marble or stone at that time.

The Lamentation of Christ is represented without a background, forcing the viewer to focus on the emotion expressed in the scene. It was intended to be the object of focus during prayer. Common in German abbeys, it is likely that the piece was placed on an altar along with other religious sculptures.

> What technique was used in creating the painting of the *Virgin (Theotokos) and Child between Saints Theodore and George?*

In the sculpture, Mary does not look optimistic, unaware that Christ will be resurrected. While she is still young, she is clothed in heavy fabric and shows intense suffering. Jesus is skinny, contorted, and his ribs are showing. This presentation of Christian thoughts was called "the patient Christ" (Ross, 2015).

Depictions of Jesus before this demonstrated his triumph, following with the Greco Crucifixion that showed Jesus on the cross with legs crossed. It was the principle that Christ's suffering not be apparent. However, this changed as artists started to believe that there was a connection to God through experiencing emotions.

Golden Haggadah

During Late Medieval Spain, around 1320 CE, the *Golden Haggadah* (narration) was created to depict The Plagues of Egypt, Liberation, and the Preparation for Passover. The artwork consisted of gold leaf and pigment on vellum (an illuminated manuscript).

Each Christian gothic image in the piece is on a golden background. It is characterized by the long-bodied figures and the small architectural details.

The series of 56 miniatures were painted in Barcelona, Spain, and were mostly used in homes. Those who owned these depictions were considered among the wealthy.

The *Golden Haggadah* depicted the Passover—the salvation from slavery—which was read at Seder and stands as a testament to the importance of Jewish culture and beliefs in Medieval Spain.

This was a piece of Jewish art in the Late Romanesque/Gothic period. Jewish patrons mostly used Christian artists to produce work in sacred books because art was justified by being didactic at the time.

4.8. Islamic Medieval Art

Great Mosque at Cordoba

Starting in 786 CE and expanding late into the 9th and 10th centuries, the Great Mosque at Cordoba is known locally as *Mezquita-Catedral.*

The mosque is one of the oldest buildings from the Umayyads—the first Islamic dynasty—still standing. It consists of a large hypostyle prayer hall filled with seemingly endless rows of two-tiered columns and arches constructed from alternating white and red voussoirs (a tapered stone). The geometric patterns make the interior seem magnified and provide a sense of monumentality.

The mosque is used for worship, where followers pray toward an exquisitely decorated horseshoe-arched niche in the wall called a "mihrab." The mihrab indicated the qibla—the direction of the Kaaba—that faces Mecca. Bands of calligraphy—inscriptions from the *Quran*—are made from gold tesserae, making it the focal point in the hall.

Furthermore, the mosque incorporates a ribbed dome—signifying the celestial canopy—above the mihrab. The dome is constructed of crisscrossed arches that reflect the Islamic civilization's architectural and mathematical accomplishments; geometry is used for artistic inspiration. The dome is decorated with a radial pattern of gold mosaic. There is a courtyard with a fountain in the middle, and an orange grove. A covered walkway circles the courtyard, accompanied by a minaret—a bell tower used to call individuals to prayer—and a minbar.

There is a steady rhythm created by a repetition of elements, such as arches, columns, and voussoirs. This also symbolizes the patterns of prayer—for example, the recitation of the Shahada—and alludes to the permanence of the mosque and religious practices.

The building illustrates Islamic mosaics and tesserae. Additionally, it represents the combination of religion and cultural fusion. The artists incorporated ancient Roman columns and horseshoe arches, the hypostyle hall was recycled from the original Christian church, and some of the original interior elements were re-used.

Art historians believe the mosque was built on the site of a former Roman temple to the god Janus. The structure was erected to symbolize the permanent presence of the Umayyads after turning the previous Christian church—built by Visigoths in 572 CE—into a mosque. This made a statement about the existence and power of the Islamic rulers of the time.

Pyxis of al-Mughira

The *Pyxis* was produced from the workshops of the artists of the
Madinat Al-Zahra—among the wealthiest cities under Ummyad
rule— around 968 CE in Umayyad-ruled Spain. It is carved from
ivory and stands six inches tall and four inches wide. The piece is
also inlaid with jade and other precious stones.

Ivory—part of the Mediterranean art tradition—was a highly-de-
sired material for the creation of pyxides (the plural of 'pyxis') as it is
durable, easily carved, smooth, and looks elegant. (A pyxis is a por-
table cylindrical container of perfume and cosmetics initially gifted
to members of the royal family during important ceremonies, such
as weddings, births, or the Mughira coming of age.) Later, ivory
objects became Caliphal gifts to allies who converted to Islam and
swore their allegiance to the Umayyad Caliphs.

Each pyxis usually contained human and animal figures that were
carved around four eight-lobed medallions depicting princely iconography. While Islamic art is often considered aniconic, figures
included animals that were hunted, birds, falcons, goats, griffins,
and peacocks, all playing an important role.

The artwork is currently held at the Louvre Museum in Paris.

Alhambra

The Alhambra is built on a hill overlooking Granada and consists of three palaces, each covered with ornamentation. It was built in the Nasrid Dynasty during 1232–1492 CE.

The palaces include the Comares Palace, the Palace of the Lions, and the Partal Palace. The structure acted as a residence of the Nasrid sultans, a citadel (Barracks), and a connection to Medina.

The Comares Palace incorporates a geometric pattern of inlaid tiles on the interior walls, an arched grill that acts as a light source, and the Hall of the Ambassadors (Salón de Comares).

The Palace of the Lions was a separate building—built by Muhammed V—that was eventually connected to the main structure. A central marble fountain is covered by an arched patio, and the structure contains residential halls with star motifs. The Hall of the Two Sisters has 16 windows and 5,000 muqarnas—ornamental vaults—that reflect light, and despite its name, was mainly used as a music room or for receptions. In the Hall of Kings, the ceiling is supported by muqarnas.

The Partal Palace is also referred to as the portico because of its main feature: a portico in the center of an arcade beside a pool.

The Generalife refers to the main vegetable and ornamental garden. The name is derived from the Arabic term for paradise gardens, "janat al-arifa."

What is unique about the Lindisfarne Gospels in
terms of its artistic style and production period?

Additionally, the site holds numerous courtyards, fountains, gardens, and water pools.

Decoration on the site includes the extensive use of geometric shapes—specifically a rhombus—and calligraphy. The walls contain rich ceramics, plasterwork, and intricately-carved wooden frames. However, the interior is decorated with false arches with no structural purpose.

Alhambra is abbreviated from Qal'at al-Hamra, which means "red fort" (Mirmobiny, 2015a).

Mosque of Selim II

Architects Koca Mimar Sinan Aga and David Aga produced the *Selimiye Mosque* in Edirne, Turkey, around 1567–1575 CE. The piece was commissioned by Sultan Selim II.

The structure measures around 623 x 427 feet. On the southeast and southwest sides of the mosque are two symmetrical square madrasas that serve as Islamic colleges. In between is a square prayer hall that is accessed through a porticoed courtyard, and inside is an ethereal dome that appears as if it is floating.

However, the ethereal dome is inferior to the grand dome, which rests on eight muqarnas-corbelled squinches supported by pillars. The piers inside the building are supported by buttresses—hidden by exterior galleries and porticoes—holding up the heavy dome.

The qibla emphasizes the open interior space, in contrast to traditional mosques. While the placement of the Muezzin's platform in the center of the dome was not traditional, its placement here signifies the surpassing of Christian architecture and created a vertical alignment. The interior of the structure was repainted and decorated with polychrome, Iznik tiles, Ottoman styles, and motifs involving leaves and Chinese clouds.

The structure represents the Ottoman Empire's wealth and power. The area was a popular passing-through place for travelers, and this was an impactful example of Islamic triumph while surpassing the Hagia Sophia and the Byzantine Basilica.

4.9. Renaissance in Europe

How is Christ depicted in *The Last Judgment* carved into the tympanum above the central entrance of the Church of Sainte-Foy?

While many have pinpointed the start of the Renaissance movement to around 140 CE, some artworks started laying the foundation for the movement during the 1200s CE.

Annunciation Triptych (Merode Altarpiece)

Created around 1427–1432 CE in Tournai, South Netherlands, the *Annunciation Triptych* is an oil on oak painting by the workshop of Robert Campin.

The overall size is an average of 25 ⅜ by 46 ⅜ inches.

The center shows a living room in Northern Europe. There is a focus on detailed objects like the aging of the door, the background, nails, rust, shadows, etc. It depicts Mary and Gabriel in a modern context, but it was not meant to secularize the scene but to bring us closer to intimate prayer. The scene depicts Gabriel coming to tell Mary about the birth of Christ. The shiny pot symbolizes Mary's purity, and many other elements suggest a connection to the incarnation. Additionally, there is a small figure coming through the window, holding a cross, representing the holy spirit.

The patrons are depicted on the left wing, and Joseph—working in his workshop—is on the right. The annunciation scene was painted first, then the wings were added.

Oil paint was used to create texture and show the artist's interest in light. There is a lot of realism, yet it is expressed differently. For instance, the perspective of the room does not make sense, there is no mathematical accuracy, and it almost brings the viewer into the image with telescoping and double perspective.

The piece can be folded up and transported. It was made to maintain an interest in physical objects turning into spiritual ideas and to aid in devotion.

The Arnolfini Portrait

Jan van Eyck produced a 32.4 x 23.6-inch oil painting on oak panel in 1434 CE.

While art historians still debate the true function of the piece, there has been documentation of a connection to a wedding. That is why it is often called *The Arnolfini Wedding Portrait*. There is evidence of a sacred event taking place, seen in their actions. Their shoes are removed, their hands joined together, one man seems to be swearing an oath, a single candle in the chandelier signifies God's presence, and a dog—symbolic of fidelity—is present to bless the ceremony.

Other religious symbolism includes prayer beads on the wall and roundels on the mirror depicting biblical scenes. There is also significance in "Jan van Eyck was here" as it seems like he was a witness to the ceremony.

Why was the Church of Sainte-Foy considered an essential stop for pilgrims on their way to Santiago de Compostela?

On the other hand, art historians argue that the scene shows a married couple showing off their wealth. Arnolfini was a rich merchant from Bruges. The image presents high fashion—the figures are wearing furs and heavy clothing, and the wife is wearing a gathered dress—and oranges, which had to be imported and were only available to the wealthy. The patrons are receiving guests in lavish bedrooms, seen in the mirror's reflection, showing off their status and taste.

The husband in the painting is most likely Giovanni Arnolfini, although that is unconfirmed. It shows individuals of a wealthy class living in a prosperous economic town in the 15th century.

The artwork is a Northern Renaissance and Italian Renaissance-inspired piece. The Northern Renaissance movement can be characterized by the lack of perspective and the obsession with human anatomy, attention to detail, and softer use of color, light, and texture. This is also due to glazing, a painting technique where translucent oil paints are layered on top of each other, creating smooth blending and gradations.

The roundels show exquisite detail in even the smaller scenes—for example, the texture of the dog's hair and the wife's gown.

Pazzi Chapel

As part of the Basilica di Santa Croce, the *Pazzi Chapel* was commissioned by the Pazzi family as a centrally-planned space inspired by the Pantheon.

The structure was mainly based on ancient Roman temples, in the revival of Greek and Roman ideals, and represents the Early Renaissance movement. It is built from Pietra Serena Stone to create spatial divisions and geometric shapes all over the floorplan.

Additionally, the artist incorporated Corinthian columns, fluted pilasters, pendentives with glazed roundels—made of clay—depicting the four Evangelists, small barrel vaults, a dome with many windows, and an oculus. The center of the chapel is the dominating space which allows for light to represent divinity entering the chapel. Overall, it feels rational and ordered.

The Pazzi Chapel was designed to be a meeting place for monks—a bench lined the wall for this purpose—and was the burial site for the Pazzi family, physically symbolic of their wealth, power, piety, and status.

David, Donatello

The five-foot bronze statue of *David* was produced by Donatello in 1440 CE. It represents beautiful intimacy and vulnerability with warm tones. Its size allows the viewer to feel closer to the subject. While this is an *Old Testament* subject, its sensuality eliminates the biblical representation thereof.

Donatello portrayed *David's* innocence instead of the gruesomeness you would expect from such events. His facial expression, nudity, and contrapposto stance—reminiscent of the Greeks and Romans—signify intimacy.

How does the *Bayeux Tapestry* portray space
perception within its design?

The statue is detached from the main structure and allows a sense of freedom, where *David* can move through the world, express himself, and communicate with a viewer. A humanistic element that was added to the piece, to be sure.

The message of the artwork is still a debate between pride and thoughtfulness. This is an unexpected representation of the story of David defeating Goliath. Although David just defeated the giant and his army, he appears thoughtful and quiet. His eyes are downcast and do not express a sense of victory; rather, they give off subtle pride. David is reflecting on his defeat and understanding that God's might made him victorious. Additionally, his relaxed contrapposto and the nonchalant placement of his hand represent pride and confidence. His sword is in his right hand as it rests on a victory wreath, signifying his pride.

Donatello was studying ancient Roman art, as he displayed knowledge of the classical contrapposto and large-scale bronze casting. The Middle Ages did not see a human-scale bronze figure until the creation of *David*, as it was the first free-standing nude figure since classical antiquity. (The Middle Ages were focused on God and did not create nude art.)

The statue was placed in a public space, in a high niche in one of the buttresses of the Cathedral of Florence. It was intended to show Christian followers that God will help with challenges. The people of Florence identified with David, as they believed they also defeated their enemy with the wisdom and strength provided by God.

Why do historians believe that the patron of the tapestry was the Bishop of Bayeux, Odo?

Palazzo Rucellai

The architect Leon Battista Alberti was responsible for the Palazzo Rucellai in Florence, Italy. The building was constructed around 1450 CE as part of the "building boom" after the Medici family commissioned the building of their palace (Zappella, 2015c). The creation of palaces at the time was seen as an addition of civic pride to Florence.

However, the Palazzo was never finished, and only three quarters of the original plan was built. It was partly based on the Medici Palace with its three-facade design.

The work aimed to emphasize harmony and intellectual delicacy. The architect filled the structure with geometric shapes and an emphasis on horizontality. The building includes four floors: the Rucellai family's center of business, the guests' residential area, the family's apartment, and the servant quarters hidden on the top floor.

The structure decoration includes the Rucellai family's seal—a diamond with three feathers around it—several times. The interior elements are also mainly based on ancient Greek and Roman ideals, including pilasters, Corinthian, Ionic, and Tuscan capitals, rounded arches, and friezes.

Madonna and Child with Two Angels

This tempera on wood artwork was created by Fra Filippo Lippi around 1465 CE.

It is located in the Uffizi and was commissioned by the Medici family to show their piety and wealth, and to act as a remembrance of Christ's story. The family wanted a humanistic depiction to allow a viewer to relate to Mary and her son, Jesus. Therefore, the artist purposefully painted them in a realistic way, representing their humanity.

Unlike Giotto and Cimabue, Fra Filippo Lippi created simple, thin, white and yellow halos. The scene has no gold or bright lights.

Mary is portrayed as youthful and beautiful, with a fair, sculptured face, blonde hair, a small mouth, a bowed nose, and delicate features. She is leaning forward with her hands clasped in prayer and seems to be looking at the smiling angel. Mary, seated on an ornate piece of furniture, is wearing a translucent cloth headpiece, a green dress with buttons and ruffles, and a thin jeweled crown.

The angels look playful, as one is smiling and the other has half of his face covered, while they are both holding Christ up as he kneels on them. Their wings appear to be wooden rather than feathers. They are wearing loose white tunics, have golden curly hair, and are cherub-like.

Christ is portrayed as a small, fair, and blonde baby looking up at Mary as his arms stretch toward her.

Florence had a lot of money at the time this piece was commissioned, as there was an increase in middle and upper-class merchants and bankers. The city was seen as an ideal city-state, where money allowed for more indulgences and freedom, and many citizens were allowed to participate in the government. Unfortunately, this freedom was threatened often, but luckily, Florence was able to avoid or win the threats. The citizens of Florence were very proud of their government because, in return, it respected their opinions, playing a huge part in humanism.

In Florence, around 1437 CE, Lippi produced a similar painting titled the *Enthroned Madonna and Child* for Corneto Tarquinia, which is currently held in the Galleria Nazionale, Rome. This artwork was influenced by Donatello's sculpture and contemporary Flemish—a portrayal of light and illusionistic details—painting.

Lippi's paintings had a sense of playfulness, and no gold or traditional Medieval elements were found. He intended for the "godly people" to seem relatable (Harris & Zucker, 2015d). The Virgin is brought forward—we see her shadow on the frame like she is in front of it—creating a sense of realism. Further naturalism is produced by making the angels look like children and the background appear earthly.

Birth of Venus

Around 1482–1486 CE, Sandro Botticello—a student of Fra Filippo Lippi—produced *The Birth of Venus*, which is currently held at the Uffizi Gallery in Florence, Italy.

The artwork depicts a golden-haired, pale-skinned, semi-nude Venus—the Roman goddess of love—standing on a white shell. Her lower body is covered to show modesty. She is accompanied by a

Why was the focus of the Chartres Cathedral on creating open spaces with thinner walls and employing perfect proportions?

servant and the wind sprites Zephyr and Aura, the latter two blowing wind from the left.

At this time, images of nude women were only allowed for educational or mythological purposes; this piece functioning as the latter. Botticello aimed at a "radical statement" by not presenting Venus in a Christian context and headed into the Renaissance movement.

Said by De Witte et al. (2015):

> In ancient Greece, although the male nude was certainly more common, the female nude eventually began to gain respectability in the late fourth century BCE. Years later, during the Renaissance, such Italian artists as Sandro Botticelli (c. 1445-1510) revived the appearance of the female nude as it had been depicted in antiquity. (p. 558)

Venus is not presented in a contrapposto stance and stands casually with an almost flexible body. There are a lot of lines that intersect with each other—seen in the waves, the shell, and her clothing—indicating movement created by the wind sprites.

The Last Supper

The *Last Supper* was painted by the painter, sculptor, engineer, architect, and scientist Leonardo da Vinci around 1494–1498 CE. This Early Renaissance painting was produced with oil and tempera—an experimental combination at the time—in Milan, Italy.

Da Vinci challenged the norm by using lead white as a base instead of traditional wet plaster, resulting in brighter colors. However, the paint immediately started deteriorating as it never adhered to the wall. He then added a double layer of dried plaster to achieve detail.

Unfortunately, many elements lead to the artwork's ruin, including its location on the side wall of the Santa Maria Delle Grazie, the materials used, the techniques used to create it, air pollution, humidity, overcrowded tourist viewings, poor restoration, and a bomb that hit the monastery in 1943 CE, during World War II, that destroyed a large section of the building. Presently, only 42.5% of Da Vinci's work remains, 17.5% is lost, and 40% includes added restoration.

Linear perspective is used, achieving perfect perspective at Christ's level, as it is viewed at 15 feet in the air. There is a strong sense of depth, and the viewer's eyes are drawn to the vanishing point behind Christ's head. The composition is mathematically unified as Christ's body also forms an equilateral triangle, symbolic of the holy trinity.

Da Vinci used the "sfumato" technique—using slightly different tones of glazing to create flawless gradients—and accurate light and shadows (chiaroscuro).

The image depicts the 12 apostles sitting at a long dining table as they react to Christ's comment: "One of you will betray me" (Zucker & Harris, 2015b). At the center, Jesus is composed—representing his ethereal nature—and his apostles are divided into four highly expressive groups around him.

During the High Renaissance Period, which was inspired by classical ideals, monks silently ate while viewing the painting, inspiring contemplation about religion. It was intended to show unity between the eternal and the mortal worlds but also represent the chaos of humanity compared to the greatness of the divine.

Adam and Eve

Produced by Albrecht Durer—who revolutionized printmaking, woodcuts, intaglio prints, and reproducible media—in 1507 as oil paintings on a pair of wooden panels.

Durer was proud of his German identity and often expressed his love of Italian and Classical traditions in his work.

The woodcut of *Adam and Eve* portrays more about the Renaissance movement in Germany than Genesis. Their stances show an understanding of classical proportions, and Durer somehow sacrifices naturalism to highlight his knowledge of Vitruvian—the distance between human features—ideals.

Sketches indicate that Durer originally designed two separate figures that present a "perfect" male and female, later experimenting with a single composition of the two engravings.

The image shows nude figures standing in contrapposto, presenting naturalism as they look at each other. Italian Renaissance characteristics are seen, including perfect physical proportions of the bodies, symmetrical frontal poses, and obvious ancient Greek inspiration.

Art historians state that the four animals represent four 'humors:' choleric, melancholic, phlegmatic, and sanguine. Around this time, it was theorized that all humans possessed all four humors and that your personality was determined by the predominant one you possessed. Durer represented choleric—easily angered and feminine—as a cat, melancholic—despondent and irritable—as an elk, phlegmatic—calm—as an ox, and sanguine—courageous and hopeful—as a rabbit. This is symbolic of how humans are connected to nature.

Erwin Panofsky deciphered Durer's artwork first. Set in a German-inspired forest scene, Adam's grasp at a mountain ash is symbolic of the Tree of Life. This is contrasted with the fig tree at the center, signifying the tree of knowledge. Eve is plucking an apple-like fruit with fig leaves from the tree, additionally depicting the seductive serpent—signifying evil—placing the forbidden fruit in Eve's hands. There are six animals and a parrot—symbolic of discernment and the antidote to evil—and a small sign (cartellino) hanging from a branch in the mountain ash. Along with the four humors, the mouse represents male weakness, while the mountain goat symbolizes damnation.

Preparatory drawings of the figures and animals show the artist's research of form and narrative.

What does the fleur-de-lis topped scepter in King Louis IX's right hand symbolize the *Bible Moralisée* dedication page?

Sistine Chapel Ceiling and Altar Wall Frescoes

Every surface of the *Sistine Chapel* is covered in Renaissance-inspired frescoes and mosaics. The chapel is where the College of Cardinals decides who the next pope is.

The ceiling is covered in frescoes depicting nine Old Testament scenes, separated by painted architectural frames. These frescoes were created by Michelangelo around 1508 for Pope Julian. His work continued for four years but came to a halt in 1510. The continuation of frescoes after that was different, as can be seen between the complex narrative and small figures of *The Deluge* and the idealized and monumental style used in *God Creates Adam*.

Michelangelo used a technique involving "carving figures out of paint," and he revolutionized this realistic painting style by making the figures appear like sculptures (Zappella, 2015a). Using bright colors and massive figures that give a sense of weight and presence, the artist showed the idealized beauty of ancient Greek and Roman sculpture, the religious optimism of the time, an emphasis on musculature, and the drama of human anatomy.

The complete layout includes nine scenes from Genesis, starting with God's division between day and night. Moving along the length of the ceiling, we see God creating the sun and planets, God dividing water from the earth, God creating Adam, the creation of Eve, Adam and Eve are tempted and banished from Eden, the Deluge, Noah's family making a sacrifice after the flood, and then Noah being drunk and disgraced.

On both sides, the scenes are flanked by prophets and Sybils—pagan future-seers that foretold the coming of Christ—sitting in the spandrels. On each of the architectural framework's four corners are ignudi, or nude males. Scenes from the Salvation of Israel are depicted in the pendentives. These scenes were painted after the break in 1510 and show a new style of monumentality.

School of Athens

Created around 1509–1511 CE by Raphael, this fresco is found at the Stanza Della Segnatura at the Vatican in Italy.

The artwork was created during the High Renaissance movement when Italy was still experiencing cultural growth. This was before the Protestant Reformation, which created uncertainty about salvation and how to reach it, as we can see in Michelangelo's painting on the Sistine Chapel's altar (c. 1530 CE).

Just before the Reformation, Raphael's *School of Athens* presented the greatness of Pagan wisdom and the papal library. It was originally titled *Philosophy* because it stood above a bookshelf containing Julius II's philosophy books.

The four walls of the Stanza Della Segnatura depict the four branches of knowledge: justice, philosophy, poetry, and theology. The ceiling portrays four allegorical figures representative of these four branches.

The architecture in *The School of Athens* was inspired by the surrounding Roman ruins, including the Basilica and the Baths of Caracalla.

The painting also shows all of the great philosophers of antiquity in a classical space. Aristotle and Plato are at the center—with the vanishing point between them—drawing the viewer's eyes toward their discussion. Plato, the most famous teacher of Aristotle, is identified by his copy of *Timaeus* in his hand—a book he wrote c. 360 BC—while he points up toward the sky. He wears purple and red robes, symbolic of air and fire, and focuses on the ethereal and theoretical. His student, Aristotle, is focused on the physical and observable, pointing toward the ground while wearing blue and brown robes, symbolic of water and earth.

This divides the painting into the theoretical philosophers, including Pythagoras, on Plato's side, and the philosophers focused on the concrete, like Euclid, on Aristotle's. Furthermore, Plato's side incorporates classical sculptures of Apollo, the god of the sun, music, and poetry. Aristotle's side depicts Athena, the goddess of war and wisdom. This division creates an almost empty space in the center and adds to the balance of the linear perspective.

This scene, among Raphael's other works, glorified the history and sharing of knowledge. He regularly emphasized wisdom in his work. This piece also demonstrates Renaissance perfection and acts as a remembrance of the harmonious and idealized elements of antiquity.

Isenheim Altarpiece

This artwork was created between 1512–1516 CE, during the German Christian period, and is accredited to Matthias Grünewald and Nikolaus of Hagenauer. It is currently housed in France.

The front of the altarpiece presents a red-robed figure standing on the far left beside a Corinthian column; Christ's crucifixion is depicted in the center. The scene is macabre and dramatic. On Christ's left side are three individuals looking up at him in anguish. The woman in white clothing is the Virgin Mary fainting into St. John's—the Evangelist—arms. On his right side, we see the lamb of God—symbolic of Christ—standing beside another red-robed man—John the Baptist—who is pointing at Jesus while holding a manuscript. The predella—base of the altar—shows Christ's dead body held by some people next to a grave. On the far right, an old bearded man in blue and red robes is holding a staff.

The back of the altarpiece depicts a woman in a black dress on the far left, next to an angel-like robed figure. The center image shows a woman in a pink dress playing a guitar-like instrument as she is surrounded by other figures playing instruments at the back. To her right is Mary and the baby Jesus sitting in a blue-skied and bright orange landscape. The far-right image shows a divine figure rising above fallen bodies, presumably the crucified Christ, as his hands and feet show similar wounds.

The altarpiece was created as the central object of devotion in a hospital in Isenheim and was commissioned by the Brothers of St. Anthony. It was intended to facilitate public prayer and inspire hope.

Entombment of Christ

Produced by Jacopo da Pontormo between 1525–1528 CE, the *Entombment of Christ* is an oil painting on wood.

It is located above the altar in the Capponi Chapel. The chapel is cubical and logically laid out. While the chapel's structure and interior frescoes are reminiscent of the Renaissance movement, the artwork in focus upon entry was created in a Mannerist style.

Mannerism directly succeeded the Renaissance and preceded the Baroque styles. It is characterized by pieces that show overelaborate distortion, elongated figures, and an imbalance that contradicts the perfect proportions of the Renaissance. Mannerism was a response to the Protestant Reformation. Mannerism is known as the art of artifice, where it is manifested through imbalanced layouts, complexity, an abandonment of convention, and the use of ambiguous space.

The altarpiece shows a mournful representation. The frescoes beside it portray the Annunciation—the beginning of Christ's life—and the end thereof. The scene shows very little background as it is packed with people, highlighting Mannerism. Whether it is a depiction of the Deposition or Entombment is unclear because there is no cross.

The artwork lacks the pyramid balance seen in the High Renaissance and presents constant movement, exaggerated emotions, and seemingly weightless figures.

Venus of Urbino

Produced by Titian around 1538 CE, the *Venus of Urbino* uses layered oil paint on canvas to depict a variety of lighting, as well as to highlight the contrast between different rich colors.

The art piece was commissioned by Duke Urbino Guidobaldo II Della Rovere as a gift for his new wife. It represented how the duke believed a wife should behave as a sexual, respectful, and motherly individual to her husband and children.

A nude female—named Venus to enable the artist to paint her nude—takes up most of the painting as she directly gazes at the viewer, drawing them into the painting.

The focus is on Venus, while there is a darker backdrop on the left and a lighter scene of a woman and a child—signifying fidelity and motherhood—on the right. Venus' body is unrealistic, given that her torso is very large, but her feet are unusually small. It acted as a symbol of beauty; therefore she was depicted naked.

While Venus is styled with many curves, the rest of the painting is very linear. The artwork portrays perfect Venetian art—art in Venice—that shows deep, rich colors and the use of lighting and shadows. Artists in this genre usually used glazing to create subtle changes in gradients as well as to create a large variety of different colors.

Allegory of Law and Grace

Finished in 1529 CE, the *Allegory of Law and Grace* is a woodcut
and letterpress piece by the most influential artist of the 16th century, Lucas Cranach the Elder.

It is currently located in Germany and was produced during the
Northern Renaissance movement when iconoclasts stormed through
the churches and thousands of religious artworks were destroyed.

The painting depicts two nude figures beside a tree in the center.
The scene shows a division between a dying tree—signifying the
law—on the left and a living tree—signifying the gospel—on the
right. At the bottom, six columns of biblical text are seen.

Furthermore, the left—law—side is symbolic of a man being forced
into Hell by Death and Satan. The image also shows Moses deliver-
ing the *Ten Commandments*, Christ in judgment, and Adam and Eve
while she eats the forbidden fruit. This highlights the association
between the law, death, and damnation. These motifs exemplify that
the law, without faith, will not get you into Heaven.

The right—the gospel—side of the painting shows Christ's cross
crushing Death and Satan, while those around the cross are covered
in the blood of Jesus. A risen Christ triumphantly stands above an
empty tomb as John the Baptist is directing a nude man—stripped
to his soul—toward Christ and the mercy of God.

This artwork was the most influential image of the Lutheran Reformation, initiated by Martin Luther in 1517 CE. It explains Luther's ideas in a visual way, including the idea that Heaven is reached through God's grace and one's faith, and abandons the Catholic ideas that good deeds—like financial contributions—play a role in salvation. Martin Luther believed that, like the law side, financial donations enriched the church and were not a way to salvation. It was due to this debate that art in Catholic churches was ultimately destroyed.

4.10. Protestants' Reformation and Catholic Counter-Reformation

Il Gesù

Il Gesù (Mother Church) and the *Triumph of the Name of Jesus* ceiling fresco can both be found in Rome, Italy. The artist was Giovanni Battista Gaulii, and the architects were Giacomo da Vignola and Giacomo della Porta. The church and the façade were built around 1575–1584 CE; however, the ceiling fresco and stucco figures were not produced until around 1678–1679 CE.

The church functioned as the original place of worship for the Jesuits and as an architectural model for future Jesuit churches. The ceiling fresco is a traditional-style illustration of the beliefs of the Jesuits. It called them to their faith by scaring them into believing. There was a strong emphasis on choosing a path and not refusing it.

The structure is a single-aisle church that allows for a space adequate for traffic flow. The floorplan is cruciform, but the transept is not overly long—like the exact proportions of a cross. The intersection of the nave is covered with a large dome, resulting in a dark interior that is mainly dependent on natural light from the outside.

There is a combination of a Baroque and a rational style. The focus is on the altar in the center, and it is surrounded by Renaissance-style—ornate Corinthian—columns made of rich materials and reused ancient materials (*spolia*).

The Jesuit religion was founded by Saint Ignatius of Loyola, and he needed a church to serve as the center. The religion was seen as a dramatic response to the reformation nearly 100 years prior, with their teachings focused on charitable work, education, and missionaries. Many religious wars were taking place at the time this religion was formed, inescapably having an effect on its ideologies and cultural activities.

The church was funded by Cardinal Farnese, the Pope's grandson, and was to be erected close to the Pantheon and Roman Forum in the center of old Rome.

Hunters in the Snow

In 1565 CE, Pieter Bruegel produced the *Hunter in the Snow* oil on wood painting in Vienna, Austria. The painting resembled the styles of the Realist period. This secular painting was commissioned by Nicaels Jonghelinck.

How does the *Golden Haggadah* represent Jewish
culture and beliefs in Medieval Spain?

The image depicts figures with their backs to the viewer in a contrapposto pose that creates dynamic movement. The viewer's eyes are drawn away from the foreground into the scene by the use of contrasting colors, sharp forms, and less gentle blending. There is a subtle sense of the atmospheric perspective of mountains and hills in the background.

The artwork intended to represent the hardships and enjoyments of winter, portraying activities of everyday life at the time. Additionally, we see a reaction to the Northern Renaissance ideals of religion and nobility.

The scene is part of a six-part series of images known as *Months of the Year*, all of which show figures and houses in warm, earthy tones that contradict the cold blues and grays represented in the surrounding weather. The faces of the figures are intentionally not shown to signify the poor and nameless (homogenized). Viewers see hunters returning from a presumably unsuccessful hunt, as they look exhausted and appear to be sulking. In the back, there are some smaller figures dancing on the ice of the frozen lake, seemingly enjoying winter. This is also in contrast to the sense of despair in the foreground.

Calling of St. Matthew

Produced in 1599–1600 CE by Caravaggio, the *Calling of St. Matthew* is an oil on canvas painting in the Contarelli Chapel in San Luigi dei Francesi, Rome.

The didactic image shows the biblical tale of the calling of Saint Matthew, a former tax collector sitting at a table while counting money. With Saint Peter at his side, Jesus walks in, points at Matthew, singles him out, and calls on him to become a disciple, to which Matthew responds with a gesture of incredulity. The scene takes place in a tavern, making it commonplace, and the characters are all dressed in contemporary—rather than biblical—clothing.

Matthew's story about the "sinner turned follower" aims to relate to the everyday citizen of Rome. Additionally, Caravaggio created the piece in regard to his own vernacular experiences.

Instead of a general ethereal glow, as seen in High Renaissance work, light has an active role in the plot of this piece. It is painted realistically, with light streaming in from an open door behind Jesus. It represents a natural light source and directs the viewer's eyes from Jesus's pointing finger to Matthew's highlighted face.

The story is told from a Catholic perspective, intended to inspire support of the Catholic Reformation. Additionally, the viewer is meant to experience the painting through Caravaggio's use of a commonplace setting, contemporary clothing, and realism, as opposed to the idealism of High Renaissance works. This was meant to create the idea that the Catholic faith was accessible to people of all lifestyles.

The Catholic church rebelled against the Protestant Reformation, started by Martin Luther in 1517 CE. They aimed to draw believers into the Catholic faith and feel an overpowering sense of emotion

> How is Hunefer depicted in *The Last Judgment of Hunefer* papyrus scroll?

to Catholic-inspired art by using drama, expressive theatrics, and shocking beauty.

The artworks followed the ideals of Baroque art, including theatrical frozen actions, high contrast, chiaroscuro, using mainly diagonal lines, and gritty realism.

The Presentation of The Portrait of Marie de'Medici

This artwork is from the Marie de'Medici Cycle created by Peter Paul Rubens in 1622–1625 CE.

The oil on canvas painting measures about 115 x 116 inches. It depicts Marie and a cherub looking at the viewer while establishing the future authority of Marie and her progeny for France. There is a strong vertical axis moving through from Hera at the top, depicting Marie de'Medici's maternal and fertile connection with ideal mothers and wives.

Ruben was inspired by Titian, the Venetian Renaissance painter. He enjoyed portraying the body in contorted and dramatic positions and often depicted historical figures in the classical Greek and Roman styles. There is an emphasis on realism and occasional eroticism in his work, and he was fond of painting exotic prints and wild animals. He was also known for creating rich Baroque-style portraits that depicted his patrons, landscapes that later influenced the Romantic style, religious works, and hunting scenes. He aimed to create a curiosity about emotional aspects in his works and included

How does the design of the Great Mosque at
Cordoba reflect the architectural and mathematical
accomplishments of the Islamic civilization?

iconography, layered allegory, and symbolism in female portraits to
provide them with equal status to the portraits of males.

In the painting, we see the winged god of marriage, Hymen, on the
left, and the god of love, Cupid, on the right, presenting a portrait
of Marie de'Medici to the enamored King Henry IV of Navarre.
Hymen is holding a burning torch in his left hand, which signifies
his passion for love. Cupid is gesturing to Marie while praising her
beauty. Henry IV is smitten and looks at the portrait in adoration.

From above, we see the blissful couple Zeus and Hera looking down
in approval as they lean toward each other with their hands touching
lovingly. The two gods are flanked by their animal symbols, an eagle
with a thunderbolt and a peacock.

A personification—a lady wearing a plumed helmet and a blue robe
with an embroidered fleur-de-lis—of France is standing behind
Henry IV to encourage him to marry for political reasons. Lady
France is whispering into Henry IV's ear to ignore his battles and
marry, that domestic matters are equally important to military ones,
and that it will preserve the monarchy.

While two cherubs (putti) are fiddling with the King's helmet and
sword in the foreground, he obliges to Lady France's encouragement.
In the background, we see a burning town, signifying the remains of
Henry's battle.

This was the sixth painting in a series of 24 pieces about Marie de'Medici's life. King Henry IV was assassinated in 1610 CE, and Marie served as regent to her son Louis XIII until 1617 CE. The biographical series was produced in 1622 CE to mark her return to Paris. She died in exile in 1642 CE.

The painting also incorporated propaganda, as it over-idealized her accomplishments and made her life seem prosperous. In reality, the painting is an idealized depiction of the marriage agreement between Florence and Henry IV in April 1600 for political and financial benefit. Henry IV did not even show up to the wedding ceremony. At nearly 50 years old, Henry had to marry and produce an heir. Furthermore, Henry IV was a Protestant being attacked by the French Catholics and decided to absolve this tension by marrying the Catholic Marie de'Medici.

Self-Portrait with Saskia

Rembrandt, the artist of *Self-portrait with Saskia*, eroded a copper plate with acid and used etching to produce his work. The etching in this piece is deeper for him than Saskia, signifying that he is closer to the viewer and more important.

The art piece comments on the private nature of their relationship, almost as if the viewer is interrupting a moment they had. The image shows a 30-year-old Rembrandt and his wife, Saskia, two years after their marriage. He was a highly experimental artist, and many of his

What does the ribbed dome above the mihrab in
the Great Mosque at Cordoba symbolize?

early etchings present the spontaneity of a rapid sketch. While his style changed greatly over the years, he is famous for his portraits.

Rembrandt rarely depicted himself as a contemporary gentleman because it was against the style of the time. This piece is the first where he shows himself as an artist in the work, allowing us to believe that it was likely etched in a mirror. However, Saskia was often used as a model for his paintings.

San Carlo alle Quattro Fontane

The San Carlo alle Quattro Fontane is a Baroque-style church dedicated to St. Charles Borromeo and the Holy Trinity. The architect was Francesco Borromini, who commenced building in 1638. The church was consecrated in 1646.

The floorplan resembles two triangles inscribed in an oval and includes a façade with three bays. This is seen when three distinct units are stacked together, incorporating an undulating lower level, a standard Greek cross for the middle level, and an oval dome with windows at the base that appears to float above the interior of the church at the top. There is a sophisticated interconnection of geometrical shapes, presenting both mathematical and musical elements, as well as a complex interweaving of rhythms to create illusionistic effects with lighting.

The façade consists of waves and concave bays on the upper part. The bays include sectioned entablature and an oval held at the center by asymmetrically-placed angels. The façade was only completed after Borromini's death. The lower stories consist of two outer concave bays and a convex center with a niche above the entrance. This niche is decorated with a statue of St. Charles Borromeo—produced by Antonio Raggi—and statues of the founders of the Trinitarian order, St. John of Matha and St. Felix of Valois.

The structure includes a series of opposites, such as lower and upper levels, the centers and edges, tall columns with small niches, concave and convex shapes, and the paradox of imagination versus intellect.

The ornamentation includes symmetrical carvings and cherubs with heads and wings but no bodies. Light unifies the white interior.

This was Francesco Borromini's first commission, and was commissioned in 1634. The construction started in 1638–1646, and the façade was not finished until 1677 by Borromini's nephew. Borromini based his design on geometric figures. He was a chief formulator of the Baroque architectural style and was considered a rival of Bernini. Borromini believed in mathematics before everything, emphasizing that geometry, light, and shapes are inseparable.

Ecstasy of Saint Teresa

Gian Lorenzo Bernini produced the *Ecstasy of Saint Teresa* around
1647–1652. The piece is located in the Cornaro Chapel in Santa
Maria della Vittoria, Rome.

This kinetic art sculpture was carved from white marble. It depicts
a canonized Teresa (of Ávila) with a golden arrow tilting downwards
toward her heart. She is accompanied by an angel who is floating
while her body is contorted, and it seems like she is about to moan.
The sun rays behind them represent the holy light of God. The
sculpture includes rock at the base that supports it and expressive
folds in their clothing that resonate with the Baroque style.

The Baroque style is characterized by religious and distorted subject
matters, no central hierarchy, unseen sources of light, dramatism,
unrealistic depictions, no real backdrop, representations of weapons
and chaotic discord instead of order and structure, and the viewer is
forcefully involved by making the artwork relatable to human experience. Saint Teresa lived in Spain in the 16th century, during the
peak of the Reformation; this artwork presents her having a vision of
an angel calling her to come to worship God.

The figures are realistic and dynamic but are not necessarily naturalistic. The flowing fabric of her robe shows the outline of her body
while also covering it. Additionally, her writhing body beneath the
heavy fabric makes it appear as if she had recently collapsed, her eyes
half-lidded and her mouth open in awe and wordless pleasure. The

angel's clothing is whipped up by the wind, adding to the expressive and emotional piece. The scene is not calm and passive; rather, it resembles the *Constanza* bust and *David*.

Bernini was very religious and aimed to help people understand divine ecstasy by using depictions of physical pleasure.

Las Meninas

This artwork was produced by Diego Rodriguez de Silva y Velázquez in 1656. The oil on canvas painting measures roughly 125 x 108 inches and is located in the Museo Nacional del Prado in Madrid. However, it used to reside in the Royal Alcazar of Madrid, specifically in the king's study.

This large painting is interesting in that it shows a painting of the same size as it is being painted. Velázquez used loose brushstrokes that still compose a clear, detailed, and realistic image. He uses an aerial and scientific perspective with the multiplication of light sources.

An informal glimpse of a moment commoners could never see, it was made for the private viewing of the king and queen. It portrays the art of painting by showing an artist at work. Velázquez created a self-portrait representing his status as he places himself in the same room as the royals. He holds a paintbrush that signifies the power in his ability to create the figures, fitting with his desire to be a knight at the order of Santiago. To add to the effect, the characters in the image are staring beyond the frame at the viewer.

How did the ancient Greeks evolve the fundamental
architectural system of post and lintel architecture?

The painting shows the use of the illusion of space, depth, and perspective. The surface of the canvas is hidden. The painting is set in
his studio.

Velázquez was the court artist responsible for art installation in the
palace and was commissioned to do several portraits of the royals.
However, this is not a typical portrait, as it demonstrates ethereal
perfection, command, and wealth. This created commentary on the
false nature of royal portraits.

Woman Holding a Balance

The *Woman Holding a Balance* was created by Johannes Vermeer in
1664.

The woman's pinky acts as the vanishing point and the center of the
balance is placed at the center of the painting. Vermeer has compo-
sitional control in color use; for example, the gold from the curtain,
the painting's frame, the pearls, and the dress.

There is a common Baroque soft-swirled painting style present in
the piece. Vermeer also uses other Baroque characteristics such as
vibrant, rich colors, intense light, dark shadows, a point of emotion and thought, diagonals, and attention to detail.

The artwork represents the need for a balance between wealth and
spirituality. Worldly possessions are depicted in the front, with Christ

behind, highlighting the idea of weighing or judgment. This presumably signified how the people strayed from religion in the 17th century.

The Palace at Versailles

The construction of the Palace at Versailles began in 1661 and concluded in 1682. The chief architect of the king, Louis le Vau, used glass, gold, marble, silver, stone, and wood. The impressive structure consists of 700 rooms, 2,153 windows, and 2,000 acres of gardens.

The palace was built to demonstrate Louis XIV's importance, hosting parties and military agreements to compare his wisdom with that of the ancient Greeks and Romans. Also, it functioned as a residential palace for him and five successive French monarchs between 1682–1789. The build took place before the Revolution began and demonstrated the shift in the government's power from aristocracy to King Louis XIV.

The palace defines the French Baroque style and highlights Louis XIV's dominance over the art and architecture of the 17th century.

Louis le Vau was also responsible for the *Grand Façade*, the king and queen's apartments, the park's orangeries and menagerie, and the Italian-style roof hidden by a balustrade railing with ornamental parapets. André le Nôtre was the landscape designer responsible for the gardens, Charles le Brun was the interior designer and decorator, Jules Hardouin Mansart was the architect during the latter part of the construction, Jean-Baptiste Colbert was the principal advisor to

What are the three primary styles of the classical
order in ancient Greek architecture?

the king, Hyacinthe Rigaud was the French king's painter, and Pierre Puget created the sculptures that are located in the palace gardens.

The most famous portrait in the palace is *Louis XIV* by Rigaud, painted in1701. The painting used to hang above Louis XIV's throne and has since been moved to the Louvre Museum in Paris. It depicts the king in his finest heels and robes.

The interior of the building contains elaborate and detailed ornamentation and a hall of mirrors (the "Galerie des Glaces") used for Louis XIV's festivals and created an illusion that became the hallmark of the Baroque style. The garden's central axis is lined with trees, terraces, pools, and lakes, and it is visible from the "Hall of Mirrors." André le Nôtre designed the landscape incorporating changes depending on the time of day, season, and location.

Fruit and Insects

This still-life painting was created by Rachel Ruysch in 1711 and is currently held at the Uffizi Gallery in Florence, Italy.

It was painted for Cosimo III as a sign of friendship and wealthy status. Ruysch had an intricate and formulaic approach that dominated the late Renaissance. Being less complex and more realistic, she painted for a widening merchant class.

At the peak of the Renaissance, artists started to challenge the norms, and many reinvented the way images were portrayed. Vibrant colors

Why did the architects of the Mosque of Selim
II choose to place the Muezzin's platform in the
center of the dome, breaking from tradition?

and uncommon subjects started to emerge more. Wealthy merchants created an advanced patronage and art market, where art was produced directly for buyers. These buyers no longer wanted historical, mythological, or religious art, instead wanting portraits, landscapes, still-life, and paintings that reflected their successes.

Rachel Ruysch was known for great floral paintings, becoming the first successful artist during the Baroque movement. She focused on still-life, art that showed the natural beauty in life, and art that reflected the time period. Ruysch produced 250 paintings in 70 years, earning titles like "Holland's art prodigy" and "Our subtle art heroine" (Harris & Zucker, 2015r).

Fruit and Insects shows elegant skill, bold colors, dynamic textures, and a representation of fall. The scene depicts a composite of the studies of fruit, vegetables, wheat, and insects. Grapes are symbolically incorporated as the blood of Christ, the animals (insects) present naturalism, and the wheat signifies Eucharist. The artwork is lively and has less symmetry than prior works of that time period. A sense of movement is created by curves, and there is a sense of energy, illusion, and realism.

The *Tête à Tête*

This artwork was created in 1743 by William Hogarth. The *Tête à Tête* is the second work from the *Marriage à la Mode* series of six.

Marriage à la Mode revolves around the monetarily-motivated marriage of a merchant's daughter to the son of a famous family, Viscount Squanderfield. It aims to portray the fatal consequences of marriage that is not based on love.

The six distinct paintings comprising *The Marriage Contract* depict the "economical deal" between the Squanderfield family, a merchant, his daughter, a lawyer, and a counselor. The scene shows pure financial and self-interest, except for the son and daughter, who are represented as not wanting to marry each other.

Tête à Tête translates to "face to face" and shows the newlywed couple looking unhappy. They are in a room lavishly decorated with art, an expensive carpet, a chandelier, and gold-outlined architecture. Viscount Squanderfield is seen on the right slouching in a chair. He is staring at the carper, possibly drunk, with a dot on his neck that indicates a mark of syphilis. He appears exhausted, presumably returning from a night of womanizing, as indicated by the dog—symbolic of fidelity—sniffing at the bonnet in his pocket. The viscountess is on the left, smirking and looking flirtatious. She has likely been intimate with another man, as seen by the top of her bodice being undone. She has a stain on her dress, sitting with her legs apart—not very ladylike or dignified—and appears ruffled. In the center, the accountant has his eyes and right hand up in the air, looking fed up with the couple and their neglect of their finances. He is holding bills and receipts in his hands. The book on Christian theology in his pocket suggests that he is a pious Methodist. Furthermore, there are several important items in the room, including a chair and a fallen instrument—

music was associated with sensuality at the time this work was painted—depicting the chaotic state of their marriage. The paintings of saints in the back of the image speak to the couple's immoral actions and the disparities between the classical life they were supposed to live and their current one. A classical sculpture with a broken nose on the mantelpiece is not valued as highly as other objects and acts as a symbol for the couple's lack of interest in classical ideals. A ruined painting of Cupid is also present, signifying that love is destroyed in money-based marriages.

The Inspection presents an examination taking place in a doctor's office. The newlywed Viscount Squanderfield is accompanied by an unknown young woman—presumably his mistress—to likely treat their apparent syphilis. The scene includes various symbols of death.

The Toilette depicts the newlywed viscountess accompanied by friends in a crowded bathroom. The counselor, Silvertongue, looks very comfortable, suggesting they are having an affair. Generally, the painting represents rebellion against behavioral societal norms.

The Bagnio—"The Brothel"—shows a kneeling viscountess begging the wounded viscount for forgiveness as Silvertongue crawls through a window. It is evident that the viscount caught his wife sleeping with Silvertongue, who then stabbed Viscount Squanderfield and attempted to flee.

The last painting depicts *The Lady's Death*. Viscountess Squanderfield had poisoned herself after Silvertongue was executed. The scene focuses on the type of greed—her husband stealing her ring and the dog stealing food off the table—that accompanies the irredeemable nature of marriages based on financial gain instead of on love.

The subjects' clothing shows that it is set in the mid-18th century, before the Industrial Revolution, when art became more accessible, causing the aristocracy to lose some power over merchants.

The artwork acted as a satirical commentary on the money-based marriages of aristocrats, appealing to the middle class, to show the difference between aristocratic ideals and the reality of their life-style in the 18th century, as well as to criticize them.

4.11. Colonial Americas: New Spain

Codex Mendoza

The *Codex Mendoza* is a pigment on paper produced between 1541–1541 in New Spain.

The codex held much information about the Aztec empire, specifically the organization, foundation, and origins of the Tenochtitlan (Aztec capital). The city and its canals are depicted as four parts intersected by blue and green diagonals. These divisions represent the city's four quadrants, mirroring the organization of the universe aligned with the four cardinal directions (north, east, south, and west).

At the center of the art piece is an eagle on a cactus growing from the middle of a lake—according to the Aztec myth—this signifies the city's founding and values. The cactus symbolizes the city's name, as Tenochtitlan means "place of the prickly pear cactus" (Kilroy-Ewbank, 2015c).

Additional images include a war shield below the cactus, symbolizing that Mexica did not settle peacefully. Above the eagle, there is a representation of a temple, perhaps signifying the Templo Mayor. There is a skull rack (tzompantli) to the right of the eagle and different plants that represent the agricultural fertility in the city. Ten men are depicted in the four quadrants, wearing white clothing and top knots in their hair, who led the Aztecs to this location. A thin black line connects them to name glyphs. There is a priest—Tenoch—among the men, seated to the left and differing in appearance with gray skin and red marks around his ear. This is representative of bloodletting from an ash-covered priest's ear as an offering to the deities. Furthermore, there are a total of 51-year glyphs surrounding the page. Below the city's diagram are two military scenes highlighting the Aztecs' superior power in battle.

The *Codex Mendoza* acts as tribute to the inner workings of the Aztec empire. It also shows their greatness, records their history, and tells important stories of the city and their beliefs.

Angel with Arquebus

This piece was produced by the Master of Calamarca sometime
before 1728.

The image shows a mixture of angels, guns, and fashion. It is
assumed that this painting is part of a series of similar artworks that
were created in the Spanish colonial region, the viceroyalty of Peru.

The paintings represent aristocratic, celestial, and military beings
and items, such as an arquebus. (An arquebus is a long-barreled
firearm that became the forefront of military technology during
the mid-15th century.) These guns were seen as supernatural by the
Indigenous, and guns represented the power the Spaniards had over
them, as well as the protection provided to faithful Christians.

While the Council of Trent (c. 1545) banned any angelic names—
except Michael, Gabriel, and Raphael—and depictions, those in
Baroque Spain and the viceroyalty of Peru did not observe the ban.
The Catholic Counter-Reformation ideally depicted the church as an
army with angels as its soldiers. Along with the cosmos, planets, and
thunder, European prints had an influence on these artworks' creation.

The imagery shows a Mannerist style that was still popular in the
17th century.

The angels with firearms represented the aristocracy, the military,
and those adorned in lavish clothing. Overall, it is believed that the

series relates to the claims of Fransico de Avíla's—a priest in Peru—that the second coming of Christ involved an army of well-attired angels with feathered hats descending from Heaven.

Screen with the Siege of Belgrade and Hunting Scene

Created between 1697–1701, the *Screen with the Siege of Belgrade* is an artwork made of tempera and resin on wood, with a shell inlay.

The piece depicts the siege on one side and a hunting scene on the other. The siege portrays the Great Turkish War of 1683–1699, and the hunting scene is based on a European print. The artwork originally included six extra panels and serves as the only work that exemplifies Mexican *biombos* (folding screens) and *tableros de concha nácar y pintura* (shell-inlay paintings).

This was commissioned by the viceroy of New Spain José Sarmiento de Valladares. It was likely displayed in Mexico's visceral palace, where it acted as a division between a ceremonial stateroom and an intimate sitting room.

Spaniard and Indian Produce a Mestizo

This artwork is attributed to Juan Rodríguez Juárez. It shows a simple composition of a Spanish father and an Indigenous mother with their baby son held by another boy. Juárez modeled the painting off the Holy family. The son of a Spanish man and an elite Indigenous woman is known as a *mestizo*.

The Indigenous mother is dressed in a *huipil* with lace sleeves and expensive jewelry. She is gesturing at her child while looking at her husband. The Spanish father wears French-style clothing and a powdered wig. He is looking at the child as the young servant holding their son looks up at him, alluding to his greatness. The family seems loving and harmonious.

This painting is part of a 16-piece series that documents the mixed population between the Spaniards, Indigenous, and Africans. These paintings, focused on the poor living conditions of racially-mixed families during the latter half of the 18th century, are known as "Casta" paintings.

The scenes show tattered, torn, and dirty individuals to discourage race mixing. On the other hand, paintings that included a European individual appeared happier, signifying that having European blood is superior. It also reflects the increase in social anxieties related to inter-ethnic mixing. Many saw intermixing more races as "dirtying European blood" (Kilroy-Ewbank & Sifford, 2015).

This is the first painting in the series, portraying the elite. As the series progresses, racial mixing increases and the scenes appear more derogatory.

Key Concepts

- **Christian art** originally evolved from classic art, but artists moved away from naturalistic representation and started to create abstract art. Artists no longer paid attention to details, modeling, perspective, or shading conventions.
- Two examples of Late Antique art are the *Catacombs of Priscilla* and *Santa Sabina*.
- There are three kinds of **Byzantine art**: *Early Byzantine* (or Early Christian), *Middle Byzantine*, and *Late Byzantine*. Examples of Byzantine art are *Vienna Genesis: Jacob Wrestling the Angel & Rebecca and Eliezer at the Well*, the *Justinian Mosaic* within the *San Vitale*, the *Hagia Sophia*, and the *Virgin (Theotokos) and Child between Saints Theodore and George*.
- Two **significant works of art during the early medieval period** were the *Merovingian looped fibulae* (an elaborate brooch for Roman soldiers) and the *Lindisfarne Gospels* (recorded Gospels with full-page illustrations of each evangelist).
- Some distinct works of **Romanesque art** are the *Church of Sainte-Foy* (a distinguished church en route to Santiago de Compostela in Northern Spain) and the *Bayeux Tapestry* (a tapestry depicting the battle of Hastings and the events that led up to it).
- The *Chartres Cathedral* and the *Bible Moralisée* dedication page are two examples of **Gothic art**.
- The *Arena (Scrovegni) Chapel* is a work of **Gothic art in Italy** that is one of the transitional works of art that lead into the start of the Renaissance movement. It is considered transitional because it is one of the first to present divine characters in humanist ways.

- Examples of notable works of art during the **Late Medieval period** are the *Röttgen Pietà* (a sculpture holding the crucified Christ on her lap) and the *Golden Haggadah* (depicting The Plagues of Egypt, Liberation, and the Preparation for Passover).
- The *Great Mosque at Cordoba*, the *Pyxis of al-Mughira*, the *Alhambra*, and the *Mosque of Selim II* are some of the noteworthy works of architecture during the **Islamic Medieval** period.
- There are several distinguished artworks and structures from and inspired by the **Renaissance**: the *Annunciation Triptych (Merode Altarpiece)*, the *Arnolfini Portrait*, the *Pazzi Chapel*, the statue of *David* by Donatello, the *Palazzo Rucellai*, the *Madonna and Child with Two Angels*, the *Birth of Venus*, *The Last Supper*, the woodcut of *Adam and Eve*, the *Sistine Chapel Ceiling and Altar Wall Frescoes*, the *School of Athens*, the *Isenheim Altarpiece*, the *Entombment of Christ*, the *Venus of Urbino*, and the *Allegory of Law and Grace*.
- There were also several artworks and structures that took place during and were inspired by the **Protestants' Reformation and the Catholic Counter-Reformation**: *Il Gesù*, the *Hunters in the Snow*, the *Calling of St. Matthew*, *The Presentation of The Portrait of Marie de'Medici*, *Self-Portrait with Saskia*, *San Carlo alle Quattro Fontane*, the *Ecstasy of Saint Teresa*, *Las Meninas*, the *Woman Holding a Balance*, the *Palace at Versailles*, the still-life *Fruit and Insects* painting, and the *Tête à Tête*.
- The following works of art were brought to life during the time of **New Spain** and the Spanish colonial era: the *Codex Mendoza*, the *Angel with Arquebus*, the *Screen with the Siege of Belgrade*, and the *Spaniard and Indian Produce a Mestizo*.

CHAPTER 5

LATER EUROPE AND THE AMERICAS

Learning objectives:

- Analyze how contextual variables result in various interpretations.
- Analyze the influence of a particular artwork on other productions.
- Describe features of tradition or change in an artwork.
- Analyze how qualities and context elicit a response.
- Justify attribution of an unknown artwork.
- Explain why and how traditions and changes are depicted.

5.1. Rococo and Neoclassicism

Portrait of Sor Juana Inés de la Cruz

In 1750, Miguel Cabrera painted a portrait of the patron Sor Juana Inés de la Cruz, a Catholic nun and sister of the Jeroimite order in Latin America. As part of the Art of New Spain movement, it shows realistic elements that were popular during the time.

This includes red curtains behind her, symbolic of her high status, as these were used in elite paintings. The religious elements on her garments signify her strong relationship with faith, and the books are connected to her love of learning. Overall, the portrait presents the subject in an intellectual sense rather than a traditional one, emphasizing its Neoclassical art style.

Considered one of the first feminists of the Americas, Sor Juana refused to marry, opting instead to become a nun. She then joined a religious Carmelite order—later a Jeroimite convent—to pursue her intellectual endeavors, and took part in debates with scientists and philosophers.

As a woman with intellectual passions, she often defended her womanly rights, which later caused some concern in the church. The church pushed her to sell her library and sign a document stating that she would cease her education. Thereafter, Sor Juana served as a nurse at an infirmary and passed away from disease. The artist, Miguel Cabrera, only painted her likeness after her death—presumably from other portraits—as a tribute to her religious and intellectual interests.

A Philosopher Giving a Lecture on The Orrery

Painted during 1763–1765, this oil painting by Joseph Wright of Derby was officially classified under the Enlightenment movement, which was somewhat different but intertwined with Neoclassicism. During this era, the English had a taste for natural styles, strong colors, and the use of lighting.

Highlights and shadows were used to enhance the realism. Heavy contrast exists between illuminated facial expressions, light from the central orrery (a mechanical replica of the solar system that depicts the orbits of the planets with the sun), and the general darkness in the surroundings. The man with the red coat is interpreted as the person with influence, presumably the lecturer.

The painting aimed to present the scientific accomplishment of the Enlightenment era. This illustrates the curiosity and demand for rational knowledge of the time. The artwork shares a focus on scientific and logical inventions with a painting of famous Classical philosophers, produced by Raphael in 1510. Similarly, navigation charts—made of wood and shells to navigate ocean voyages—were built in the 19th century in the Marshall Islands, Micronesia. Surrounding the orrery are women and children, suggesting their involvement, as well. While the identities of each person are unclear, they each depict a real person. There is a debate about whether the lecturer in red is a representation of Isaac Newton or a member of the Lunar Society of Birmingham.

The strong light source is meant to signify the sun and is also symbolic of the search for meaning during the Enlightenment. The art piece captures the vibrant learning atmosphere and philosophical thoughts that shifted from the traditional and religious ways of living during the former eras. Additional themes highlighted in the painting include nature, the passing of time, how the world works, location, scale relationships, and technology.

Although scientists and philosophers were essential at the time, creatives such as Joseph Wright of Derby were unofficially known as the artists of the Enlightenment.

The Swing

The Swing is a portrait painting by Jean Honore Fragonard in 1766. The piece is part of the Rococo movement and uses elements like an overall lightheartedness, naturalism seen in the background, the use of soft colors, ornate details presented in the woman's dress, and the strong use of lines and sunlight that had been popular during the era.

The oil painting depicts a woman on a swing while a bishop and her love interest are standing nearby. The swing is located in a lush garden with multiple flowers and Cupid statues, all representative of the lavish lives the wealthy lived in France during the 18th century.

While the French population was struggling with a multitude of issues, the wealthy women often "escaped" by becoming patrons of art. Artworks became exclusive to the higher class and were frequently used by nobles to express their status.

Monticello

Located in Virginia, United States, the Monticello, designed by Thomas Jefferson, was built between 1768–1809.

The structure includes a Greek-like marble porch that runs into the cross-form building. A dome was constructed near the center—closer to the entrance—of the building. Marble fencing—known as the balustrade—had been placed around the roof to give a strong sense of horizontality, and the viewer's eyes are then drawn down to the long rectangular windows on the walls. Furthermore, the layout is symmetrical around the central vertical axis.

Inspired by Classical and Neoclassical style of architecture in France, Thomas Jefferson remodeled the original two-story structure—

inspired by the Hôtel de Salm in Paris—and aimed to reinforce Classical ideals, such as civic responsibility, democracy, education, and rationality.

The porch contains two Doric columns that hold a triangular pediment decorated with a circular window looking over the west French-imitation gardens. The structure was also partly inspired by the Classical Basilica, with colonnades, a dome, pediments, Persian windows, steps inspired by ancient Etruscan temples, and a transept—intersecting like gothic churches—plan.

While Thomas Jefferson studied at William & Mary, a public university in Virginia, he was never trained officially as an architect. He loved French, Greek, and Roman architecture and lived by their ideals of strength, power, and pervasiveness of culture.

The Oath of the Horatii

Showing French royalty, *The Oath of the Horatii* was produced by Jacques-Louis David in 1784, a time in which France was approaching the Revolution and the end of the monarchy. It is a French Neoclassical style oil painting on canvas.

The artwork presents elements that had been popular among French Neoclassical artists, like the rejection of the Rococo style, simplicity, the use of symbolism, and structural organization. The male figures were constructed with geometric shapes, and the female figures presented organic shapes.

The image shows three sons swearing an oath to their father—allegedly depicting a Roman myth—and grieving women sitting on the right side of a columned hall.

The myth involves the *Legend of Horatii,* which speaks about the conflict between Rome and Alba. Three representatives—the brothers of Horatii—were sent to settle the disagreement instead of starting a war. The story held moral value in Rome, as sacrificing oneself for the defense of one's city was considered a noble cause at the time.

George Washington

The marble sculpture of George Washington was produced by the French artist Jean Antoine Houdon from 1788–1792. This was during the prime of the American Neoclassical era.

The sculpture shows the first U.S. president in a contrapposto stance with symbolic details, such as his fatherly expression—wearing street clothing—and his power and authority suggested by his sword. However, not holding his sword in his hand signifies the end of his military and presidential career after the American Revolution.

During this time, it was common to depict war heroes in art. This sculpture was ordered by the governor of Virginia, who was inspired by George Washington's decision to retire to work on a farm and allow his country to develop.

Self-Portrait, Elisabeth Vigée Le Brun

Inspired by the Rococo movement, French artist Elizabeth Vigée Le Brun painted a self-portrait in 1790. She aimed to return to the naturalistic ideas of the Renaissance era, showing herself in a natural, active pose.

The image shows the artist wearing a traditional black dress with a red-colored sash. It shows Elizabeth Vigée Le Brun painting a portrait, presumably of Marie Antoinette, because she mainly worked for the crown of France.

There were not many female artists at the time, and this artwork presents the greatness, freedom, and intelligence of the artist, who was considered revolutionary herself. Due to her work, she was forced to leave France during the French Revolution but became very rich from her beautiful paintings.

While there was an emphasis on beauty and color at the time, the artist also highlighted the main themes of independence, intelligence, women, and work.

5.2. Romanticism

Y No Hai Remedio (And There's Nothing to Be Done)

Plate 15 from *Los Desastres de la Guerra*—"The Disaster of War"—was produced by Francisco de Goya between 1810–1823 and was finally published in 1863.

The piece shows a black and white etching of a blindfolded man in white, tied to a pole by his hands to the back. Overall the scene is dark, but the landscape has some depth. Behind the central figure is a firing squad aiming at other people tied similarly to poles. The central character tied to the pole is referred to as Alter Christus. To his right, a grotesque body is lying on the ground, presumably dead. Further to the right are rifle barrels pointed at the central figure, not showing the individuals holding the rifles.

The artwork was created to express the brutality of the French against the Spanish. The first group of plates—*Y No Hai Remedio*—presents some of the inhuman acts of the French troops. In total, 82 plates were produced in protest against the French occupation of Spain by Napoleon Bonaparte and the brutality that went with it. After Napoleon tricked the king of Spain into allowing the French troops to cross their border, the king was usurped, and Napoleon's brother took the throne. The French were eventually pushed out after the Peninsular War of 1808–1814. This was a very bloody affair and later resulted in extreme poverty for the French as well as for the Spanish, who had reclaimed their home.

The first plates were based on the effects of conflict; the middle plates were based on the effects of famine; and the last plates were based on the demoralization of Spain.

Francisco de Goya worked as a painter for the Spanish and French royals, producing controversial work. He made the images by first etching them into metal, then using a dry point technique—scratching uneven lines with a stylus—after the metal plate was dipped into acid, ink was poured over the image (which only remains on the incisions burned by the acid), and the plate is then run through a press with a moist paper placed on top for transfer. These prints were intended to install Spanish nationalism, focusing on the main themes of art as a form of protest, authority, the human psyche, power, violence, and fear.

Goya later lost his hearing and became a recluse.

La Grande Odalisque

Painted in 1814 by the prominent artist Jean-Auguste-Dominique Ingres, *La Grande Odalisque* shows a reclining nude woman, which had been the subject matter for centuries. It was also common to refer to paintings of nude women regarding classical mythology: for example, calling them Venus.

However, Ingres refused to cloak the female figure in his artwork and instead presented the woman as a female slave used for the sultan's sexual pleasure.

The image depicts a woman who is wearing nothing but jewelry—a pearl and ruby brooch and a golden bracelet—and a turban. Her back is to the viewer as she seductively looks over her shoulder, presumably at someone who had just entered the room. Her surroundings show luxurious damask and satin fabrics. Lying behind her is a facedown bejeweled mirror, and she is also holding a peacock feather fan in her hand, symbolic of wealth.

Ingres strayed greatly from the Neoclassical style as he presented an almost exaggerated female form to appear more elegant. When looking at her back, it seems that there are two to three extra vertebrae, and the anatomy of her lower left leg is inaccurate, as her knee is unlikely to be at the center of the painting and attached to her hip.

Tension was created between Neoclassicism and Romanticism, an approach to the canvas which would continue throughout the first half of the 1800s.

Liberty Leading the People

The French artist Eugène Delacroix created an oil on canvas artwork presenting a personification of liberty from September to December 1830.

As a bare-chested 'Liberty' is seen marching over dead bodies, she is leading the way to freedom. She is holding a musket in her left hand and a flag of revolution in her right. To her side is a young boy with two pistols, representative of sacrifice, and an upper-class man in a top hat holding a rifle, representing the inability of the wealthy class to stay out of a war.

The piece was created during the Romanticism period. It is mainly based on the three-day revolution of July, 1830. The painting includes Romantic elements such as realism, dramatic lighting, emphasis on the softly-rounded lines of the figures instead of the sharpness in their weapons, and a background clouded in fog, presumably for theatrical effect.

Eugène Delacroix aimed to glorify the people—the citizens of France—who were involved in the war and to acknowledge the sacrifices made for the sake of revolution against a corrupt regime. It depicts French people of all ages and social classes bravely protesting against the government thus becoming one of the most prized possessions of the Louvre Museum in Paris.

The Oxbow

Also known as *The View from Mount Holyoke, Northampton, Massachusetts, after a Thunderstorm*, this artwork was painted by Thomas Cole in 1886.

Currently held at The Metropolitan Museum of Art in New York, the style of work is realistic but cartoon-like, almost a caricature, even, of the bend in the Connecticut River.

The artist used warm hues—green and yellow—for the presentation of nature and cool colors—blue and gray—for the weather.

Common among other works of Romanticism, the image symbolizes the insignificance of humans in comparison to the greater scheme of things. This is highlighted by the near lack of presence of the artist in the lower center, also being the only interaction the scene has with humans. Simultaneously, it discusses political ideology as it talks about Western expansion. Looking at the untamed, unruly, and wild part of the landscape, it is seemingly untouched by humans.

How does *The Oath of the Horatii* reflect the French Neoclassical style in its portrayal of figures and the overall composition?

A diagonal separation—showing two unequal sections—is made from the lower right-hand corner toward the upper left-hand corner. The bent tree is symbolic of nature being at mercy to itself as it has been beaten by the weather, and the gloomy storm clouds in the foreground enhance the contrast of the clear skies—assuming a storm has passed—in the distance.

Still Life in Studio

Created in 1837, *Still Life in Studio*—also called *The Artist's Studio*—was painted by Louis Daguerre.

Inventing the daguerreotype technique, the artwork is presented as a highly-polished photographic image on a silver-plated sheet of copper. The anatomy of the daguerreotype includes a handful of still-life images, Parisian scenery, and portraits of other artworks accompanying the invention of photography.

Each daguerreotype is a one-of-a-kind black-and-white photographic image with remarkable details. They are created by sensitizing the silver-plated copper sheet with iodine vapors, exposing it in a large box camera, developing the image in mercury fumes, and then stabilizing the final product with salt water or sodium thiosulphate. Unfortunately, after a devastating fire on March 8, 1839, less than 25 of Louis-Jacques-Mandé Daguerre's photographs survived.

While this became not only a medium of artistic expression, but also an impactful scientific tool, artists feared that photography might replace painting.

Slave Ship

This painting can be best described by its other name, *Slavers Throwing Overboard the Dead and Dying* or *Typhoon Coming On*. It was painted by Joseph Mallord William Turner in 1840 and is currently held at the Museum of Fine Arts in Boston.

The image depicts a slave ship sailing into a storm as slaves are being thrown overboard to drown. There are some gruesome elements, including fish with their teeth on the chained legs of the slaves, a fiery sunset, writhing foamy waves, and a high wall of water below grey clouds that allow us to believe nature is taking revenge on the ship for abandoning the slaves, and will ultimately result in a shipwreck.

An entry from Gateways to Art states (DeWitte et al., 2015):

> In his dramatic painting in the Romantic style, Slave Ship (Slavers Throwing Overboard the Dead and Dying, Typhoon Coming On), Turner condemns the slave trade. Although slavery was illegal by this time throughout Britain, Turner was highlighting the injustice of the slave trade and protesting against any consideration of its renewal. His powerful canvas portrays an infamous incident aboard the slave ship Zong in 1781. It was common practice for slave-ship captains to fill their vessels with

more slaves than they would need, knowing that disease might spread amongst them. The captain of the Zong knew that he would be paid for any slaves lost at sea, but not for those who were sick when they arrived. He, therefore, had sick slaves thrown overboard while still far from land. (p.505)

J.M.W. Turner started using techniques that would only become popular 20 years later during the Impressionist movement. He used the popular 1700s–1800s theme of man vs. nature, and while slavery was banned in Britain, it was not in colonized countries like the United States of America.

The image uses abstract forms that make it difficult to recognize the subject matter and what is taking place in the scene.

The main function of the artwork is to protest any reconsideration of slavery becoming a normalized practice in the future, to create a shock factor so viewers can take note of the brutality of slavery, and to communicate both sympathy and judgment. It shows that those who participate in such horrific practices—such as the slave ship and its captain—are morally damned.

Palace of Westminster

Produced by the architects Charles Barry and Augustus Welby Northmore Pugin (A.W.N. Pugin), between 1840–1870, the *Palace of Westminster*—among the *Houses of Parliament*—is situated across from the River Thames in London. It was built during the early

Victorian—19th century English—Era after the original building
burned down in 1834 and had to be rebuilt.

A competition was held to determine the best architects for the job,
and Charles Barry and A.W.N. Pugin won.

While the building resembles a Gothic-style structure on the outside
with stained glass windows as part of the interior design, the architects
originally intended to base the design on the Elizabethan style, too.
However, only Gothic elements—of Shakespearean times—are used.

The main function of the building is for practical reinforcement
of traditional values instead of serving aesthetically. Presently, the
structure is still being utilized by the British government and is also
referred to as the *House of Commons* and the *House of Lords*.

5.3. Late 19th Century Art

Why did Jean Antoine Houdon choose to depict George Washington in his sculpture without holding his sword in his hand?

The Stone Breakers

During the Realism movement, around 1848–1900, Gustave Courbet painted *The Stone Breakers* (c. 1849).

The artwork was a reaction to the labor unrest of 1848, during which people protested for better work conditions, and it was submitted to the Parisian Salon of 1850.

The focus is on two central figures that appear to be destined for a lifetime of poverty. The two men are breaking down the stone into rubble for the production of pavement. The viewer is faced with multiple signs of poverty, tattered clothing, and smithing tools (hammers). This signifies the unforgiving circumstances of the working-class individuals in Europe in 1850, the passing of time, and the lack of social mobility for them at the time.

The importance of the "common" people was highlighted by Gustave Courbet as he rebelled against the fact that they were never represented. He painted the image on a large canvas, which, at the time, was only used for significant historical subject matter.

Nadar Raising Photography to the Height of Art

Nadar was known for taking aerial photographic images of Paris, France, in 1856. In 1862, Honoré Daumier created a lithograph published in *Le Boulevard*—a French journal—that served as a commentary on the court's decision to permit photography to be considered a form of "high art" (Barber, 2021).

The lithograph—mass imagery produced by printing from a smooth metal plate or stone—shows a daring Nadar taking photographs from a hot air balloon. The city's buildings below all have "Photograpie" written on them. Daumier highlights the bizarre excitement as the photographer's hat is flying off, and he nearly falls from the balloon. The purpose of the ironic imagery is to mock the notion that photography can be considered equal to high art.

The piece shows that ridiculous means and dangerous endeavors need to be used to elevate photography to the standard of high art. Furthermore, the artwork foreshadows modern aerial-surveillance photography, as Nadar's balloon was used for intrusive photography during the 1870 Siege of Paris.

Olympia

Édouard Manet produced a salon painting—an academic painting—in 1863 that received extremely negative critique for its rebellion against traditional ideals.

Olympia—a common name for prostitutes at the time—depicts a reclined nude woman in an imperfectly harsh style that defies all Classical rules and ethereal views of the female body. While the painting presents elements of Realism, it was intended to be a shift toward impressionism. Manet created an artistic revolution with his

How does Francisco de Goya use depth and contrast in
the artwork *Y No Hai Remedio (And There's Nothing to
Be Done)* to emphasize the brutality of the scene?

choppy, flat, badly-contoured style with abrupt tonality shifts and lack of depth. Furthermore, there is no understanding of space as there is no sense of perception.

The scene includes a small black cat lying at the feet of a chaise lounge. At the back, a Black female servant is standing and holding a bouquet of flowers, presumably a gift from a client. The reclining female figure—Victorine Meurent modeling a prostitute—is staring at the viewer with an indifferent and cold expression.

The main themes of the painting speak of the harsh realities of Parisian life at the time, including prostitution and the division among racial and social classes. French colonial mindset and systemic injustice are highlighted, and racial division specifically is emphasized by the stark contrast between the black and white skin.

The artwork was seen as scandalous, and many found it insulting to Parisian tradition. Édouard Manet presented viewers with a defying prostitute and a Black woman, both seen as inferior and presented with an animalistic sexuality. Viewers were unnerved by Manet's shameless use of contemporary subjects, his rejection of controlled brush strokes, and his Classical Illusionism. He stated that it had no relevance in the modern—the time of the Industrial Revolution—world. Manet became the "father of impressionism," and inspired modern works with his technique and subjects.

The Saint-Lazare Station

Wanting to be remembered as a painter of the "modern world," Claude Monet produced an oil painting of *The Saint-Lazare Station* in 1877 (Ostergaard, 2016).

Monet lived in the rural area of Argentuiel, from which he traveled into Paris via the Saint-Lazare Station. This commute represented modernity and industrialization, as the roads and railway stations of Paris had only just been modernized by Baron Haussmann. It had been an unusual subject for Monet because he was famous for painting water lilies.

The image presents a locomotive train pulling into the triangular-roofed station as steam is released into the air. The realism of the train is depicted by perspective and foreshortening.

The painting shows a gritty texture that follows traditional techniques in landscape painting, such as diagonal lines running from the roof into the background and trees framing the central focal point.

Monet had to challenge his abilities in the artwork's creation to establish his relevance in an industrialized society. He captures the comings and goings of a busy day in France.

The Horse in Motion

In 1878, photography reached an advanced stage that allowed it to
capture moments in stills.

As part of Eadweard Muybridge's take on Realism, he set up multiple cameras—a setup specifically called a 'zoopraxiscope'—at even
distances on a racehorse track to create the "illusion of continuous
motion" (Belden-Adams, 2021a).

Muybridge studied the movement of a horse and jockey in addition
to establishing the potential of photography. This study bridged the
gap between still photography and videography.

The artwork shows a rectangle with four rows and four columns.
Each block depicts a still image of a jockey racing a horse, capturing
the horse's stride. When the 16 images are viewed as a series, a sense
of movement is created. It appears as if the horse is running past a
bystander, looking at its profile view. The images tell a story, and
when multiplied, they elevate photography from still to motion.

The Valley of Mexico from the
Hillside of Santa Isabel

As an academic landscape painter, José María Velasco produced an
image of *The Valley of Mexico from the Hillside of Santa Isabel* during
his studies of the panoramas of the Valley of Mexico.

The artist meticulously observed clouds, foliage, rocks, water, and everything else in nature. Velasco rebelled against the Realism of Courbet and Turner's Romantic landscapes.

The painting shows off the valley's blue skies, puffy white clouds, the lake, mountains, and trees, as well as human figures. This was painted from the mountaintop village, Guadalupe, where the artist stood above looking down at the scene. The main purpose of the artwork is to glorify the Mexican countryside.

The Burghers of Calais

Following the Realism movement, late-1800s-style sculptures emerged, and the bronze depiction of *The Burghers of Calais* was created by Auguste Rodin between 1884–1895.

Showing six middle-class people—"burghers"—from the village, the content speaks of how burghers promised their lives to the English king to keep their villages safe during the Hundred Years' War.

The central focus shows a man with large swollen hands awaiting his execution with a noose around his neck. The man is Eustache de Saint-Pierre.

Rodin aimed to depict the severity of the war and the English king who made the burghers wear sack clothes and carry the key of Calais.

The French Council of Calais rejected Rodin's sculpture, wanting a single metaphorical figure instead.

What event inspired the creation of "Liberty Leading the People"?

Each emaciated figure represents a different emotion—fearful and forlorn—that was sculpted individually and arranged for maximal effect. The overall close-up impression of the figures is their depravity, as Rodin aimed to make them relatable by placing them at ground level.

The Coiffure

Part of the Post-impressionist movement, *The Coiffure* is a dry point and aquatint image on paper. It was created by Mary Cassatt in 1890.

The artist was inspired by Japanese-style prints with light brushstrokes and a sketchy appearance that can easily be reproduced on paper.

Cassatt aimed to make art accessible to all social classes but was advised against producing art with widespread availability because it would make her art less valuable. However, she insisted on creating less expensive art for the masses. She knew that photography would soon enable more people to have access to art and decided that it would be smart to develop with technology rather than resist it.

The image shows a nude woman fixing her hair in front of a mirror. The Asian influence is noted in the decorative patterns in the background. A truer, more intimate representation of the female nude is created by Mary Cassatt, as females were mainly painted by male artists and were drawn intended for the male gaze. The scene is de-eroticized, made functional, personal, and intended to be seen and understood by women.

Around 1890, trade between Europe and the East became popular. European artists were fascinated by the characteristics of Japanese prints, including the two-dimensionality, water-like brushstrokes, faded colors, and leafy ornamentation.

Starry Night

After the start of Post-Impressionism (c. 1885), Vincent Van Gogh painted *Starry Night* in 1889.

Post-Impressionism is characterized by dynamic strokes, exaggeration, vibrant colors, non-naturalistic representation, and painterly quality.

The oil painting depicts the view from Van Gogh's room in a hospital in St. Rémy.

The composite landscape shows the exaggerated steepness of the mountains, a Dutch church, Mediterranean cypress trees, a crescent moon, and wave-like movements that lead the viewer's eyes from left to right. There is a vertical break in these lines by the cypress trees—symbolic of death and eternal light—and the church steeple.

The artist experimented with stylized techniques. Van Gogh was known for his short, thick brushstrokes, yet he did not need to fill every inch of the canvas, and some parts of it can be seen behind the paint.

Art historians believe the nightscape depicts Van Gogh's inner struggle with his mental illness. After his hospitalization, he had a breakdown and cut off his own ear.

This piece inspired the later movement called Fauvism.

Where Do We Come From? What Are We? Where Are We Going?

Between 1897–1898, Paul Gaugin produced an oil painting incorporating a continuous narrative, similar to frescoes or friezes.

The piece was characterized by a Symbolic style, where color is key, the piece is expressive and symbolic, and it appears two-dimensional and non-naturalistic. The background has a strange multi-perceptiveness to it.

The scene shows the stages of life of the Tahitian natives from left to right (infant, adult, and elderly). The figures are presented in non-Western, partial clothing.

While the artwork's meaning was mostly private to Gaugin himself, there are various philosophical interpretations.

Mont Sainte-Victoire

The representation of the 3,317 feet high limestone peak of Mont Sainte-Victoire was created between 1902–1904 by Paul Cézanne.

Why was there a fear among artists that photography might replace painting upon the invention of the daguerreotype?

Cézanne lived in a town called Aix-en-Provence, just below Mont Sainte-Victoire. He became known for his oil and watercolor paintings of the mountain. While his earliest paintings did not have the mountain as the main element, he later explored and presented different points of the mountain, specifically during the Impressionist movement. This included studying the mountain's relationship to changing elements in the surrounding environment, like weather, trees, fields, bridges, buildings, etc.

The main one we are looking at is currently in the Philadelphia Museum of Art. This artwork shows three nearly-equal horizontal divisions with a band of houses and foliage closest to the viewer. The foreground is then extended into a middle ground of roughly-colored patches, including emerald, viridian green, and yellow ochre. Above that, the mountain is surrounded by a sky of blues, grays, and purples.

Cézanne skillfully used subtle adjustments to evoke a sense of depth in the panoramic scene.

Carson, Pirie, Scott and Company Building

At the birth of the Art Nouveau movement, this steel-frame skyscraper with its terracotta exterior and cast-iron entryway was designed by Louis Sullivan in 1899.

Constructed in Chicago between 1903–1904 and originally called The Sullivan Center, the structure incorporates an easily-accessible, open ground level, and decorative first floor. Above that, it holds

multiple similar-styled stories of office space, an attic, and a distinct
cornice (ornamental molding below the ceiling). This set the tripartite (involving three parts) building apart from others in the city.

The ground floor is highlighted, given larger windows to showcase
a decorative, welcoming, and aesthetically-pleasing shopping space.

Art Nouveau—characterized by intricate, flowing curves inspired by
natural forms—cast-iron decorations cover the entrance in the corner and the exterior of the ground level. The organic floral design is
depicted on industrial materials.

Instead of emphasizing the height and vertical lines of the building,
the department store highlights the entrance on the ground floor
to attract shoppers. This is where the term "form follows function"
emerged in the divergence from traditional skyscrapers (Herman,
2015).

The Kiss, Gustav Klimt

The Kiss by Gustav Klimt shows a couple kissing on a precipice.

The scene is very passionate, and little of the human form is visible. Only some parts of the woman's face are seen, such as her calm
expression and closed eyes, and only the neck of the man is shown,
creating a sense of desire and physical attraction. There is a large
pattern on their clothing, the male's being more rectangular and the
female's more circular.

> Why did Jospeh Mallord William Turner choose to highlight the incident aboard the slave ship Zong, despite slavery being illegal in Britain by the time he painted Slave Ship?

The artwork emphasizes the permanence of all-consuming love and passion.

The Kiss is associated with the time between 1890 and World War I and the modernization of Barcelona, Brussels, Paris, and Vienna. The piece is characterized as having an Art Nouveau style, with many floral patterns, vegetal elements, a complex design, and wave-like surfaces.

Klimt sought to combine artistic mediums into one, connecting with the idea of portraying a universal kiss in a time of chaos.

5.4. Early 20th Century Art

Goldfish

This artwork, produced by Henri Matisse in 1912, uses vibrant colors to evoke an emotional response and a contemplative relaxation for the viewer.

It is a still-life painting with violent contrasts of color that are thinly applied, as we see the white of the canvas showing through the energetic brushwork. Art historians presume it had been influenced by Asian art.

The *Goldfish* shows characteristics of the Fauvism art movement that debuted in Paris in 1905. It was named after a critic who commented that the paintings looked like they had been painted by "Wild Beasts" (Wilkins, 2015).

> What architectural style does the exterior of the
> Palace of Westminster primarily resemble?

The movement was inspired by Van Gogh and Gauguin, both Post-Impressionists who like who emphasized a painterly surface with broad flat areas of strongly contrasting color. This maximized expressive effects.

Matisse was a French painter and was also one of the biggest figures in the development of modern art. He loved to experiment with the expressive potential of color and its relation to form. Matisse believed that colors are emotions. He was famous for his decorative style, expressive forms, and bold use of color.

It is believed that the piece was inspired after Matisse went to Morocco, "where everyone would stare at goldfish contemplatively all day long" (Wilkins, 2015). It signified a relaxed lifestyle, and goldfish became a symbol for a tranquil state of mind. Matisse explained it as "an art that could be a soothing, calming influence on the mind, something like a good armchair that provides relaxation from fatigue" (Wilkins, 2015).

The Scream

In 1910, Edvard Munch produced *The Scream* as a Symbolism-style piece of art during the Expressionism movement.

Munch combined traditional, high-quality tempera paint with industrial cardboard. He incorporated vibrant color contrasts, skewed proportions, non-naturalistic elements, and a lot of uncertain movement to represent the symbolism of the moment.

The painting depicts an elongated, androgynous face, with its hands pressed against its face as it screams. In the background, two figures are walking across the bridge. In addition, the sea swirls into the air, and the natural forms draw the viewer's attention with everything that is blended and sketch-like.

Art historians argue that the piece is semi-autobiographical, as Munch regularly expressed themes of life, death, relationships, and dread in his work. Presumably, he is recounting a former personal experience where he was struck with melancholy while walking with friends during a sunset. Furthermore, there is a sense of synesthesia—the synthesis of the senses—where some visual elements are associated with remembering the moment.

The Scream is part of a series called "The Frieze of Life" involving Munch's study of various mediums. The series includes four renditions of the same scene, each using different materials and surfaces. The artist experimented with how mediums presented the moment differently.

Edvard Munch aimed to express internal emotions through external matter. The key elements are dream-like and colorful, and purposefully overshadow the less important aspects of the image.

Improvisation 28

Improvisation 28 was produced by the Russian artist Vasily Kandinsky in 1912.

Kandinsky wanted the audience to respond to a painting in the same manner that they would an abstract musical piece, like a concerto or sonata. The piece's title is derived from musical compositions, and the artist often gave musical titles to his works like *Composition* and *Improvisation.*

The artwork shows a movement towards abstraction, representing objects as suggested rather than depicted, the use of strong black lines, and colors shaded around the shapes.

It was created as part of the Expressionist movement and was inspired by the Fauve movement, the *Die Brüke* (The Bridge) movement (which saw itself as the bridge between traditional and modern painting), the German *Der Blaue Reiter* (The Blue Rider) movement that was based on the fondness of horses and the color blue, and abstraction.

Kandinsky's idea was to portray the natural world in a way that went beyond representation. He believed that if there are recognizable shapes, then our conscious minds will take over, and there would be a link between the emotional effects of sound and color. He was one of the first artists who produced a non-objective, abstract painting.

The Kiss, Constantin Brancusi

Constantin Brancusi's *The Kiss* was created from limestone between 1907–1908.

Brancusi was a Romanian-born French sculptor. He incorporated the long Romanian tradition of stone carving and devoted himself to finding the simplest and most elegant way to express his subjects.

The artist wanted to express the subject in its most pure form and depicted two intertwined figures with interlocking forms through sculpture. The woman is on the right, as she is slightly thinner, her eye is slightly smaller, and a bulge signifies her breasts.

The limestone's surface is left raw and archaic, suggesting an artistic return to a primitive form after the Renaissance and Baroque periods of the 19th century. It appears that Brancusi is rejecting the academy.

The style of art uses elements of Cubism, where the human form is broken into angles and shapes.

The Portuguese

The Portuguese was painted by George Braque in 1911.

The artwork intends to show all sides of the artist's subject. The style is neither naturalistic nor conventional. There are fractured forms and clear-edged surfaces on the picture plane, it is nearly monochromatic (acting as an exploration of shapes), and the only realistic elements are stenciled letters and numbers.

This art style is known as Analytical Cubism, which occurred between 1907–1912. It was the first phase of Cubism, so imagery was highly experimental. Most works had jagged edges and sharp, multifaceted lines.

Braque worked with Picasso to develop this style.

The Migration of the Negro, Panel no. 49

This artwork, produced by Jacon Lawrence in 1940–1941, consists of casein tempera on hardboard, and acts as a return from the Italian masters.

The image depicts simple, flat shapes, unmodulated colors, geometrical forms, tilted tabletops to show the surfaces, and forms that hover in large spaces.

It is part of a series that represents the migration of African Americans from the rural south to the urban north after the First World War. The artist incorporated a public restaurant in the north that is deeply segregated. This is shown through the yellow pole dividing the races.

Lawrence created the piece in the Harlem Renaissance period, during which large numbers of African Americans migrated to the New York City neighborhood, Harlem. This happened in the early 20th century.

What is depicted in Monet's *The Saint-Lazare* Station painting?

The Two Fridas

Surrealism started around 1920 and sought to portray an unseen world of dreams, subconscious thoughts, and unspoken communication.

It goes in two ways: the abstract tradition of biomorphic forms and the veristic tradition of using subjects based on reality put together in unusual ways. It aimed at puzzling, challenging, and fascinating viewers and was not to be clearly understood.

The Two Fridas was painted by Frida Kahlo in 1939 and is presently held at the Museum of Modern Art in Mexico City.

This artwork shows the juxtaposition of two self-portraits. We see a Spanish lady in white lace on the left and a Mexican peasant on the right. There is a sense of stiffness and provincial quality of Mexican folk art that served as the artist's inspiration. It shows her two hearts intertwined by veins and severed by scissors at one end. They lead the viewer's eyes to a portrait of Kahlo's husband. The artist Rivera painted it at the time of their divorce.

Furthermore, we see infertile land in the background, figures against a lively sky, and blood on her lap that suggests she had many abortions, miscarriages, and surgeries because of polio.

Frida Kahlo rejected the Surrealism label.

What architectural elements in the Palazzo Rucellai can be traced back to ancient Greek and Roman ideals?

The Jungle

This gouache-on-paper art piece was painted by the Cuban artist Wilfredo Lam in 1943.

The artwork is significant to modern art and Latin American art. Lam was influenced by his many encounters and experiences in different cultures. During the 1920s and 1930s, he was in Madrid and Paris. In 1941, he returned to Cuba when Europe took part in the war. After the war, he left his native country and returned to Europe. Art historians believe his inspiration came from his "consciousness of Cuba's socio-economic realities, his artistic formation in Europe under the influence of Surrealism, and his re-acquaintance with Afro-Caribbean culture" (Bravo, 2015c). This resulted in *The Jungle*.

Acting as a game of perception, the imagery shows seemingly randomly constructed figures from a wide variety of shapes. This includes the suggested rounded backs, thin limbs, enlarged hands and feet, and crescent-shaped faces that resemble African masks. There is a tight sense of no direction, creating an unorthodox landscape. The painting intended to communicate a psychic state. The sugarcane that is included in the flora of the scene reminds the viewer of Cuba's unrepresented hardworking past. There is an incorporation of symbols from Santería, an Afro-Cuban religion with Surrealist elements.

Dream of a Sunday Afternoon in the Alameda Park

This fresco was produced by Diego Rivera in 1947 and was housed in the Hotel Del Prado in Mexico City.

The artwork shows more than 400 characters through the ages of Mexican history, joined together on a stroll in the gardens.

Some light-hearted and playful elements are also included, like the colorful balloons and bright foliage. Additionally, Rivera includes darker elements, where we see an argument between a policeman and an Indigenous family and a smiling skeleton directed at the viewer.

While Rivera's work was never officially associated with Surrealism, this painting depicts some characteristics of the Surrealist movement. He depicts subjects that came from his dreams. Thus, the fresco is appropriately named *Dream of a Sunday Afternoon in the Alameda Park*.

A type of chronology takes place from left to right. On the left, the conquest of Mexico by the Spaniards is taking place. Then, the fight for independence and Mexican Revolution are portrayed in the center. Lastly, modern achievements are shown on the right.

Both the nightmares and dreams of every period are depicted. This includes the oppression of the conquest and the dream of democracy, religious idealism and intolerance, lavish lifestyles versus the effect of a fiscally-divided nation, and Rivera's love for Frida Kahlo, accompanied by her declining health.

The figures overlap with each other while not interacting, but they are not separate.

Rivera is seen in the middle, front, and center. He is accompanied by Frida Kahlo and *La Catrina*. La Catrina—depicted here as a smiling skeleton—was the 20th-century nickname used to describe upper-class women who dressed in elegant European clothing.

La Catrina is uniting the two great artists, Rivera and Posada. Frida Kahlo holds a yin and yang symbol that represents opposite yet interdependent forces, femininity, and masculinity, as well as Kahlo and Rivera's relationship. Initially, she mentored him, but they later married and divorced. Nonetheless, they remained political comrades who often painted each other even after that.

Rivera uses imagery from Mexican history, including a feather boa around La Catrina's neck, reminiscent of the Mesoamerican serpent god Quetzalcoatl.

Frescoes were famous in Mexican history. They were initially considered to be propaganda for the post-revolution government, but then artists began to use it for their own purposes.

5.5. Mid-20th Century Art

Woman I

This artwork represents Abstract Expressionism, which became the first American avant-garde art movement as a reaction to the Minimalist version of abstraction.

Woman I was painted by Willem de Kooning around 1950–1952, and is currently held at the Museum of Modern Art in New York.

The scene shows an angry woman with large eyes baring her teeth. Her large breasts are represented satirically to reflect those on magazine covers. Her fierce smile is influenced—and cut out from a magazine—by the woman selling Camel cigarettes in an advert. She has a large frozen grin and a blank gaze.

> How does the portrait of Mary differ in appearance and attire
> in the *Madonna and Child with Two Angels* compared to typical
> depictions of her during the period the artwork was created?

The artist produces the piece by slashing paint onto the canvas, creating an overpowering image with jagged lines. The background is vague.

Willem de Koonng intended for the artwork to act as an ironic comment on the stereotypes used by the movie and advertising industry. Furthermore, this woman—the first in a series of six—is inspired by Paleolithic goddesses.

The Bay

The Bay was painted by Helen Frankenthaler during 1963 in Detroit, Michigan. It is part of a series of color field paintings.

Frankenthaler preferred painting on unprimed canvas to better absorb the very runny paint she used. There is no set function of the piece; she created art for art's sake.

The scene shows a very two-dimensional landscape as the base of the imagery, lacking any depth seen in prior artworks.

The artist's color field paintings were very popular in the 1960s.

Fountain

Marcel Duchamp produced this porcelain piece of art in 1917.

This sculpture depicts an upside-down urinal.

> What does each emaciated figure in the *The Burghers of Calais* sculpture represent?

Duchamp was inspired by the Dada movement and had the ready-made sculpture signed by R. Mutt as a pun. Dada translates to "hobby horse," but was meant as a random reaction against the horrors of the First World War.

The artwork was intended to present irony, both in the sense of being upside down and the signature as a play on the cartoon strip of the time, *Mutt and Jeff.*

Dadaists shunned traditional methods and manners, eschewed oil and canvas in favor of ready-mades and worked on glass, and accepted the precedence of the artistic concept over the execution of the piece.

The Steerage

Alfred Stieglitz's gallery showcased photography next to the avant-garde in modern works because photography quickly became its own art form. Being one of the United States' most progressive galleries, they displayed *The Steerage* with pieces captured between 1902–1917. Influenced by the Cubist movement, the photo was also published in *Camera Work* in 1911.

Mainly intended to represent photography as a form of fine art, this piece also shows the social divisions of society.

How did Mary Cassatt present the female form in *The Coiffure* differently than her male counterparts?

The image shows diagonals and framing effects of objects like ladders, sails, steam pipes, etc. Poor travelers on a ship from the U.S. to Europe are depicted.

The name is derived from its meaning, being the part of a ship reserved for passengers with the cheapest tickets.

Stieglitz arranged little in his photographs. He took pictures of life as it happened and emphasized clarity and realism. His focus was on the composition and the art of the photograph rather than the subject matter. Stieglitz neglected to talk about the subject matter because his political opinions on immigration were conflicting. He also used photos to argue that photography is a fine art.

Composition with Red, Blue, and Yellow

Acting as a big contributor to the De Stijl movement, Piet Mondrian created this artwork in 1930.

Mondrian evolved a non-representational form called Neoplasticism. He was taught drawing by his father at an early age, went to an art academy, and became a teacher. In 1911, he moved from the Netherlands to Paris and started to experiment with Cubism. However, Mondrian saw Cubism as a "port of call" on his artistic journey rather than a destination (Chadwick, 2016).

Around 1917-1918, back in the Netherlands, Mondrian published *De Nieuwe Beelding in de Schilderkunst* (The New Plastic in Painting).

This was his first major attempt to express his artistic theory in writing. Mondrian's best and most often quoted expression of this theory, however, comes from a letter he wrote to H. P. Bremmer in 1914 (Mondrian et al., 1986):

> I construct lines and color combinations on a flat surface, in order to express general beauty with the utmost awareness. Nature (or, that which I see) inspires me, and puts me, as with any painter, in an emotional state so that an urge comes about to make something, but I want to come as close as possible to the truth and abstract everything from that, until I reach the foundation of things. I believe it is possible that, through horizontal and vertical lines constructed with awareness, but not with calculation, led by high intuition, and brought to harmony and rhythm, these basic forms of beauty, supplemented if necessary by other direct lines or curves, can become a work of art, as strong as it is true. (p. 224)

In 1919, he went back to Paris, where he began to create his grid paintings, for which he is most famous. This painting is an example of one of these grid paintings. It uses unique brushstrokes and layering of each color. Mondrian's style was very influential and appeared in mediums like fashion, pop culture, architecture, and music album covers around the world.

How does Paul Gaugin incorporate the Symbolic style into *Where Do We Come From? What Are We? Where Are We Going?*

Seagram Building

The Seagram Building was designed by architects Ludwig Mies van der Rohe, Philip Johnson, and Robert Allan Jacobs. The building officially opened in 1958.

The architecture of this building consists of a steel frame with a glass curtain wall and bronze veneer that gives it a monolithic look. This skyscraper model became the template model for buildings of its kind after World War I.

The architect wanted the structural elements to be visible and to depict the idea of "less is more." There reflects the minimalist movement in the interplay of vertical and horizontal lines.

The Seagram Building became the international style of architecture. Architects across the globe incorporated its clean spaces and white lines, internal structures that are skeleton systems holding the building up from within, and abandoning ornamentation and paint applied to the exterior.

Spiral Jetty

This is an earthwork sculpture by Robert Smithson that was completed in 1970.

The sculpture incorporates mud, salt crystals, rocks, and a water coil on the Great Salt Lake in Utah. The area was abandoned and is extremely remote.

Smithson had to use a tractor with native stone to create the jetty.

Jetties are supposed to be piers, but here it is in the middle of nowhere.

Smithson was very interested in the blood-red color of the water due to the presence of the bacteria that live in the high salt content, and created this example of "Site Art." It is sometimes referred to as "Earth Art," depending on its location.

The original environment must be fully intact to understand the work fully.

House in New Castle County

Designed by the architects Robert Venturi, John Rauch, and Denise Scott Brown, the House in New Castle County was built between 1978–1983.

This was a response against the international style and emphasized ornamentation, conventional architectural expressions, and references to earlier styles in a modern context. It was made to capture a viewer's attention.

Why was it significant for the Medici family to
depict Mary and Jesus in a humanistic manner in
the *Madonna and Child with Two Angels*?

The house was designed for a family of three in rural northern Delaware. It is surrounded by rolling hills and a forest. The house has an elaborate and well-stocked music room for the wife, who was a musician. The husband was a bird watcher; thus, large windows looking out at the trees were implemented in the design.

This is a post-modern mix of historical styles, using many geometrical shapes. The front façade incorporates a floating arched screen used to identify the structure as a residence. The rear façade is dominated by a prominent arched screen that is framed by the roof, and has Doric colonnades to create a grand and whimsical feeling.

The interior is simple and cozy, with plenty of wood décor, many painted jagged arches, and quirky chandeliers.

Marilyn Diptych

The *Marilyn Diptych*, produced by Andy Warhol in 1962, is a combination of oil, acrylic, and silkscreen enamel on canvas. It is housed at the Tate Gallery in London.

As a reaction against Abstract Expressionism, this exemplifies the Pop Art movement that glorifies and magnifies the commonplace. The style bridges the gap between "high" art and pop culture. It was often centered around mass production.

The canvas shows 50 rectangular screen-printed photographic images of a film still from *Niagara 1953* on a rectangular background. The

How does Sandro Botticello depict the movement
created by the wind sprites in the *Birth of Venus?*

left uses color, representing Marilyn Monroe's life, and the right is grayscale, signifying her death.

Repetition is employed to make the image emotionally and physically flat and to rob it of its meaning. This goes against the notion that art must be unique. The grid makes the piece appear too automatic.

Warhol used this artwork to mock the "cult of the celebrity" and people's tendency to care too much about famous people. Bold and artificial colors are utilized to put emphasis on Marilyn's media-based facade.

The large-sized canvas demands the viewer's attention.

"Diptych" is used intentionally in the title to draw on connotations of triptychs from Medieval times.

Lipstick (Ascending) on Caterpillar Tracks

Another popular example of Pop Art includes the *Lipstick (Ascending) on Caterpillar Tracks*, created by Claes Oldenburg.

The Pop Art movement gathered momentum in the 1950s, reaching its peak in the 1960s. Materials from everyday life—items of mass popular culture—were used in artworks. The pieces glorified the commonplace and brought the viewer face-to-face with everyday reality.

This artwork is not satirical and serves as a reaction against Abstract Expressionism. It was made between 1969 and 1974 out of cast resin, aluminum, and corten steel that had been painted with polyurethane enamel. It was initially set up in New Haven's Beinecke Plaza.

The piece served as a platform for public speakers and as a rallying point for anti-Vietnam protests. It was put up secretly.

The tank-shaped base signifies the idea of "anti-war."

Male and female forms unite—tank and lipstick—symbolizing death, power, desire, and sensuality.

Oldenburg initially used cheap, brittle materials like plywood tracks and vinyl balloon tips. Later, the artwork was refurbished with steel, aluminum, and fiberglass and was reinstalled in front of Morse College, Yale, in 1974.

Key Concepts

- Some notable examples of **Rococo and Neoclassical art and structures** are the *Portrait of Sor Juana Inés de la Cruz, A Philosopher Giving a Lecture on The Orrery, The Swing, the Monticello, The Oath of the Horatii, George Washington, and the self-portrait of Elisabeth Vigée Le Brun.*
- Distinguished artworks and structures from the **Romanticism period** include *Y No Hai Remedio (And There's Nothing to Be Done), La Grande Odalisque, Liberty Leading the People,*

The Oxbow, Still Life in Studio, Slave Ship, and the *Palace of Westminster*.

- Not only did the **Late 19th Century** artists create art that was influenced by and relevant to their time period, but photography was also starting to be recognized as a form of art. For instance, Nadar attempted to elevate photography to the level of high art, and *The Horse in Motion* is one of the first artworks that used photography to capture moments using stills. Aside from these, other artworks, prints, and structures from the Late 19th Century include: *The Stone Breakers, Olympia, The Saint-Lazare Station, The Valley of Mexico from the Hillside of Santa Isabel, The Burghers of Calais, The Coiffure, Starry Night, Where Do We Come From? What Are We? Where Are We Going?, Mont Sainte-Victoire*, the *Carson, Pirie, Scott and Company* skyscraper, and *The Kiss* by Gustav Klimt.

- Works of art from the **Early 20th Century** include *Goldfish, The Scream, Improvisation 28, The Kiss* by Constantin Brancusi, *The Portuguese, The Migration of the Negro, Panel no. 49, The Two Fridas, The Jungle*, and *Dream of a Sunday Afternoon in the Alameda Park*.

- Examples of art and structures from the Mid-20th century include *Woman I, The Bay, Fountain, The Steerage* (a photograph), *Composition with Red, Blue, and Yellow*, the *Seagram Building*, the *Spiral Jetty*, the *House in New Castle County*, the *Marilyn Diptych*, and the *Lipstick (Ascending) on Caterpillar Tracks*.

CHAPTER 6

INDIGENOUS AMERICA

Learning objectives:

- Describe features of tradition or change in an artwork.
- Justify attribution of an unknown artwork.

6.1. North America

What is the significance of the term "form follows function" in
relation to the Carson, Pirie, Scott and Company Building?

Mesa Verde Cliff Dwellings

Discovered in Montezuma County, Colorado, the Mesa Verde Cliff
Dwellings consist of sandstone structures erected by the Ancestral
Puebloan (Anasazi)—stationary farmers—around 450–1300 CE.

A total of 600 structures were built directly into the cave, on top,
and along the mesas.

The materials used to create these structures include stone and mud
mortar that is supported by wooden beams inserted into the natural
clefts of the cliff face. The sandstone was shaped with hard stones,
and pieces thereof were used to fill gaps in the mortar. Additionally,
new building techniques were utilized using an adobe brick, which
was made of clay, sand, straw, and sticks.

The mural paintings were pigmented with clay and other organic
materials. These plastered and painted artworks mostly contained
animals, plants, and geometric patterns that depicted the geography
of the land.

The structural plan incorporated kivas—circular underground
rooms used for rituals—and architectural units. The kivas had
wooden roofs supported by sandstone columns, a central fire pit with
a deflector vent, and a small hole in the ground called a "sipapu."
The Mesa Verde—meaning "green tables" in reference to the mountains—was used for residential and ceremonial purposes. While
they were initially covered, the structures currently have no roofs.
The spaces around the main buildings were used as a small plaza,

How did Leonardo da Vinci achieve depth and
direct the viewer's focus in *The Last Supper?*

the circular and square rooms were for living, and the units that faced the plaza were used for family gatherings. Furthermore, the site includes smaller rooms at the base of the mountain—presumably used for storage—and a circular tower of which the purpose is unconfirmed.

Great Serpent Mound

The Great Serpent Mound was allegedly created by the Fort Ancient peoples of the Middle Ohio River Valley around 1070 CE. It remains in its original location in Adams County, Ohio. The serpent's head is directed to the cliff over the Ohio Brush Creek.

Native American tribes lived in the valleys of the Ohio, Missouri, Mississippi, and Illinois Rivers before settlers of European descent came to the region in the 19th century. The creators of the serpent likely lived in settled agrarian communities of 100–500 residents, farming beans, maize, and squash and living in rectangular and circular houses; however, they did not leave behind any written records to confirm this. It is believed that some tribe members also traveled in hunter groups, often hunting bears, deer, elk, and other small game, and lived alongside the indigenous Mississippian culture responsible for the Cahokia, heavily emphasizing the rattlesnake's symbolism. This suggests that the mound was at least in part influenced by their rattlesnake worship.

The tribes of the Upper Midwest commonly created effigy mounds of animal figures. Unfortunately, the majority of mounds were destroyed by the plows of European settlers.

Snakes were believed to have supernatural powers—being a powerful deity of the underworld—and were used in spiritual ceremonies. The tribes often made copper serpentine figures. Therefore, it is believed that the serpent is astrologically aligned—the head is in line with the sunset of the summer solstice, and the tail aligns with the sunrise of the winter solstice—and used to mark the seasons. The serpent's body follows the curves of lunar phases or equinoxes, and the snake is swallowing the ovoid shape at its head that represents the sun, symbolic of an eclipse.

Additionally, the North Star lines up with the first curve of the serpent, suggesting that the artwork may have served as a natural compass. It is connected to the constellation Draco, which includes the Pole Star.

The serpent was created around the time Haley's Comet appeared, suggesting that it marked this astronomical event.

While there is no archeological evidence, many historians also argue that the serpent was related to the nearby burial sites from the early Adena culture. The mound's true purpose is continually debated by scholars.

At over 1,300 feet long, an average height of 4–5 feet, and an average
width of 20–25 feet, the serpent mound is the largest in the world.
It is thought to resemble a rattlesnake swallowing an orb. The head
faces east, and the tail faces west. It is a national historic landmark.

Templo Mayor

The Main Aztec Temple was constructed by the Mexica (Aztec) people in Tenochtitlan, Mexico. The 90-foot high structure was built
around 1325 CE and, thereafter, was rebuilt six times.

The structure follows the characteristics of the post-Classic and
Mesoamerican styles. It was constructed of volcanic stone and covered in stucco. The structure included a large symmetrical building
with two staircases leading up to twin temple towers. It was the focal
point for the Mexica people because it was much larger than the
other buildings.

The temple was inspired by Mexica mythology, and either side represented the two primary gods. Inside each temple was a wooden
statue of its dedicated god, including the god of war and sun—
Huitzilopochtli—in one half and the god of agriculture and rain—
Tlaloc—in the other.

The south side of the temple, dedicated to Huitzilopochtli, includes
a sacrificial stone, standard bearer figures, and serpents. It represents
snake mountain (Coatepec). This half of the temple is also painted
red to signify the dry season during the winter solstice, and the steps

were painted in bright red to symbolize blood and war. The stairs
had sculptures of snakes and feathers.

Tlaloc's side of the temple includes an altar with a sculpture of frogs
and chacmools to receive offerings. It symbolizes the mountain
which produced rain and allowed crops to grow (sustenance). The
north side was painted with blue stripes to signify the wet season
during the summer solstice, and the stairs leading to the temple were
painted in white and bright blue to represent water. The stairs held
sculptures of snakes with blinders.

While the halves contradict each other, there is a sense of balance
and harmony of opposites in nature.

The temple was originally mainly used as a place to worship the two
gods, hold ceremonies, and reenact myths, such as Panquetzaliztli—a
performance of banner raising to honor Huitzilopochtli's triumph
over Coyolxauhqui—and a representation of Aztec warfare.

Tenochtitlan was known as a sacred precinct of the Mexica empire
on an island in the lake of Texcoco. The Templo Mayor—meaning
"Greater Temple"—is currently a UNESCO World Heritage Site.
In 1521, the temple was destroyed by the Spanish, and the remains
were buried. Only after the Coyolxauhqui stone was discovered did
the temple become an excavation site of ruins.

Many ritual objects have been uncovered here, including those from
other cultures that show Mexica influence, such as the Olmec mask.

Because Tenochtitlan established itself as the capital around the 12th century, it incorporated the constant threat of military invasion to maintain order in the smaller surrounding cities. It soon became a trade center of food, gold, and pottery and also allowed the spread of the Mexica ideals and traditions.

The Coyolxauhqui stone (c. 1500) is made of volcanic stone and was found at the base of the Huitzilopochtli side of the temple in 1978. It is a monolith relief carving initially painted blue, orange, red, and white. This sacrificial stone is related to warfare and the sun. It depicts the Aztec goddess Coyolxauhqui, the sister of the patron god Huitzilopochtli, who was killed by her brother when she attempted to murder their mother. The graphic imagery shows her beheaded and dismembered body, highlighting themes of chaos and death. During Panquetzaliztli, captives were killed, rolled down the temple, and landed on the stone as a reenactment of the defeat of Coyolxauhqui, who fell off the snake mountain. This ritual was to assert authority over the enemies of Mexica.

The Calendar Stone—also known as the Sun Stone—from 1502–1520 was discovered in 1790. It is made from basalt and was originally painted to highlight an angry face, resembling the sun with an open mouth and ear spools. The piece is related to the Aztec mythology regarding the five suns created through the different eras; for example, the modern era is connected to the fifth sun. The stone incorporates 20 symbols, each representing the days of a calendar, and arrows pointing in different quadrants that signify the universe. This tells the story of the cosmos under Aztec belief.

The Olmec-style mask from 1200–400 BCE is a small jadeite sculpture that had been discovered at Templo Mayor. The sculpture depicts a baby-like face with a distinct Olmec—before the Aztecs—style and was an offering to the Aztec gods. The Aztecs collected many objects from different cultures, indicating the vast trade of Mesoamerica and how Aztecs cared about history and past cultures.

Ruler's Feather Headdress

Presumably that of Moctezuma II, the *Ruler's Feather Headdress* (c. 1428) is an Aztec artwork that contains gilded brass, gold, leather, paper, plant fibers, wood, and feathers. It is 3.8 feet in height and 5.75 feet in width.

The headdress incorporates small plates of gold and 450 tail feathers—mainly birds from the Yucatan peninsula—that are mounted on wooden sticks, layered in semi-circles, originally including a bird beak in gold. The vibrant colors signify importance and high status. Extensive trade and time were required to create the headdress and the amantecas—feather workers—who produced it were so highly skilled and regarded that they lived in a special quarter of the capital.

The ruler most likely carried the headdress through town during ceremonies. Art made with feathers symbolized wealth and was part of warriors' clothing, shields, and fans. Rare feathers were even given as payment in this culture.

> How were the Templo Mayor's two halves decorated to represent the two primary gods, Huitzilopochtli and Tlaloc?

Bandolier Bag

The Bandolier Bag, recorded in 1850, was the creation of the Lenape people of the Delaware tribe in the Eastern Woodlands, a cultural area of the Indigenous people of North America. The Lenape people consisted of three communal clans—turkey, turtle, and wolf—that traced lineage through their maternal ancestry.

The bandolier—a belt with pockets worn over the shoulder—and bag are connected. The long rectangular bandolier has a red trim around the black, blue, green, and pink floral-patterned cloth and has trapezoidal extensions ending with blue, green, red, and tan tassels. However, only one side is decorated, whereas the other side is brown. Trade cloth, like cotton and wool, and leather are used as the base materials.

The bag has the same color schemes as the bandolier, with shorter and thinner tassels decorating its opening. It is rectangular in shape, large, and rests on the hip. The bandolier bag is worn as a cross-body bag. Thousands of tiny glass beads cover the surface of the bandolier bag, indicating mastery of technical skill and trade with Europe. The beads were prized for their color. It was also reminiscent of the bags European soldiers carried to hold ammunition for their rifles.

The overall prairie-style design is characterized as asymmetrical and abstract, as each side is different. White beads act as contour lines, and contrasting colors were used to represent the sky and the underworld.

At the time, bags were merely ornamental, and even some with pockets never carried anything. While women made them, men wore them—often multiple at a time—to express their social status and identity. These bags were called "Aazhooningwa'on" in the Ojibwe language, meaning "worn across the shoulder (Green & Zucker, 2020).

The Lenape people were forced from their homeland by American President Andrew Jackson's Indian Removal Act, signed into law on May 28, 1830 (National Geographic Society, 2022), but continued their traditions through art. The bandolier bags serve as the perseverance of their culture.

Transformation Mask

The *Transformation Mask* is made of painted red cedar and string. It was produced by the Kwakwaka'wakw people of the Northwest coast of Canada.

The form resembles an exaggerated eagle head with a large beak that opens—by pulling cords—to show a human ancestor's face. The open mask looks more like a bird spreading its wings. The hair is made of string, and it includes multiple bright colors.

The mask was mostly worn during powerful dance ceremonies and Potlatch—a ceremony where wealth is given away—where the host displayed their high social status. Some masks conveyed family crests that presented a family's genealogy often passed between family members within a clan. The mask was opened while the people were dancing. The Kwakiutl people wore transformation masks with a red cedar bark cloak.

The artwork is characterized by using form line style elements, like bilateral symmetry, calligraphic lines, and many waves, ovoid, "S," and "U" shapes.

This Indigenous community was based on fishing. Men hunted, and women were gatherers, also responsible for weaving and doing wood-work. Their wealth was determined by the number of material goods and slaves they had. Their ancestry was traced through their mater-nal side. The community also consisted of a primogeniture—the right of succession belonging to the firstborn—political structure of four classes, including nobility, aristocracy, commoners, and slaves.

Painted Elk Hide (Cadzi Cody)

A painted elk hide attributed to Cotsiogo, thus named *Cadzi Cody* after his American name, was discovered at Wind River Reservation, Wyoming. It dates back to 1890–1900.

The elk hide is one of numerous animal hide paintings by the artist. He often painted on deer, elk, and buffalo hide with natural pig-ments like red ochre and charcoal, mainly combining free-hand pen-ciling and stencils. Cotsiogo was a member of the Eastern Shoshone tribe, and this artwork was traditionally a recording of their history.

Such pieces represent the transformation from tribal methods into modern Western society. The artworks were multifunctional in assisting the economy—this was an era of intense poverty in Wyoming—and cultural representation of the Wind River Reservation. This resulted in economic development after tourist sales. Tourists also took part in the community's Sun and Wolf Dances, where they spent more money. This piece can be seen as a "cultural survival statement" for the tribe (Kilroy-Ewbank, 2015b).

Artworks like this combine the history of Indigenous tribes and contemporary tradition. Important rituals and dance ceremonies in honor of deities are displayed, in addition to the daily life on the Wyoming reservation. Men—and warriors with feathered headdresses that show their honor—were seen hunting on horses, and women sat at fires, presumably cooking their meals.

Black-on-Black Ceramic Vessel

Dating back to 1939, Maria Martínez and Julian Martínez claimed the creation of a *Black-on-Black Ceramic Vessel* in New Mexico.

The Pueblo vessel is made of blackware ceramic, volcanic ash, and pigment. The ceramic was mixed with the volcanic ash to make it black, and the pot was built up with coils as opposed to being formed on a pottery wheel.

Puebloan rituals were based on women's reproductive ability. Ironically, females did not have official ceremonial authoritative roles but were afforded respect in the domestic sphere.

Word of Maria and Julian Martínez's artworks spread, and they were sold as fine art. However, the original function was to be ollas—a widemouthed earthenware vessel—that held water, seed, and grain or to be used in cooking.

The imagery on the ceramic vessels mainly depicted natural phenomena, challenging tradition and cultural identity. The artists transformed traditional Puebloan pottery into symbols of their culture and the status of American collectors.

6.2. South and Central America

Chavín de Huántar

This archeological site in the Andes of Peru—the capital of the pre-Inca civilization—involves an architectural complex constructed by the Chavín Cult.

It consists of roughly-shaped stones used for the walls and floors and smooth stones for its artistic elements. The first temples usually did not have windows and rather made use of numerous tunnels to bring in air. *The Lanzòn* and other sculptures are made of granite and the jewelry from gold alloy, which was a more expensive material compared to that used in the production of other structures at the time. This highlighted the size of the population producing the pilgrimage, as well as the spiritual importance of their culture.

The U-shaped structure was mainly used for religious worship of a god—a supernatural anthropomorphic being that was depicted in the sculptural art—through spiritual rituals and acted as a popular pilgrimage site that attracted many people to unify the previously distant pre-Inca Peruvian society. This is evident from the range of artifacts from all over.

The structure was intentionally developed at 10,330 feet above sea level at a very popular geographical location. The Ancash region allowed for a lot of Southern Highland and Coastal migration. Easy access was created through the site's connection to two of the largest rivers in Peru. Additionally, the mountainous region enabled agricultural development and growth of potatoes and maize. The majority of the construction took place in 900 BCE and had continuously been occupied by Incan descendants until the 1940s.

The transportation of ceramics, textiles, and other elements frequently took place.

The temple was developed in 500 BCE when it was made larger and incorporated the addition of a sunken court. Inside, there is a large sculpture of the god for whom the temple was initially built. Furthermore, there are other mysterious and supernatural art carvings; for example, the serpent motif that was often worn as a nose ornament by the elite of the Chavín Cult to demonstrate their powerful status.

The main themes of the building include the civilization's religious beliefs, being in a central cultural and spiritual capital, the relationship between humans and nature, and authority or power through legend.

Yaxchilán lintel 25, structure 23

Located in Chiapas, Mexico, the Yaxchilán is near the Usumacinta River and Piedras Negras.

The site was built to show dominance against their rivals—showing high contrast to the architectural styles—and is defended on all sides by a looped hole, except for a small road to approach from the south of the river.

The site holds over 100 structures and monuments and is well-known for its exquisite high-quality relief carvings, carved doorway lintels, hieroglyphic inscriptions, and stele on the stairs.

Structure 23 holds the most famous lintels. These Yaxchilán lintels were carved with great detail and were originally painted, but only a few red and blue traces remain. The lintels of Structure 23 narrate different ritualistic moments in the life of Lady K'abal Xook. Lintel 24 shows bloodletting—she is pulling a thorny cord over her tongue to bleed into a basket of paper on the ground before her—while her husband, Shield Jaguar II, is holding a lit torch above her. Diamond patterns decorate Lady Xook's garment (huipil).

Lintel 25 also depicts bloodletting, but here Lady Xook is kneeling in front of a serpent with a figure emerging from its mouth. She is wearing an elaborate headdress, bracelets, earrings, and a jade necklace and is holding a bowl in her left hand, looking up at the rising serpent. The bowl in her hand contains bloodstained pieces of paper. The figure that is emerging from the serpent's mouth is wearing a helmet and is holding a spear and shield. Similar to Lady K'abal Xook, the figure is decorated in an elaborate headdress, a breastplate, and ear spools. The corner is inscribed with glyphic text—written backward—stating the date of Shield Jaguar II's ascension to the throne: October 681. Shield Jaguar II's heir, Bird Jaguar IV, continued building structures and sculptures before the city collapsed in the 9th century.

> How is the *Transformation Mask* operated
> to display its two distinct faces?

Bloodletting was a common ritual among the Mayan elite and was often depicted in their artwork. Both male and female rulers believed that their blood fed and honored their gods, as well as maintained order in the cosmos. As rulers were believed to be descendants of the gods, they were tasked with taking care of the community. Additionally, bloodletting was connected to rejuvenation. During this ritual, the loss of blood and burning of the bloodstained paper, together with incense, allowed the elite to hallucinate and attract the vision serpent.

The focus on Lady Xook was intended to symbolize the promotion of the ruler's lineage, using his most favored wife. This was important to represent his power and the role of the royal women in the Mayan culture.

City of Cusco

The City of Cusco (c. 1440) with the Inca main temple (Qorikancha), the Spanish colonial convent Santo Domingo (dating dated 1550–1650), and the Walls at Saqsa Waman (Sacsayhuaman) are located at the central highlands of Peru at an elevation of 11,200 feet.

The structures mainly comprise andesite stone. The buildings are close together and contain red roofs. They are built on a flat valley between a mountain range, which made them ideal for settlement as the land was fertile and fed by surrounding rivers. The structures are organized into an urban layout of technical construction.

This was the capital of Tawantinsuyu—the Inca empire "Land of the Four Quarters"—in Quechua, which was divided into four divisions representative of the specific people associated with each section of the empire. The two main sections consisted of 'hanan' (upper) and 'hurin' (lower).

The City of Cusco was also referred to as the "center of existence" (axis mundi), where the Inca rulers and nobles lived. Men went to Cusco for education, whereas women went to become "acllas," meaning "chosen women," who would weave cloth for the nobles, be chosen for marriage, or make 'chicha' (corn beer). Furthermore, mummies and gods were kept in the capital to maintain control over followers.

The Qorikancha was at the center of the hurin, and it was known as the most sacred shrine dedicated to the Incan sun god, Inti. The monastery of Santo Domingo was later built around it. The Sacsayhuamán acted as a fortress but was left unfinished due to colonization.

The city is supposedly laid out in the shape of a puma—symbolic of strength—and shows advanced ability with stone construction and aesthetic values. The noble homes were separated from the other canchas (houses) in the city, also solidifying the political power's importance in the city.

The city became known for its monumental architecture, road networks, use of knots for communication (quipu), agricultural advancements, and political ideals. While they had no money system, exchanging goods and labor were forms of payment. People

How did Cotsiogo incorporate natural pigments
in his artwork, the painted elk hide?

also paid their taxes and the access to land and celebratory events in the form of labor. Men and women were seen as equal, where men contributed to farming and herding—sometimes also to combat—and women were responsible for domestic work and weaving. This changed after the Spanish invasion of the 16th century because the Spanish saw women as slaves.

The Spanish Conquest led to a visual juxtaposition between the cultures as monasteries and Baroque-style houses were built over the Inca city. Presently, it is a cultural heritage and monument site.

Maize Cobs

Maize Cobs is an Incan artwork dated c. 1440–1533 and is currently housed at the Ethnological Museum in Berlin.

Metalsmiths from the Inca culture combined silver and copper to imitate actual corn's internal and external lifelike proportions. This was produced on sheet metal (repoussé) with alloys. The husk was thinner and the corn was thicker, and the kernels were sculpted individually. The sculpture was life-sized and mimicked ripe corn ready for harvest, also referred to as Zea mays (more commonly referred to as maize, and a member of the grass family). Corn was an important source of nutrition and for making chicha, and this sculpture honored that.

The metal sculpture was on display in the Inca temple Qorikancha in Cuzco. Incan art like this portrayed their love of naturalistic forms.

> Why can the painted elk hide be viewed as a "cultural survival statement" for the Eastern Shoshone tribe?

Maize Cobs was intended for ritual offerings by the Inca government and state religious officials. Gold and silver objects were often used as sacrifices that helped to retain Inca officials' power and their divine right to rule. Furthermore, these offerings signified the supernatural origin of the Incas in the sun god and their control over nature as descendants of this deity.

City of Machu Picchu

Consisting of individual granite stones shaped to fit together, Machu Picchu was built by the Inca people around 1450–1540 in the Andes Mountains of Peru.

Presently, the site is referred to as the ruins of an Inca city near the Inca capital, Cuzco. The area incorporated houses and terraces, initial steps that were built into the side of the mountain. These aimed to slow the process of erosion and provide ideal land for agriculture.

There are 16 stone channels that drain excess water from the houses into fountains, one of which acted as a ritual bath for the emperor. The walls are decorated to mimic mosaic, wood and thatch are used for roofing, the entrances, windows, and niches are trapezoidal, and the structure includes an observatory made of a stone enclosure above a cave. The stones each have a protruding and concave side that fit into each other like a puzzle while allowing for movement during earthquakes. The outward-facing sides are smooth.

The site was originally used as a palace for the emperors—Pachacuti Inca Yupanqui—during the mid-15th century. It overlooks the Urubamba River and is located about 3,000 feet lower than Cusco in a fertile climate. The emperor Pachacuti believed he was the direct descendant of the sun god and, thus, named it the "temple of the sun."

The buildings and layouts were divided according to social hierarchy, and the structures for the people of a lower class were crude and not in the elite Inca style. The buildings in the northeast were dedicated to the higher classes, and the emperor—symbolic of his status as ruler—lived in the southwest, with the observatory—used for astronomical studies and mythological narration—next to his residence.

Additionally, Machu Picchu presented the importance of religion and rituals to reinforce the relationship between the Incas and the supernatural forces of existence. This is highlighted by the Intihuatana, the carved boulder in a ritual structure of Machu Picchu. The boulder reflected and reinforced the belief in spiritual connections. It also used the sun and shadows to tell time.

The site was discovered by Hiram Bingham, who excavated it. Unfortunately, present-day visitation makes it difficult to maintain the traditional integrity of the site.

Why do art historians believe that *The Scream* might be
a semi-autobiographical piece by Edvard Munch?

All-T'oqapu Tunic

Created by the Inca people around 1450–1540 in Peru, the *All-T'oqapu Tunic* is a rectangular piece of cloth—camelid fiber and cotton—folded into a square with a slit in the middle and red woven squares as decoration.

The red squares (t'oqapu) and geometric motifs that compose the tunic are meant to be worn around the neck and over the shoulders. A band of motifs is found near the neck or waist. This particular tunic is made of dyed camelid wool that is warped over cotton, representative of high status.

The dye includes cochineal red and indigo blue. The fibers were collected, spun, and dyed before the weaving process began. Red was one of the most difficult colors to produce, as it required collecting and grinding thousands of bugs from cacti. These vibrant colors represented the apex of the resources required for production, as well as the social and political power of those that wanted them. The amount of time and skill was only reserved for high-status textiles.

The tunic incorporated the two techniques of warp and weft thread. Warp thread acted as a vertical background, and weft thread was the dyed vicuna wool that is weaved horizontally, as visible in the final product. The threads—approximately 100 threads per centimeter—were spun from cotton plants found on the Andean coast and the silky wool of alpacas. This ensured a light but strong weave and allowed for brightly-colored textiles.

> What materials were predominantly used in the creation of the *Black-on-Black Ceramic Vessel?*

Tunics were worn to depict various ethnicities, places, and social roles. Tunics like this represent the Sapa Inca's (ruler) ability to command the taxation of the empire, their access to luxury, and the mastery of the women chosen to weave for the elite (acllas). The Inca warriors wore a tunic that displayed a black and white checkerboard pattern, signifying the Sapa Inca's military power. It was also believed that the cloth had a spirit (camuc).

Key Concepts

- Some notable examples of architecture and art from **North America** are the *Mesa Verde Cliff Dwellings*, the *Great Serpent Mound, Templo Mayor*, the *Ruler's Feather Headdress*, the *Bandolier Bag*, the *Transformation Mask*, the *Painted Elk Hide (Cadzi Cody)*, and the *Black-on-Black Ceramic Vessel*.
- There are also several distinct artworks and structures from **South and Central America**: the *Chavín de Huántar*, the *Yaxchilán lintel 25, structure 23*, the *City of Cusco*, the *Maize Cobs*, the *City of Machu Picchu*, and the *All-T'oqapu Tunic*.

CHAPTER 7

AFRICAN ART

Learning objectives:

- Identify an artwork.
- Analyze form, function, content, and context to explain the intentions of the artwork's creation.

7.1. West Africa

What specific role or function did the ceramic
vessels serve in the Pueblo community?

Great Mosque of Djenné

The Great Mosque of Djenné was founded in 1200 and rebuilt between 1906–1907 on the Bani River in Djenné, Mali.

The structure is made of cylindrical adobe mud brick and was made by the hands of the entire society. The building is rectilinear, supported by pillars topped with ostrich eggs that are symbolic of fertility, contains a mihrab, and is partly enclosed by a wall.

The mosque was a sign of the chief's religious devotion to Islam, acting as a center for prayer and community. The congregation is still practicing there. It also acts as a political symbol to Europe and is the location of Crepissage, the festival dedicated to the communal plastering effort of the mosque.

The structure includes three minarets, an earthen roof, a Qibla that faces Mecca, and terracotta that covers over the roof. Timber poles are seen over the roof, called torons, which are used for climbing the mosque during the plastering and decoration that occurs annually. The stairs symbolize the transition between the sacred place and the marketplace.

Djenné is the oldest known city in Sub-Saharan Africa, and the mosque is the largest mud brick building in the world. It had been rebuilt three times after the French had colonized Djenné in 1836. The current version was rebuilt and completed in 1907, led by the architect, Ismaila Traoré.

How did Vasily Kandinsky's approach differentiate from traditional artists in representing the natural world?

African chiefs adopted Islam when the mosque was built by the first converted Muslim ruler, Koi Konboro. Islam had a large impact on the region at this time, and Mali emerged as a powerful and prosperous empire.

Adjacent to the mosque, there are tombs of great regional Islamic scholars.

Benin Plaques

The *Benin Plaques* are cast brass relief plaques that were created by the Beninese people.

Brass was a valuable material in Benin, and it took a high level of technical skill to do brassworking.

These plaques were used as ornamentation on walls and were created in pairs that were attached to the pillars in the Oba's palace. An Oba is what the Nigerians call their chief or king.

The images depict court rituals that took place in the palace and the history of the kingdom. It expresses royal power and presents a large Oba. Additionally, the plaques portray the results of British imperialism during the Scramble for Africa, with a focus on the trade between Benin and Portugal after the British conquest. We can see the king at the center, attended by several court attendants, emphasizing his power. As Beninese artists had not used a sense of depth yet, the smaller figures around the king signify that they are less important, and not just because they are further away. The king is wearing expensive jewelry and rides a horse. His jewelry is similar to the beads worn traditionally by an Oba, his horse is similar to the horse an Oba rides, and the hierarchical scale shows the relative importance of the Oba compared to the surrounding figures. Distinct proportion is used where the Oba's head is unusually large because he was referred to as the "Great Head," symbolic of his wisdom and power.

At the time of the plaque's creation, the Beninese traded under a new system with the Portuguese empire. The Portuguese empire started declining around the 18th century and inroads were created by the British. They sought mutually-beneficial trade, while the British wanted to dominate the people and extract resources. The Oba's palace was raided and looted by the British in 1897 while they burned the city around it.

The *Benin Plaques* were among the valuable artifacts that the British stole and are currently displayed in a British museum. Ownership thereof is under debate.

Sika Dwa Kofi

The Asante people of South-Central Ghana produced the *Sika Dwa Kofi* around 1700.

This artwork contains traditional Asante carved wood layered with gold and cast-gold attachments. The 18-inch high, 24-inch long,

What role does the Great Mosque of Djenné serve in the local community beyond being a place of worship?

and 12-inch wide pieces were carved from a single block of wood. The wood has a seat shaped like a crescent and is held off the ground by a flat base.

The stool is the divine throne of the Asante people. The bells on this stool warn the king of danger and it is used in celebrations and processions. The Asante people believed that it embodied the spirit of the Asante Nation (sunum). Therefore, nobody was allowed to sit on it, so it was kept on its side.

It represents the soul and identity of the people and gives meaning to the society's existence and a place in history.

For initiation rituals, new kings were lowered into and raised over the stool, although the stool itself could not be touched. Less sacred stools were handed to both men and women at reaching adulthood, and they adopted the soul of the person throughout their lives.

Two bells are tied to each end of it, depicting divine spirits or kings, and it has elaborate designs in the midsection, linking the seat to the base. Small figures are fastened to the seat. The gold symbolizes royalty.

The Asanti make up the majority of the population in Ghana. Their king, Osei Tutu, merged numerous formerly independent chiefs into one kingdom in the 17th century. After assembling the chiefs, the priest Okomfo Anokye allegedly lifted his arms toward the skies, after which a golden stool then descended to Osei Tutu, and the chiefs devoted themselves to the king as the divine symbol.

The stool is so sacred that it has never been placed on the ground or sat on. Some say it is more important to the Asante people than the king (Asantehene), despite the king being viewed as a divine medium between his people and the spiritual realm.

Portrait Mask (Mblo)

The *Portrait Mask*—also referred to as *Mblo*—belonged to Owie Kimou in the early 20th century.

This is a wooden mask decorated with pigment. It is attributed to the Baule people that resided in Côte d'Ivoire (Ivory Coast).

The mask shows a black elongated face with brown triangular symbols and traces of orange and red pigment near the lips, eyes, and nose. The nose is long, and the mouth is closed. Rounded ears are carved into either side of the face. Markings are carved around the hairline, representing hair. A crown-like object is attached to the head, and a rectangular shape has a cross-like set of curved triangles at the center, with circles on either side carved into it. Six shapes are located at the top of the rectangle.

The mask is a bit over 14 inches in length.

The Baule people's masks were used during a masquerade event called Gbagba, held in the village of Kami during the early 1900s. The masquerade included drummers, singers, and dancers. Those who wore the masks hid until a climactic moment when the artworks worn on the faces of the entertainment were revealed.

What is the main narrative being depicted in *The Last Supper*, and how are the apostles arranged around Jesus?

The masks are hidden while they are not utilized, and were not, like other masks, hung on walls for the mere appreciation of their physical appearance.

Over time, their meaning and function changed for the Baule.

Many believed these masks had the power to communicate with ancestors and spirits, and they were created in honor of the respected members of the Baule community.

The mask's creation was inspired by Moya Yanso's portrait. Yanso was a woman from Kami idealized for her beauty and incredible dancing. Moya Yanso continued to dance with this mask until her physical ability came to an end. The mask displays her at her prime, with small lips and a high forehead that convey posture and intelligence, and her left eye is slightly higher than her right eye, giving an impression of complexity. The tubular pieces above her head are purely decorative. The folds near her mouth convey a sense of aging, the brass surface represents health as it reflects sunlight, and there is a slight representation of animals with the horns.

The Baule people were known for wood sculptures and ceremonial masks. The majority of communities are farmers that live in matriarchal family units.

Sadly, these traditional masquerade events ended in the 1980s.

How did the artists of Benin convey the importance of figures
in the *Benin Plaques* without using a sense of depth?

Bundu Mask

The *Bundu Mask* and similar pieces were created by the Sande
Society—Mende people of the West African forests of Sierra
Leone—during the 19th to 20th centuries.

The mask was created from dark wood, cloth, and fiber. It resembles a thimble-like shape, holding a very small face with small features at the center and bottom of the head. There is an upward point
extending from the face that forms the forehead. The pointed forehead is decorated with geometric patterns on either side that fold to
the back of the head. The geometric shapes are separated by a ring
that grows from the top of the head. This area contains multiple
perpendicular points arranged on the face. A wild hairstyle is represented by fibers that extend down from the head.

These masks were used in a masquerade celebrating a girl's matura-
tion. A female dancer wore the costume and resembled Sowo, the
water spirit of the Sande Society. This is intended for young girls to
strive and mimic Sowo's image.

The Sande Society believed that the mask highlighted wifely ideals
and spiritual knowledge through dancing.

While the mask was not worn during a ritual, it was safely stored
away.

The full costume includes a gown of raffia fibers, completely covering the girl's body and the 24-pound mask that represents Sowo. During the ceremony, the woman's body is painted with white clay to make her unattractive because she is not a woman yet. The mask's deep black and smooth surface shows the ideal aesthetic in contrast to the white clay. A coat of palm oil allows the surface to reflect light, also representing healthy and beautiful skin.

It was believed that the mask embodied an ideal moral and physical beauty. Fertility, good health, and high status are represented through stylized rings around the neck. The eyes are closed and downcast, indicating a sense of reservation. The small mouth signifies the dismissal of spreading gossip; the small ears indicate that women should not listen to gossip; and four lines under the eyes show the ideal aesthetic of scars.

Girls are referred to as chrysalis—or inactive pupa—during the initiation, as they are transforming from girls into women. This is echoed in the shape of their necks.

Ikenga

The *Ikenga* is a sculpture made of carved wood within the masculine sculptural genre. It has both animal attributes and a human face (anthropomorphic and zoomorphic).

All *Ikenga* are noticeably taller than they are wide. Ikenga figurines have a set of ram horns that vary in size, and the main carvings of the figures are covered in intricate designs.

The artworks honor the Igbos' belief in the value of individual accomplishment. It serves as a source of power for the owner, and it highlights the strength of the right hand. This is why a sword is typically held in the right hand.

While Ikenga figures resemble the people for whom they were created, they are meant to represent that individual's importance in society or any previous achievements. Ikenga illustrates the value of a person's earned status in Igbo culture and establishes their status as a warrior.

It is always kept in some kind of sanctuary in the home of the owner. Figures were placed in their own personal shrines, and men made sacrifices to it.

Horns were a symbol of aggressiveness and ambition because they believed that rams battle with the heads and the head initiates all good action. Most *Ikenga* carvings grip their swords in the right hand.

These figurines are made by the Igbo people of modern Nigeria. The Igbo civilization dates back to the 19th century, and they lived in a remote area where they were very isolated and independent from surrounding tribes. They lacked any form of government or a chief. This created a welcoming society that celebrated personal achievement and success. Today, the Igbo people make up the second largest ethnicity in southern Nigeria.

Opo Ogoga

The *Opo Ogoga* is one of four carved wooden posts painted with an
unknown pigment. It was created by Olowe of Ise.

It serves as a veranda post, the structural support for the palace at
Ikere.

The focal point depicts a seated king. The senior wife is standing
behind him, crowning him. Her large scale and pose show her
importance in participating in the coronation and as a political advisor to the king. The small figure at the king's feet signifies a junior
wife. The trickster god Esu plays the flute, and there is also a fan
bearer.

The artwork reflects Olowe of Ise's style. It has exaggerated proportions, an interrelationship between the figures, and spaces between
them. The technical composition depicts the intimate bond between
the king and his wives. The line of the senior wife's jaw continues by
a bird's tail. A diagonal line of breasts goes into the king's jaw and
is seen again in his arms. The king's crown shows a pattern of beads
from the senior wife's bracelet.

The *Opo Ogoga* exemplifies the influential style in Yoruba culture.
Olowe was considered the best Yoruba carver until his death in 1938.

7.2. Central Africa

Ndop of King Mishe miShyaang maMbul

The artwork shows an anthropomorphic figure with an enlarged head. The calm, expressionless face reflects dignity, while a man—presumably the king—is sitting cross-legged on a raised platform. The figure holds a royal drum and wears a crown. The head is the most important part of the body because it is considered the center of intelligence.

The sculpture is carved out of wood and is polished, giving it a shiny and reddish appearance. The artist includes intricate detailing on the arms, drums, face, and platform. The king has bold facial features with a strong brow and closed eyes. While it is not an exact likeness of the king, it captures the ideal king.

Certain objects identify an individual king, like the drum and belt, and various geometric motifs and emblems (ibol) distinguish each reign. Other symbols capture the king's wealth and royal lineage.

The *Ndop of King Mishe miShyaang maMbul* was commissioned in 1710 by the Kuba King Mishe miShyaang maMbul at the height of his reign. Kuba refers to 19 different factions who follow the same leader, the nyim. The Kuba kingdom was prosperous between the 17th and 19th centuries.

It is intended to celebrate his generosity and a great number of loyal subjects. A Ndop is a record of the king's reign and commemorates his accomplishments. The Kuba people did not have written historical records; instead, they used Ndops. It was also believed to hold the king's spiritual essence and was carefully protected for those who would reign in the future.

The artwork was purchased in 1961 by the Brooklyn Museum in New York.

Nkisi n'kondi

The *Nkisi n'kondi* is known as a power figure that was made by the people of the Kongo (the Democratic Republic of the Congo) in the late 19th century.

The figure is made of wood, resin, ceramic, and metal and it serves as a somewhat magical carving resembling a human. There is a dramatic sense as the figure is leaning forward in a wide stance. Simultaneously, this signifies strength and importance. The carving contains a variety of materials, such as nails, pegs, and sticks. Each of these has a different meaning.

The figures are only a few inches tall because they are meant to be small and transportable.

A strong sculptural tradition exists among these people. Power figures were often used as reminders of their obligations within society and to enforce proper behavior. The figures also brought protection and healing to the community, served as a mediator between the ancestral spirit world and the living world, and symbolized honoring contracts and agreements.

The figure has an elongated belly button created from a cowrie shell that had been placed on the abdomen. This is symbolic of fertility and wealth. The figure also acts as a connection to the ancestors. The wide, staring eyes and imposing stance aim to ward off negative forces that would interfere with its ritual function. This is enhanced by medicinal combinations—covered by a piece of glass—contained inside the figures. The glass's reflective surface symbolized contact with the supernatural.

The figures are also used as nkisi (plural minkisi), containing sacred substances—activated by supernatural forces—that summon positive spirits into the natural world. Spiritual importance and protection were very significant to the Kongo people.

However, the figures were destroyed by missionaries of the late 19th century because they were feared as evidence of sorcery and heathenism.

The figures were carved by a spiritual specialist—called a nganga—who summoned the spirits by inserting blades, nails, and other metal objects into the wooden surface to make them "angry" and call them into action. The spirits were also activated by a shaman who stored medicinal combinations—called bilongo—in the heads of the figures. This made a connection between the spiritual and physical world.

Female (Pwo) Mask

Pwo Mwana is the founding mother and deity who represents the fertility of the Chokwe people.

These masks showed a woman's face in a realistic manner, complete with elaborately styled hair, earrings, and tattoos.

They portrayed the ideal female features, including wide foreheads, small noses, serene demeanors, glowing reddish-brown complexions (considered healthy), and delicately rounded ears, mouths, and chins. The artists employed symmetrical shapes, circles, and clean lines. The masks, crafted with very delicate carvings, captured a peaceful expression. The triangles of the tattoo (cingelyengelye) are on the left cheek and forehead. There is also the temple tattoo mitelumuna (knitted eyebrows), and tattoos under the eyes signify tears.

These creations serve to honor the ideal Chokwe woman who had successfully given birth.

Two performers, one wearing the Pwo mask and one wearing a mask of her male counterpart, Chihongo, would dance and perform rituals meant to give the tribe fertility and prosperity.

The masks were also utilized during male initiation rituals to teach young men about proper behavior as well as to show them the ideal type of woman (who is like Pwo) to take as their wife.

Lukasa

A lukasa is a wooden plank that has beads made of metal and other materials that are specifically placed to make patterns to visualize the history of the Luba people. These memory boards varied in size but were small enough to hold. They were popular with the Luba in the Democratic Republic of Congo during the 19th and 20th centuries.

A lukasa was utilized to document important times and events in Luban society. The Luba people, emerging as a powerful nation in central Africa in the beginning of the 1500s, wanted to find a way to preserve their history so their culture would not become lost. Specific people were chosen by Luban kings and were instructed to memorize patterns and colors in order to tell the story to the people.

However, only a few specially trained people were able to do this. This shows hierarchy and class consciousness, as only the most accomplished and senior members of the council were able to read the memory boards. These people were known as "men of memory" (Moss, 2015). Readers would hold the boards in their left hand and follow patterns with their right index finger.

It is hard to keep the stories of the Luba alive because they are carried on in the oral tradition, and trained readers are dying and not passing down the stories; thus, culture is lost.

Aka Elephant Masks

Aka elephant masks hail from Bamileke (Cameroon, western grasslands region) c. 19th to 20th centuries.

The wooden masks are composed of colorful cloth and beads. They have hoodlike faces with round eyes of white cloth and red beads. There are also vibrant navy-blue tones in the fabric. The face and the rest of the mask are covered in cowrie shells. Two long panels of woven raffia fiber—that represent the elephant's trunk—adorn the edges. Isosceles triangles and other geometric designs are used. Two circles represent the elephant's ears.

This piece of art was meant to be used in performance, with the wearer also donning a tunic and decorative headdress. It is very dramatic, and many people would wear these masks while emerging from a large palace compound. To adorn these outfits, people frequently added bracelets made from ivory and rare leopard pelts. The headdress symbolized privilege. It was made of red feathers from the African gray parrot and left the audience in awe.

Its purpose was to highlight the Bamileke king's total power and dominance.

The elephant was always regarded as a representation of regal might and was meant to be worshiped. Beads imported from Venice and the Middle East symbolized great wealth and status, while black beads represented the link between the living and the dead. White beads represented ancestors and medicines. Red beads signified life and women, and the triangular bead design, resembling leopard spots, symbolized power and authority.

Byeri

The *reliquary figure (byeri)*, a carved wooden figure, belonged to the Fang peoples of southern Cameroon (Equatorial Africa) during the 19th and 20th centuries.

The Abstract style is emphasized by the geometric shapes of the object. This depicted the idea of a guardian figure instead of a realistic human figure. This figure is male, but female byeris were made as well.

Figures had elongated torsos, downcast eyes, closed mouths, and powerful musculature.

These were used to guard family reliquary boxes against the "forbidden gaze of women, uninitiated boys, and evil spirits" (Harris & Klemm, 2015).

Holy relics, such as the bones of revered ancestors and potent substances, are kept in reliquaries. They served as a talisman or an object with supernatural properties that kept them safe from harm and provided good fortune.

Sometimes the figures were consulted when making crucial decisions, and at times, they were used as puppets to teach their ancestry
to young males in the community.

The body depicts that of an adult, while the head symbolizes that
of an infant. This highlights the cycle of human development. An
enlarged head represents intelligence. The infant's characteristics
include a high forehead and a protruding belly button. Infants
establish a link between the living and the dead. It also reflects the
significance of ancestors.

Bulging muscles contradict a calm, expressionless face, and a symmetrical pose is utilized to emphasize the physical traits the Fang people
valued. Muscles represent readiness to defend reliquaries from spirits
or humans attacking them. The patient expression suggests honor,
serenity, vigor, and the ability to hold opposites in balance. The figures
are essentially abstract geometric representations of the human form.

7.3. Southern Africa

Conical Tower and Circular Wall of Great Zimbabwe

Built between 1000–1400 by the Shona people, the Conical Tower
and Circular Wall of Great Zimbabwe are located in Southeastern
Zimbabwe.

The structure is made of coursed granite blocks. Ashlar masonry was
applied, eliminating the use of mortar by using carefully cut stones

instead. The wall is an 820-feet-long stone-walled structure punctuated with turrets and monoliths.

The granite materials were extracted from hills in the region and took decades to transport. It took over 30 years to complete the structure, which represents the remarkable skill of the builders.

A sculpture made of soapstone shows a seated bird resting on a panel of zig zags. It was found in the circular nook of a wall. The sculpture is thought to symbolize the strength of Shona kings. The Conical Tower was built as a place to worship the supreme all-creator god, Mwari.

The construction took place during a time Great Zimbabwe was wealthy and successful, and the structure was representative of their pride.

The tower is 30 feet tall and 18 feet in diameter, incorporating impressive geometric shapes and detailed patterns.

Smaller structures and towers are enclosed within the greater walls. The circular wall of Great Zimbabwe around the Conical Tower has used the same kind of stone.

It reflects a distinct style because of the location, uninfluenced by Islamic architecture.

This was a royal center where kings exercised their power. The wall separated the common people from the royal families and showed their power. Additionally, it acted as protection for the houses and the commercial markets in the area.

The Conical Tower functioned as a granary, which symbolized that the ruler was responsible for a bountiful harvest. The amount of grain was indicative of a Shona ruler's power and wealth.

Furthermore, the circular plan enabled panoramic views of the country and allowed residents to see whether enemies were approaching.

The Shona are still the largest ethnic group in Zimbabwe.

Key Concepts

- Examples of notable structures and artworks from **South Africa** include the *Great Mosque of Djenné*, the *Benin Plaques*, the *Sika Dwa Kofi*, the *Portrait Mask (Mblo)*, the *Bundu Mask*, the *Ikenga*, and the *Opo Ogoga*.
- The *Ndop of King Mishe miShyaang maMbul, the Nkisi n'kondi*, the *Female (Pwo) Mask, lukasa, Aka elephant masks*, and the *byeri* are some of the significant works of art from **Central Africa**.
- The *Conical Tower and Circular Wall of Great Zimbabwe* is a noteworthy structure located in **Southern Africa**.

CHAPTER 8

ASIA

Learning objectives:

- Identify an artwork.
- Explain why and how traditions and changes are depicted.
- Analyze form, function, content, and context to explain the intentions of the artwork's creation.
- Analyze relationships between artworks based on differences and similarities.

> How does the *Ndop of King Mishe miShyaang maMbul* depict the significance of the head in their belief about the center of intelligence?

8.1. West and Central Asia

Tombs at Petra

The Tombs at Petra are iconic rock-cut façades that make up an ancient city. The site was built between 400 BCE and 100 CE by the Nabateans. They were the inhabitants of the city, and the most famous monument they produced is known as the Khazneh Treasury.

The city's style resembles the Hellenistic Era and shows the influence of the great Eastern Mediterranean city, Alexandria. The architecture incorporates a broken pediment with a circular building at the center of the upper level. Corinthian columns ornate the spaces. Two obelisks' bases are located above the pediment and stretch up into the rock.

With all the necessary facilities, this was a functioning city. The primary buildings were utilized as a temple, a treasury, and tombs. In addition, major trading took place here because of its centrally-located geographical position in the landscape of early civilization.

Some of the tombs at Petra are dated by inscriptions and align with another Nabataean site, Egra, where there are 31 dated tombs.

The tombs were presumably constructed when the Nabateans were at their wealthiest between the second century BCE and the early second century CE.

Buddha of Bamiyan

The *Buddha of Bamiyan* is located in Afghanistan and dates from around 400–800 CE. Unfortunately, it was destroyed in 2001.

This high-relief sculpture was cut from rock and sculpted with plaster and polychrome paint. The sculpture included two figures that were carved into the cliff face facing the Bamiyan valley, while the feet and heads are round, allowing worshippers to circulate around it.

The western Buddha stood at 175 feet tall, and the eastern Buddha stood at 120 feet tall.

There is a clear combination between the Hellenistic style and Indian images. This can be seen in the Greek drapery in their robes and the way in which the statues are painted similarly to ancient Greece sculptures.

Bamiyan Valley in the center of Afghanistan was known as a destination on the Silk Route, preferred for its fertile land and its ideal location for merchants and missionaries to stop.

Masjid-e Jameh

The Masjid-e Jameh is a rebuilt mosque made of additions, expansions, and modifications that took place over 1,000 years.

The site incorporates a large courtyard at the center, surrounded by a two-story arcade, brick piers, and columns that support the roof system. The mosque is a four iwan—open on three of the four sides—design.

One area is primarily used as a private space by the sultan and opens up to the courtyard. The structure includes centrally planned inscriptions on the walls and uses a combination of blue and gold.

The Masjid-e Jameh intended to bring people together in prayer and away from the surrounding busy streets. The aim was to unite the community (umma), making the mosque's location in the heart of the city ideal for gathering and transportation. Overall, it became much more than just a space for prayer.

When were the tombs at Petra most likely constructed?

Folio from Quran

The Qur'an is the sacred text of the Islamic religion. One of the most important artworks in history is an analyzed folio from the Qur'an.

The sacred text was written with black ink on parchment with a broad-nibbed reed pen. The type of calligraphy used in this manuscript is known as Kufic, and being written in Arabic, it is read from the right to the left.

The text is divided into chapters—referred to as surahs—which contain verses called ayahs by triangles consisting of five gold circles located at the end of each verse. Each surah's title is written in gold ink and is surrounded by a rectangle filled with golden vines. This indicates the beginning of each surah and allows for readers to maneuver through the manuscript easily.

Like other religious texts, the Qur'an is used for sacred rituals and recitations. The Islamic faith revolves around this book. The Arabic text speaks of the divine revelation of the Prophet Muhammad.

The scribes who created the illustrations for this book were highly regarded in their society for their stylistic abilities.

The Ardabil Carpet

The *Ardabil Carpet* is an Iranian carpet from the Safavid Dynasty that dates back to 1539–1540. It is inscribed with the words "Maqsud Kashani."

This piece of art consists of silk warps and wefts with wool, and the dyes used to color the fabric include pomegranate rind and natural indigo.

The carpet acts as one of the prominent examples of Islamic art. Carpets made of silk and wool were frequently exchanged or sold throughout the Islamic lands, China, and Europe. Iranian carpets were highly prized, as these carpets were used to decorate homes, mosques, and shrines. They were also hung on some walls to preserve warmth.

The visual design depicts geometric shapes, floral patterns, scrolls, and other typical Islamic art. A golden medallion at the center dominates the carpet, and is surrounded by an intricate ring of multi-colored ovals. The carpet's border consists of rectangular spaces where calligraphy is used and filled with decorations.

The *Ardabil Carpet* mainly served as a funerary shrine for Safi al-Din and for prayer ceremonies. It was named after the town of Ardabil in Northwest Iran, the home of the shrine of the Sufi saint, Safi al-Din Ardabili. Safi al-Din Ardabili was also the leader who introduced his followers to Islamic practices. His followers expanded after his death in 1330, and their descendants became Islamic influencers in the community.

> How was the sculpture of the *Buddha of Bamiyan* constructed in terms of materials and technique?

8.2. Indian Art

Lakshmana Temple

The Lakshmana Temple is attributed to the Khajuraho group in the Chhatarpur District in Madhya Pradesh, India. The temple dates back to 954 CE.

The structure consists of fine sandstone and uses ashlar masonry in a Nagara style. It acts as a Hindu temple.

The temple includes a shrine—referred to as a "vimana"—and an entryway—known as a 'mandapa'—on a flat-roofed porch. Nagara-style shrines often include a large superstructure—known as sikhara—on a platform that can be seen from a great distance.

Additionally, it is a Chandela-style temple, suggesting that the structure does not act as a hall for congregational worship but the residence of a god instead. The temple is used for cultural events and festivals as a way to spread cultural values.

There is a sculpture of the deity, Vishnu—in his three-headed form, known as Vaikuntha—at the center of the temple. This area is referred to as the temple's inner womb chamber, implying that the sculpture has a harmonious integration with the structure.

Additional sculptures of loving couples—known as "mithuna"— are added as symbols of the divine union and the final release from samsara, the cycle of death and rebirth known as' moksha.' The couples' erotic poses represent regeneration. However, they were not intended to be provocative but served a ritual and symbolic significance to the builders, devotees, and patrons instead.

The Chandella rulers, who ruled over the capital Khajuraho, erected numerous temples, the first of which was the Lakshmana Temple. Yasovarman, the head of the clan, served as this temple's first patron. Yasovarman maintained control over territories in the Bundelkhand region of Central India, which was once a part of the larger Pratihara Dynasty.

Many Hindu temples have been dedicated to the gods Shiva, Vishnu, and Surya. Temples were also built to honor the divine teachers of the ancient Indian religion, Jainism.

Why was it important for the Masjid-e Jameh
to be situated in the heart of the city?

Taj Mahal

The Taj Mahal is located in Agra on the banks of the Yamuna River in Uttar Pradesh, India. Its construction included marble workers, masons, decorators, and mosaicists working under the direction of Ustad Ahmad Lahori, the emperor's architect. The structure was built between 1632–1653.

You would enter the building from the forecourt that was accompanied by shops. Next, you passed through a gateway decorated with inlaid red sandstone and a long water channel leading to Taj. Taj is located on a raised panel at the northern end of the gardens.

Taj is encircled by symmetrical buildings, like the guest house and the mosque. The exterior shows a bulbous dome and four equally tall minarets. The interior has a "hasht bishist" (eight levels) floor-plan that alludes to the eight levels of the Muslim paradise. Many side rooms and eight halls connect to a central space in a cross-axial form. The center holds Mumtaz's—for whom the Taj Mahal was initially built—remains in a raised cenotaph. Shah Jahan was buried next to her decades later.

The walls are inscribed with verses, and white marble is carved and decorated with semi-precious stones, as the Mughal architecture tended to utilize red stone for exteriors and white marble for decorations or interiors of tombs or holy places.

> What type of calligraphy is used in the
> analyzed folio from the Qur'an?

The mausoleum and gardens were for Mumtaz Jahan and were commissioned by Shah Jahan, the fifth Mughal ruler. The structure was a tomb for his favorite wife Mumtaz, who died in childbirth, and it was known as the 'Luminous Tomb' during the Mughal rule.

The building is based on Humayun's tomb and can be interpreted as a symbol of love, but it may have been built even if Mumtaz had not died. Overall, the building glorifies the Mughal emperor and his rule.

8.3. Southeast Asian Art

Angkor

The temple of Angkor is located in Cambodia. The structure was erected in honor of the 800–1400 CE Hindu Angkor Dynasty.

Angkor Wat is the greatest religious monument worldwide, spanning nearly 400 acres of land and with a height of 699 feet. It includes various Khmer Empire capitals from the 9th to the 15th century, including the Angkor Wat temple in Angkor Thom.

Not only does the site consist of temples and monuments, but it very successfully incorporates hydraulic structures like basins, dykes, reservoirs, and canals, as well as communication routes. The villages spread throughout the park are still inhabited, and Buddhist monks and nuns still worship there today.

What are surahs and ayahs, and how are they
differentiated in the folio from the Qur'an?

The entire structure is made of stone, and high-relief ornaments and pictures in bas relief adorn nearly every surface.

Vishnu, the protector or preserver, was honored in the Angkor temple.

As stated in ancient Sanskrit and Khmer texts, temples should be built in harmony with nature. Therefore, it was planned according to the calendar of the year as well as the sun and moon. The central axis is aligned with the planets, the plan of the universe, or the mandala.

The temple is separated from the moat by an expansive wall. The plan shows three passageways—referred to as galleries—that run around the temple and a sanctuary marked by five stone towers at its center. The stone towers are representative of the mythical home of the gods in both Hinduism and Buddhism, called Meru. Meru is considered an "axis-mundi," or a connection between Heaven and Earth (Rod-Ari, 2015a).

A carved relief of 12,916 square feet represents eight different Hindu tales. This includes the beginning of time, or what is thought of as the creation of the universe. We see the powerful 'devas'—gods— fighting 'asura—demons—to reclaim order. There is a depiction of gods and demons churning the sea of milk while using Naga—the snake—in a game of tug-of-war to churn the oceans. It is believed that once the elixir is released after churning, Indra—the king of all gods—descends to collect it and save the world.

What does the *Ndop of King Mishe miShyaang maMbul* aim
to represent or commemorate about the king's reign?

The structure has become a Cambodian national symbol. The name
means "City Temple" in Khmer, the national language of Cambodia.
It was built by King Suryavarman II (1113–1150 CE), the "protector of the sun" (Rod-Ari, 2015a).

Chinese Art

Terracotta Warriors

These sculptures—along with the entire burial complex—were created for emperor Qin Shihuang during his reign from 221–209
BCE.

How were the dyes used to color the *Ardabil* Carpet derived?

The *Terracotta Warriors* were intended to later guard the tomb of the emperor, as he was the first to unite China. This unification was the greatest symbol of the Qin dynasty's influence. During his reign, currency, measurements, writing, and more were introduced as the standard. Emperor Qin Shihuang connected cities and states with advanced systems of canals and roads. He is also credited with the construction of the Great Wall of China. While his strategies were extremely violent and destructive, Qin was referred to as a military genius.

An entire complex has been found underground, consisting of gardens, jade jewelry, stables, ritual vessels made of bronze, and many gold and silver ornaments.

Emperor Qin ensured that his burial complex was decorated with precious stones intended to represent the stars, sun, and moon. As someone who looked at the cosmos for guidance, he was deeply concerned with the universe as a means of crossing over to the afterlife.

Qin ascended to the throne at age 13 and immediately began to plan the burial site that would carry him into an immortal world. His terracotta army included chariots pulled by horses that carried warriors and infantrymen with all their armor and weaponry.

Funeral Banner of Xin Zhui

The *Funeral Banner of Xin Zhui*—the person also referred to as Lady Dai—was painted on silk in the second century BCE. It was found in the nesting caskets of Lady Dai.

These caskets consist of wooden—with varnished exterior and interior—coffins placed inside one another. The dimensions of the outermost coffin are roughly 100 x 46 x 45 inches. While the casket did not survive in good condition, it preserved the funeral banner extraordinarily well.

Historians are uncertain of its exact function, but the banner presumably held some connection to the afterlife. Its potential use was to identify the deceased during their burial ceremony. Other theories involve its use as a burial shroud that led the soul to the afterlife successfully. However, only the most elite could afford such banners, and thus they were a clear display of wealth.

The banner consists of four registers, including the heavenly register, depicted wider and longer than the others. The heavenly register has a god with a dragon's body and a human head, two men who are depicted as the gatekeepers of Heaven, a pink sun, and a crescent moon. This likely represents the supernatural aspect of the heavenly realm.

Lady Dai and her attendants are seen in the second horizontal register. The scene includes a portrait of Lady Dai wearing an expensive embroidered silk robe while she is standing on a bi—a disk with a hole that represents the sky—with two servants in front of her. White and pink colored dragons surround the register.

The body of Lady Dai is depicted in the third register along with two rows of mourners, sacrificial funerary rites, large receptacles, and vase-shaped jars that were used to present food and drink to the gods. Lady Dai is seen wearing a similar silk robe as in the register above.

> How is the structure of the Lakshmana Temple built
> in terms of materials and architectural style?

The fourth register depicts the underworld, two enormous black fish, a red snake, two blue goats, a deity that resembles a human, and beings that represent water and death in the underworld.

Lady Dai was known as an elite member of the Han Dynasty. This powerful dynasty was wide and stretched as far as the Roman Empire, where the elite were housed in gated villages near the emperor.

It is an early example of one of the earliest natural works in China. It has the earliest known portrait in Chinese art history, with containers in the background that are smaller than the ones in the foreground. These act as attempts at the earliest display of depth on a two-dimensional surface.

The David Vases

The *David Vases* are produced in the 1351 Yuan dynasty. They are found in Jiangxi province of China.

The vases are made of blue and white porcelain with intricate designs modeled after bronzes.

They were created as an altarpiece, along with an incense burner, to honor a commander who had just become a god, thanks to his extraordinary strength, wisdom, and ability to see and tell the future. They were also intended for the altar of a Daoist temple.

The vases are tall and white, decorated with blue stylized dragons, clouds, birds, and floral patterns. The handles are designed like an elephant's head, and the vases' necks and feet are decorated with flowers and leaves. On the side of the necks of the vessels, there is a dedication that is thought to be the earliest blue and white porcelain dedication ever discovered. They were made as an altarpiece along with an incense burner to honor a general who had recently been made into a god due.

The central section shows Chinese dragons with scales and claws and traditional long bodies and beards, set in a sea of clouds.

The blue porcelain was imported from Iran. The Chinese expansion into Western Asia made the cobalt blue available.

With their distinctive blue glaze on white porcelain and its dragon, floral, and other curvilinear motifs, these porcelain vases demonstrate the classic Chinese porcelain-making methods.

Forbidden City

The main palace for the Chinese emperors over the centuries is what many know as the Forbidden City. The site was the political and ritual center of China for over 500 years.

Final improvements were added to the site, located in the center of Beijing, in 1420.

The precinct consists of red walls with yellow-glazed roof tiles. The 98-building city stretches 1,050 yards long, 820 yards wide, and contains a moat 55 yards wide.

The Forbidden City was intended as a ceremonial, residential, and ritual space. Therefore, the architects based the design on the ideal cosmic order in Confucian ideology. This layout design ensured that all activities adhered to the participants' familial and social roles. Thus, an individual's social status determined where their family lived in the Forbidden City.

The palace served as the home to the Chinese emperors and their court. The court was separated from the city on an island, strengthening the emperor's influence.

The palace consists of an inner and outer court. The outer court was utilized for state affairs—only men were allowed inside—and the inner court comprised living quarters where the focus was on domestic life. The main building located in the outer court—also known as the Hall of Supreme Harmony—was where the important decisions of the state were made, and the main buildings in the inner court were the emperor and empresses' residences. They are known as the Palace of Heavenly Purity and the Palace of Earthly Tranquility.

Operating for over 500 years, the site saw many political, technological, and other changes over its lifetime. It was originally built to solidify power from a coup d'état—the fourth son of the Ming emperor who usurped power from his older brothers and seized

control—when he moved the capital from Nanjing to Beijing and
began building a new home.

After the Ming dynasty, the Qing dynasty ruled and continued to
use the Forbidden City as the headquarters of the royal court.

After its closure in 1925, the site became the National Museum of
China.

8.5. Korean Art

Gold and Jade Crown

The crown of the Silla kingdom is from the second half of the fifth
century. It was excavated from the north mound of the Great Tomb of
Hwangnam. It is made from gold and jade.

The crown was placed in Chinese burial mounds when royal family
members died. People of high ranking wore it on special occasions
to show their influence and power.

The crown was discovered in the Silla Kingdom. This kingdom
occupied most of the southeast after Korea was divided into three
kingdoms.

The Gold and Jade Crown highlights the connection between Korea
and the Eurasian steppe, which spans thousands of miles of grassland

from central Europe through to Asia. The same Chinese burial techniques were used throughout, resulting in many pieces of gold and precious items being found with the dead kings.

Three branches form around the headband, which stand in for the sacred tree that previously stood in Gyeongju's ritual precinct. It also demonstrates a link between Heaven and Earth. Two antlers represent the reindeer, an animal native to the Eurasian steppe. Gold disks and jade pieces (gogok) are also on the branches, depicting the ripe fruits that show the fertility of the land.

Portrait of Sin Sukju

The *Portrait of Sin Sukju* is made during the second half of the 15th century. It is a silk-based, hanging scroll created with color and ink. The portrait was a part of the Goryeong Sin Family Collection in Cheongwon, Treasure no. 613.

The full-length portrait has a slight rightward tilt. It uses a lot of angular lines.

The portrait was commissioned in honor of the court member—and future prime minister's—accomplishments. Sin Sukju was a scholar and politician who attained the position of prime minister in 1445. The scene gives a sense of the loyalty Sin Sukju had to the king, whom he believed was deserving of respect. This is shown through the official robes and rank badge he is wearing on his chest. This rank badge is typically made of embroidered silk and features two peacocks surrounded by plants and clouds.

The pictured scene also served as a ritualistic site where Sin Sukju's family was guided in worship. However, it also acted as propaganda and was allegedly used to reflect the government's superiority over the Korean people.

The portrait shows the full-length view of a seated Sin Sukju, with his head slightly turned to only show one ear. This was common during that time period. Dignity and wisdom are reflected in his wrinkles and solemn expression. This detail on his face contrasts with the simplicity of his attire.

The Koreans believed that the face revealed important clues about the subject reflected in the portrait. So the interest and detail on his face were improved when the Jesuits introduced Koreans to Western painting techniques in the 18th century.

8.6. Japanese Art

How were the *Terracotta Warriors* and the burial complex constructed during Emperor Qin Shihuang's reign?

Tōdai-ji

The *Tōdai-ji* is located in Nara, Japan. Various artists were involved in creating this piece, including the sculptors Unkei and Keikei as well as the Kei School.

The piece dates back to 743 CE and was rebuilt in 1700.

Todai-ji means the "Great Eastern Temple." This refers to its location in the city of Nara, on the eastern edge.

The Kokubun-ji is known as a national system of monasteries in Japan. Its chief temple was the Todaji-ji. Commissioned by Emperor Shomu, it was a way to promote religious harmony among the Japanese provinces, unifying them under his reign and showing the authority, prestige, and piety of the Japanese imperial court.

At its core is a huge hall called a "hondo," which is supported by 84 cypress pillars. Later, monks erected two nine-story pagodas, a lecture hall, and living quarters.

On either side of the gate are the guardian kings or Nio guardian statues. They are shown as two enormous wooden statues almost 25 feet tall. The figures are shown with complex swirling drapery, intimidating expressions, powerful gestures, and dynamic bodies. These men stand guard over the Buddha. The figures were initially painted.

There is also a bronze Great Buddha (Daibutsu) statue atop a bronze lotus-petal pedestal. This captures the refined naturalist design of the Nara period.

Images of Shaka and Bodhisattva are engraved in the interior. Shaka is the historical Buddha, and Bodhisattva is a god who refuses to enter nirvana to help others.

The current building is a reconstruction of the original, which was destroyed by a 12th-century fire.

The structure was the largest building project to that date in Japan and was, at one time, the largest wooden building in the world.

It illustrates the combination of Buddhism and politics in early Japan. Buddhism gained popularity in the Nara Era after it was introduced in the 6th century under Emperor Shomu and the Empress.

It promoted Buddhist thought in political policies and architecture.

Red and White Plum Blossoms

This artwork was created by Ogata Kōrin on a pair of fold screens made of watercolor and gold leaf on paper.

A sense of mastery is seen in the interplay of forms, the use of colors and texture, and the unconventional methods of ink painting that are executed.

How did the artists of the *Female (Pwo) Mask* emphasize
the ideal features of a Chokwe woman?

The *Red and White Plum Blossoms* established Kōrin's reputation and preserved the ideal values of the Rimpa Movement. The artist produced a piece that successfully matched a traditional Japanese folding door's function.

Both abstract and realistic elements are noted in the artwork. The viewer is denied any sense of time or geographic location by the overbearing gold leaf background. While the stream is a non-naturalistic metallic color, its swirls present a movement in the water. A further non-naturalist upward tilt is created within the scene by the use of sharp, tapered lines. The colors are muddy and do not have a naturally distinct outline. However, there is a clear indication that Kōrin understood how plum trees grow, as seen from the accuracy in their shapes.

Each screen is hinged at its central hinge. This enables the two-dimensional painting to appear as three-dimensional.

As an epitome of Japanese art, this piece was part of the Rimpa Movement or the "School of Kōrin." This movement is known for the combination of dynamism, monumental presence, naturalism, and a sense of sensuality. It was first inspired by Chinese literature but eventually evolved to depict naturalistic Chinese elements.

How are the four registers on the *Funeral Banner of Xin Zhui* distinct from each other in terms of their depiction and themes?

Kanagawa Oki Nami Ura

This piece, produced between 1830–1833, is a polychrome woodblock print with ink and color on paper. It was created in the Ukiyo-e print style.

The artist, Hokusai, is responding to the rise in domestic travel and the corresponding market for images of Mount Fuji. The woodblock prints were bought as souvenirs.

The arrangement of the piece framed Mount Fuji. The viewer's eye is drawn directly to the peak of the mountain top diagonally by the white top of the large wave.

There is a juxtaposition of the large wave in the foreground and the small mountain in the distance, along with men in their boats amid strong waves.

It represents nature's intention to drown the people on the boats in person. One of the waves appears to be Mount Fuji.

The striking design contrasts the water and sky with large areas of negative space.

The piece was a part of Kasuchika Hokusai's *Thirty-Six Views of Mount Fuji* series. Hokusai discovered Western prints from Dutch trade and developed Japanese versions of linear perspective. The low horizon line and Prussian blues show Dutch influence.

What do the tattoos on the Female *(Pwo) Mask represent?*

Mount Fuji, the highest mountain in Japan, is considered sacred.

The prints are recognizable for the emphasis on line, pure bright colors, and the ability to distill form down to the minimum.

Ukiyo-e prints are extremely popular in Europe.

Key Concepts

- Examples of distinguished structures and works of art from **West and Central Asia** include the *Tombs at Petra*, the *Buddha of Bamiyan*, the *Masjid-e Jameh*, an *analyzed folio from the Quran*, and the *Ardabil Carpet*.
- Two prominent **structures in India** that are appreciated for their architecture are the *Lakshmana Temple* and the *Taj Mahal*.
- The temple of *Angkor* in Cambodia is known as the greatest religious monument worldwide. It is one of the most noteworthy structures in **Southeast Asia**.
- The *Terracotta Warriors*, the Funeral Banner of Xin Zhui, the David Vases, and the *Forbidden City* are some of the most well-known and appreciated structures, sites, and works of art in **China**.
- Two distinct pieces of **Korean art** are the *crown of the Silla kingdom made from gold and jade*, and the *Portrait of Sin Sukju*.
- The *Tōdai-ji, Red and White Plum Blossoms*, and *Kanagawa Oki Nami Ura* are some of the most notable works of **Japanese art**.

CHAPTER 9

PACIFIC ART

Learning objectives:

- Explain how choices about art making shape an artwork.

9.1. Micronesia

Nan Madol

Nan Madol is in Pohnpei, Micronesia. This structure is one of the early examples of a centralized governmental system in the Western Pacific.

It acts as a tribute to the Saudeleur Dynasty of 700–1600 CE, who believed there is a high value in agriculture and gods.

The Nan Madol includes boulders made of a fine volcanic rock called basalt and prismatic columns. The basalt stones were carved from lava necks.

The Nan Madol's construction was considered an early engineering masterpiece because the builders had to transport the stones— roughly 5–50 tons in weight—from the mountains to the reef without assistance from animals or the little machinery available at the time.

A system of canals runs between the ruins, resulting in the name of Nan Madol, which translates to "spaces between."

The builders did not use concrete; instead, they made use of a crisscrossing pattern incorporating horizontal logs called stretchers and perpendicular logs on top of them, known as headers. This is similar to the post and lintel technique first seen at the creation of Stonehenge.

How were metals combined to achieve the lifelike
appearance of the *Maize Cobs* sculpture?

The site's remote location allowed them to concentrate on building a unique capital city complex that served as a home to over 1,000 inhabitants. Its residents referred to the city as the "Reef of Heaven."

Sadly, the Saudeleur Dynasty started to fail because of increasingly oppressive rulers who were believed to have offended several deities, and eventually, they fell in 1628. Presently, the site is an abandoned city with no preservation.

Female Deity

The *Female Deity* is a wooden sculpture made from the breadfruit tree (Artocarpus altilis). While the exact artist is undetermined, the figure was produced by the Nukuoru from the Caroline Islands, Micronesia.

The wooden figures were carved using an adze with blades of tridacna shell in combination with traditional European tools. The figures all had ovoid heads, very few or subtle facial features, flat buttocks, and long-stretched legs.

The *Female Deity* and similar wooden works were created for religious purposes. Each figure represents a specific deity. All of these include the deity's name, and every deity was attributed to a different family, a priest, and a temple.

The figures are also used as part of an annual harvest ritual where they are offered food during the ceremonies.

During this time, old figures that were rotten were also replaced. The Nukuoru people believed that the deity's spirit lived inside the wooden sculpture during the festival. Nukuoro deities were also believed to inhabit animals and other objects. This was referred to as 'tino aitu.'

Offerings to the figures took place during the annual harvest and included arrowroot, banana, breadfruit, coconuts, pandanus (a fibrous fruit), sugarcane, and taro.

The subtle facial features and flexed legs suggest a "blank vessel" that is ready to take on a deity's spirit. In addition to representing Nukuoro deities, these figures signified their ancestors.

Nails were attached to the figures to allow people to place pieces of clothing—representative of the deities' identities—on the sculptures at the festivals.

The female figures were designed with a triangular shape of the pelvis, indicative of a mandatory tattoo—te mata—given to the elite women of the tribe.

This Micronesian ring-shaped coral reef is located in the Western Pacific. According to archaeologists and art historians, Nukuoru was settled in the 8th century by Polynesians that traveled from Samoa using canoes. Although it is geographically placed in Micronesia,

Nukuoro's culture emphasizes Polynesian influences, including social structures and carving wooden human figures.

The area was ruled by a religious and a secular chief who passed down the reign hereditarily within a family without regard for gender. Thus, Nukuoru chiefs could be male or female.

Navigation Chart

This piece of art was found in the Marshall Islands, Micronesia, around the 19th–20th century.

The *Navigation Chart* is made up of wooden sticks bound to palm leaves and connected with shells, representing the Marshall Islands.

Creators used an array of fibers, shells, and wood arranged to indicate the different regional Marshallese geographic locations, such as the ring-shaped coral reefs.

The *Navigation Chart* is a form of a rebbelib—a chart that covers the Marshall Islands—used by travelers to navigate between the islands in Eastern Micronesia. The chart is composed of horizontal and vertical wooden sticks, which acted as a support system, and the diagonal and curved sticks were representative of the wave swells. Small shells represented the location of all the islands.

This artwork signifies the inventiveness of the Marshallese ri-metos, despite the initial European belief that they were primitive.

Micronesians in the Northwestern Pacific are known for their excellent navigational skills and their use of these navigation charts. The Marshallese navigators had the ability to use natural ocean swells to navigate around vast island chains.

The *Navigation Chart* had important information that served as a mnemonic tool for skilled ri-metos, which enabled them to achieve high status and social influence. The chart was not brought on the canoes, but instead, they memorized it.

6.2. Polynesia

Easter Island, Ahu, and Moai

Easter Island is referred to as "Rapa Nui" by the residents. Ahu means "platform," and Moai means "statue."

The figurines were originally displayed on a stone platform. This was at Orongo, a stone village on Rapa Nui that was the site of ceremonial rituals.

The religion shifted when the environment on the islands started to change, which led to the end of the creation of the Moai statues. These statues started being torn down in 1600; the last ones were destroyed in 1838.

The Moai was carved out of stone. While 14 were made from basalt, the rest were constructed out of volcanic tuff. When the statues' creations were completed, they were transported to the coast by large groups of people—tens to hundreds—who used ropes and levers to move the statues.

A total of 887 Moai have been discovered on Easter Island. Originally, they had red and white designs. All of the statues have their backs to the water around the island. The area also has lots of open space on grassy hills near the coast.

Similar features that can be seen on the majority of the statues include a stern expression, a heavy eyebrow ridge, oval nostrils, elongated ears, thin lips in a downward curve, a prominent clavicle, protruding nipples, thin arms laid against the body, and barely any hands. The eyes were initially filled with coral and red stones.

The Moai signify the human spirit. They served to honor the ancestors of the people, and each sculpture was presumably created by an individual with high status and significant skill in carving because the hard rock the sculptures are made of is difficult to work with.

ʻAhu ʻUla

The *ʻAhu ʻUla* was produced with feathers and olona (shrub) fibers.

The feathers were attached in overlapping rows to the netting. Coconut fiber was used as a base. This allowed for an exterior that shows red feathers from the ʻiʻiwi bird, and black and yellow feathers from the ʻoʻo bird. Overall, the process utilized roughly 500,000 feathers, while some birds only had seven usable ones.

During ceremonies and battle, the noblemen wore cloaks and capes made of feathers. However, only high-ranking leaders and highly skilled warriors were allowed to wear *ʻAhu ʻUla*, and the additional cloaks and capes were given to sea captains and their crews as it was believed to shield the wearer from danger.

During the 18th century, feather capes were symbolic of power and social standing in Hawaiian culture.

The identity of the person who brought this cape to England is unknown because many of the gifted items were passed onto wealthy patrons to finance voyages. However, this particular item was presumably in the possession of Captain Cook's widow and was later inherited by the descendants of her cousin, Rear Admiral Isaac Smith. Captain Cook traveled to Kealakekua Bay, Hawaii, on

January 26, 1779. This was around the same time as the Makahiki seasonal festival, and Kalaniopuu (the chief) ceremonially greeted Cook by giving him his own cloak.

Hiapo (tapa)

Hiapo (tapa) is the traditional creation of the people of Niue, Polynesia.

It incorporates fine lines and detailed geometric designs, like circles, spirals, squares, triangles, and motifs that appear to shrink. Along the edges of the cloth, detailed representations of native plants are added, and an animated drawing represents supernatural or magical power, referred to as 'mana.'

Bark cloth is used in the process that is performed by women only. This includes pounding bark with a wooden tool until it is flat and sticking several pieces of bark together with a paste made of plants like arrowroot. The designs are then either added with a carved beating tool or by utilizing a stencil.

Hiapo is used for bedding, clothing, and wall hangings, or it was displayed at special events. Some pieces still exist today as parts of funeral and burial rituals. These pieces could function as a type of currency, and they were exchanged for food and services.

They serve to designate status during ceremonies, are worn during rituals, are exchanged in important life events, and are often wrapped around babies and sacred objects for protection. A family was considered poor if they did not have tapa to give away.

Particular designs and textiles were incorporated into the Hiapo for people with high social ranking. Important figures often wore this decorated clothing during the prominent stages of their lives.

Similar pieces of clothing were seen between different cultures and islands, and these were often distributed to places they traveled to by boat. Bark cloth has symbols that represent the local wildlife and marine animals and occasionally has portrayals of people.

The designs on each tapa are unique to the maker's island, township, or region. Thus, all pieces of this type are one of a kind.

The cloth is from the small Polynesian island 1,500 miles northeast of New Zealand, Niue. It was discovered next to Tonga, Samoa, and the Cook Islands, allowing mass trade with Christian missionaries in the region. The making of the Hiapo cloth was mainly considered a women's art because the technique involved weaving with soft materials. Women's art often incorporated materials such as flowers and leaves; in Polynesia, textiles signify a woman's wealth.

Tapa cloth is still used across many Pacific islands, such as Tonga, Samoa, and Fiji.

How were the feathers attached to the netting of the *'Ahu 'Ula*?

Tamati Waka Nene

This painting, created by Gottfried Lindauer around 1890, shows a figure known as *Tamati Waka Nene*. The subject was the chef of the Ngāti Hao people in Hokianga.

Tamati Waka Nene is seen wearing feathered robes, with veined, muscular arms holding a weapon. The weapon resembles an ax of wood, often including feathers hanging from the head of the weapon and an eye carved into its center, below the grip.

The figure is clothed in a cloak covered in kiwi feathers, a single earring hangs from his right ear, his hair is a light to dark gray ombré color, and green tattoos cover his face. The tattoos incorporate swirling patterns that end at the figure's jawline. The background portrays mountain foliage and an overcast sky.

Lindauer introduced the presence of ancestors into the present in an effort to preserve the person in history. According to his beliefs, the painting did not just depict the image of Tamati Waka Nene but physically embodied the chief.

The attire shows his status as a Māori man who acted as a rangatira—chief—of the Ngāti Hao people in Hokianga. He was an important war and peacetime leader of the Ngāpuhi tribe.

> Why were the David Vases created as an
> altarpiece, along with an incense burner?

Presentation of Fijian Mats and Tapa Cloths

This grayscale photograph from 1953–1954 shows a parade of women wearing skirts, presenting Queen Elizabeth II with Fijian mats and tapa cloths.

The women walk in procession while holding mats and decorative skirts painted with geometric patterns. They are moving through groups of men across an open grassy area. The men are seen wearing primarily white clothing.

All the women have similar hairstyles and share similar face paint or tattoos on their cheeks.

This depicts a celebration in 1953 where the visit of Queen Elizabeth II was honored.

The skirts are made of bark cloth—also known as 'masi'—and in their arms are tapa mats. Tapa mats are produced from the bark of the paper mulberry tree, and while men tend to the trees, only women can produce the fabric. The decorations are hand-painted onto the cloth.

Tapa mats were often used as capes, cloth, sheets, and gifts for important ceremonies and tributes. The mats are often gifted to important people.

Simplicity in design indicates the importance of the owner.

Key Concepts

- The *Nan Madol, the Female Deity*, and the *Navigation Chart* are three examples of **Micronesian structures and pieces of art**.
- Some notable pieces of **Polynesian art** and clothing/fabric include the *Easter Island, Ahu, and Moai*, the *'Ahu 'Ula, Hiapo (tapa), Tamati Waka Nene*, and the *Presentation of Fijian Mats and Tapa Cloths* (grayscale photograph).

CHAPTER 10

CONTEMPORARY ART

Learning objectives:

- Analyze relationships between artworks based on differences and similarities.
- Justify attribution of an unknown artwork.
- Analyze form, function, content, and context to explain the intentions of the artwork's creation.
- Describe how context influences artistic decisions.
- Explain how decisions about art making shape an artwork.

10.1. 20ᵗʰ Century

Narcissus Garden

The *Narcissus Garden* is a masterpiece created by Yayoi Kusama in 1966, and it involves large plastic silver balls.

Yayoi Kusama is among the most popular female artists born in Japan.

Having a lifelong history of mental illness, she voluntarily lived in a mental health facility in Tokyo. Kusama arrived in New York City in 1958 and began to advance as an impactful artist. Her first exhibit was launched in 1965, which was a room full of mirrors with phal-lic-stuffed pillows covering the floor. It appeared as though there was a continuous "sea of multiplied phalli expanding to its infinity" (Shang, 2015).

The *Narcissus Garden* was the most famous of her exhibits. It consisted of 1,500 mass-produced plastic silver balls tightly arranged on the lawn outside of the Italian Pavilion of the 33rd Venice Biennale. The balls reflected images that were projected, distorted, and repeated. This work of art was compared to a fortune teller's ball.

Many art enthusiasts have frequently interpreted the exhibition as Kusama's own self-promotion and a protest against the commercialization of art. The goal thereof was to be an interactive performance between the artist and the viewer.

Summer Trees

Summer Trees is an ink-on-paper art piece produced by Korean artist Song Su-Nam in 1979. Song painted the piece with a traditional Korean method of ink on paper.

The artwork shows large vertical lines that differ in thickness and "sumukhwa," an ink painting technique used by highly skilled artists.

The artist used broad, vertical strokes of parallel ink blends and bleed from one to the other. He utilized a stark palette of blacks and diluted grays. Some strokes have feathery edges that indicate washes were applied to very wet paper, whereas the ink and paper were somewhat dry when he created the darker strokes.

The shapes overlap and stop near the bottom edge of the paper. This creates a sense of shallow space. The ink is skillfully utilized with simplicity and impact.

The painting gives a sense of psychological power but also has relatively modest proportions. It gives new life to ink painting in a modern world where artists have begun to use computers, revolutionizing the creative spirit of fine art.

At the time, artists who preferred the classics still used oil paints, marble carving came to an end, and there was a rise in mixed media installations involving three-dimensional art made from materials such as cloth, paper, wood, and miscellaneous objects.

Androgyne III

Magdalena Abakanowicz created *Androgyne III* in 1985. She used resin, burlap, nails, string, and wood.

Magdalena Abakanowicz is a Polish artist known for making headless figures without arms and has created sculptures, in groups and alone, since 1974.

Androgyne III is placed on a short, wooden frame that acts as an extension of the legs of the figure. The figure is hollowed out and has a surface made of plaster that resembles wrinkled human skin.

The art piece was made to be seen from all sides. There is an emphasis on space and mass. The figure is androgynous and ambiguous—suggesting that it should be viewed as a human rather than a man or woman—to allow for multiple interpretations.

Abakanowicz aimed to express dehumanization and suffering in a modern context. This is also based on her own experiences with war and totalitarian states.

Untitled #228

The 1950s introduced acrylic paint as a new medium. Although acrylic paint dries faster than oil paint and does not change color during the drying process, it cracks faster. Therefore, oil paint is still preferred.

Many abandoned a canvas for a computer screen, and modern forms of sculpture are faster to produce and reproduce that way.

Cindy Sherman created *Untitled #228* from the *History Portraits* series in 1990. The artwork is a photograph held at the Broad Art Foundation in Santa Monica, California.

Sherman is not just a photographer but the subject, costume designer, hairdresser, and makeup artist for each piece.

> Why did Magdalena Abakanowicz choose to create
> an androgynous figure for *Androgyne III*?

Untitled #228 talks about gender, identity, society, and class distinction. The artist shines a modern light on great masters by using old master paintings as inspiration. This scene shows Judith decapitating Holofernes.

There is a richness in the costume design and set—decorative drapes in the background—which acts as a commentary on the late 19th-century version of the story.

Judith lacks emotion or any reaction to the murder. Holofernes is a mask-like, alert, and nearly bloodless subject.

Electronic Superhighway

The *Electronic Superhighway* was created by Nam June Paik in 1995, a South Korean artist who lived in New York City at the time. Paik was one of the first artists to use televisual materials in his creation and referred to it as video art.

He was interested in American culture, maps, travel, and the U.S. interstate system. In his projects, Paik intended to reflect on how we interact with technology and imagine new ways of doing so.

The art piece shows a map of the U.S. with vibrantly-colored neon lighting outlining the states. Each state has its own video feed, and there is a total of 50 different video clips chosen based on the relevance to the state they are shown in. (For example, Kansas is *The*

What themes does *Untitled #228* address?

Wizard of Oz, and Iowa shows political candidates.) A total of 313 television monitors make up the artwork, and the clips made the *Electronic Superhighway* a prominent representation of the culture of the 1990s.

At the New York exhibition, there is a hidden camera that allows the spectator to become a participant, as the video feed is actually the viewer.

Paik uses neon to evoke connotations of hotel and restaurant window signs, while the use of multiple colors intends to mimic the design of many U.S. maps. The work of art compares the use of highways for the transportation of people and goods with the use of technology that spreads ideas.

Trade

Jaune Quick-to-See Smith created *Trade (Gifts for Trading Land with White People)* in 1992.

The artwork is an oil painting combined with mixed media, collage, and miscellaneous objects on a canvas. It is currently located at the Chrysler Museum of Art in Norfolk, Virginia.

Smith is from the Confederated Salish & Kootenai American Indian tribes of the Flathead Indian Nation.

This piece commemorates the Quincentenary Non-Celebration of the European occupation of North America, and places a focus on the social issues of alcoholism, disease, poverty, and unemployment within the Native American community, all of which can be traced back to the European occupation. It highlights the lack of equality between Europeans and the Indigenous people in both the past and present.

Smith stated that if *Trade* could speak, it would say: "Why won't you consider trading the land we handed over to you for these silly trinkets that so honor us? Sounds like a bad deal? Well, that's the deal you gave us" (Fricke, 2018).

The canvas is divided into three sections, like a triptych. This is reminiscent of Medieval devotional triptychs. The artist included a large mixed-media abstract expressionist painting with collage elements like newspaper clippings, images of the conquest, and geometric shapes. These are layered to emphasize the history of the occupation and the complexity of the situation.

Trade includes many items that represent how the Indigenous people have been represented by the Europeans, including emblems of sports teams, toy arrowheads, tomahawks, pages from comics, gum and tobacco wrappers, etc. The artist utilizes images of Native American men in historical clothing while smoking and photos of deer and buffalo. The canoe is representative of the possibility of trade and cultural connections, but it is depicted as stuck and motionless. The red paint represents Native American blood and the violent actions of the Europeans during the conquest. It also signifies warfare and Smith's anger. She also includes green, white, and yellow in her artwork.

How did Jaune Quick-to-See Smith utilize the canvas to divide *Trade* into three sections reminiscent of a Medieval devotional triptych?

10.2. 21st Century

Lying with the Wolf

Lying with the Wolf was composed of ink and pencil on paper by the German-American artist Kiki Smith in 2001.

The artwork incorporates a large wrinkled drawing pinned to a wall, reminiscent of a bed sheet or cloth.

The artist aimed to show a woman's strength and depicted a scene of a nude female figure lying down with a wolf. The subject's strength is highlighted as it seems that the wolf is tamed by her grasp. A wolf usually symbolizes evil and danger, but not here.

The piece speaks about the different stereotypes—that women are seen as pitiful and wolves are fierce. The woman is portrayed as strong, whereas the wolf is representational of the innocent and pitiful.

Lying with the Wolf is part of the Modern Art movement and adds to the changing of traditional forms of painting—oils to acrylics—and sculpture.

Stadia II

Julie Mehretu produced *Stadia II* in 2004. The artwork involves ink and acrylic on canvas. It is currently located at the Carnegie Museum of Art in Pittsburgh.

The scene is connected to the Ethiopians who live in New York City. The artist incorporates large-scale paintings with abstract elements and titles that place a viewer's attention on the meaning. The work of art includes stylized representations of a stadium-like architecture, using forms that suggest excitement, and speaks of a competition held in a circular space, surrounded by depictions of the world.

There is a dynamic balance between the sweeping lines that create vibrancy and the multi-layered lines that add to the animation of the work. In addition, the sweeping lines add depth, and there is a focus around the center where colors, flags, and symbols originate.

Preying Mantra

Preying Mantra is a mixed media on mylar—a polyester resin in heat-resistant plastic sheets—art piece by Wangechi Mutu, produced in 2006. Mutu is a Kenyan-born artist based in New York.

The artist used the medium of collage to produce a female figure composed of human and animal materials, miscellaneous objects, and machine parts.

It acts as a commentary on the female persona in art history.

The figure is presented in a relaxed, reclined position, accompanied by a green snake that interlocks with her fingers, bird feathers on the back of her head, and her left ear lobe has chicken feet, insect legs, and pinchers. Mutu created an ironic twist on the praying mantis associated with religious rituals. Mantis means "prophet" in Greek and uses camouflage. Overall, this figure seems camouflaged like an insect.

Shibboleth

Doris Salcedo is responsible for the production of *Shibboleth* from 2007–2008. The installation is held at Tate Modern in London.

Doris Salcedo is a female Colombian sculptor, and one of her main goals is to create a change in perspective.

Shibboleth is a word that suggests a person unfamiliar with a language may mispronounce its words, and it is used to identify foreigners or individuals that belong to a different class. The purpose of this custom is for them to be excluded.

The piece is titled accordingly because it visually depicts the gaps in foreign relationships and the invisible barriers placed between people. Thus, it references themes like racism and prejudice. Salcedo said that *Shibboleth* portrays the experience of immigrants in Europe.

This artwork incorporates an installation that features a large crack in the floor. The crack starts small and widens as it moves across the room. The artist created it by opening the museum's floor and inserting a cast of Colombian rock wired with mesh. The crack is 548 feet in length but varies in width. The smallest sections are as little as one inch wide, whereas the larger sections are nearly two feet wide.

Salcedo's work of art was on display for seven months. After that, it was sealed and currently exists as a scar that commemorates the lives of those who are prejudiced against and excluded. In addition, it signifies that the past cannot truly be erased, but this action also represents the possibility of healing.

The installation represents the middle ground of the relationship and interaction between the sculpture and the space in addition to the relationship between the artist and the viewer.

This is a piece of conceptual artwork and one whose meaning is purposefully left up to interpretation.

Key Concepts

- Some examples of **20th Century art** include the *Narcissus Garden, Summer Trees, Androgyne III, Untitled #228, the Electronic Superhighway*, and *Trade*.
- *Lying with the Wolf, Stadia II, Preying Mantra*, and Shibboleth are notable pieces of **21st Century art**.

REFERENCES

Disclaimer: The provided list contains external links to sources and references. These links have not been activated by the publisher, and therefore, we cannot guarantee their accuracy, relevance, timeliness, or completeness beyond the date of publication. The content on these sites is subject to change over time. Though our intention in providing these external links is to offer additional references and potential sources of information, we highly encourage readers to exercise discretion and independent judgment when accessing these links, as the nature and content of the sites may change over time. We are not liable for any errors, omissions, or damages resulting from the use of or reliance on the information found on these external sites. By accessing these links, you acknowledge and accept all associated risks.

Agnani, S. (2005, June 9). Trajan's Column and Forum: Immortality and Memory. University of Washington. https://depts.washington.edu/hrome/Authors/shivali/TrajansColumnandForumImmortalityandMemory/pub_zbarticle_view_printable.html

Allen, W. (2015a, August 8). Hagia Sophia, Istanbul. Smarthistory. https://smarthistory.org/hagia-sophia-istanbul/

Allen, W. (2015b, August 8). Hagia Sophia, Istanbul. Smarthistory. https://smarthistory.org/hagia-sophia-istanbul/

Allen, W. (2015c, August 8). Virgin (Theotokos) and Child between Saints Theodore and George. Smarthistory. https://smarthistory.org/virgin-theotokos-and-child-between-saints-theodore-and-george/

Anda, L. (1965). The Pleistocene Carved Bone from Tequixquiac, Mexico: A Reappraisal. American Antiquity, 30(3), 261-277. doi:10.2307/278808

Arnold, R. D. (2015, August 9). Ndop Portrait of King Mishe miShyaang maMbul (Kuba peoples). Smarthistory. https://smarthistory.org/ndop-portrait-of-king-mishe-mishyaang-mambul-kuba-people/

Augustyn, A., Nirala, S., Kuiper, K., Gaur, A., Goldberg, M., Prine Pauls, E., Sampaolo, M., & Editors of Encyclopedia Britannica. (2019, April 10). Mesolithic | Definition, Technology, & Facts. Encyclopedia Britannica. https://www.britannica.com/event/Mesolithic

Barber, K. (2021, June 6). Honoré Daumier, Nadar Elevating Photography to the Height of an Art. Smarthistory. https://smarthistory.org/daumier-nadar-elevating-photography/

Becker, J. A. (2013). Forum and markets of Trajan. Khan Academy. https://www.khanacademy.org/humanities/ap-art-history/ancient-mediterranean-ap/ap-ancient-rome/

Beetham, S., Zucker, S., & Zygmont, B. (2021, November 5). Jean-Antoine Houdon, George Washington. Smarthistory. https://smarthistory.org/houdon-george-washington/

Belden-Adams, K. (2015, August 9). Alfred Stieglitz, The Steerage. Smarthistory. https://smarthistory.org/stieglitz-the-steerage/

Belden-Adams, K. (2021a, June 6). Eadweard Muybridge, The Horse in Motion. Smarthistory. https://smarthistory.org/eadweard-muybridge-the-horse-in-motion/

Belden-Adams, K. (2021b, June 6). Louis-Jacques-Mandé Daguerre, The Artist's Studio / Still Life with Plaster Casts. Smarthistory. https://smarthistory.org/daguerre-artists-studio/

Boffa, D. (2015, December 11). Pieter Bruegel the Elder, Hunters in the Snow (Winter). Smarthistory. https://smarthistory.org/pieter-bruegel-the-elder-hunters-in-the-snow-winter/

Bravo, D. M. (2015a, August 9). Diego Rivera, Dream of a Sunday Afternoon in Alameda Central Park. Smarthistory. https://smarthistory.org/rivera-dream-of-a-sunday-afternoon-in-alameda-central-park/

Bravo, D. M. (2015b, August 9). Doris Salcedo, Shibboleth. Smarthistory. https://smarthistory.org/doris-salcedo-shibboleth/

Bravo, D. M. (2015c, August 9). Frida Kahlo, The Two Fridas (Las dos Fridas). Smarthistory. https://smarthistory.org/kahlo-the-two-fridas-las-dos-fridas/

Bravo, D. M. (2015d, August 9). Wifredo Lam, The Jungle. Smarthistory. https://smarthistory.org/lam-the-jungle/

Brennan, K. L. (2015a, August 9). Gold and jade crown, Silla Kingdom. Smarthistory. https://smarthistory.org/gold-and-jade-crown-silla-kingdom/

Brennan, K. L. (2015b, November 22). Portrait of Sin Sukju. Smarthistory. https://smarthistory.org/portrait-of-sin-sukju/

Brennan, K. L. (2016, January 26). Liu Chunhua, Chairman Mao en Route to Anyuan. Smarthistory. https://smarthistory.org/liu-chunhua-chairman-mao-en-route-to-anyuan-2/

Brey, A. (2015, August 8). Folio from the Qur'an. Smarthistory. https://smarthistory.org/folio-from-a-quran/

Brown, K. T. (2015, August 9). Fort Ancient Culture: Great Serpent Mound. Smarthistory. https://smarthistory.org/fort-ancient-culture-great-serpent-mound/

Bruckbauer, A. (2021, February 26). Jean-Honoré Fragonard, The Swing. Smarthistory. https://smarthistory.org/jean-honore-fragonard-the-swing/

Camara, E. (2015a, August 8). Peter Paul Rubens, The Presentation of the Portrait of Marie de' Medici. Smarthistory. https://smarthistory.org/rubens-the-presentation-of-the-portrait-of-marie-de-medici/

Camara, E. (2015b, November 28). Michelangelo, Last Judgment, Sistine Chapel. Smarthistory. https://smarthistory.org/michelangelo-last-judgment/

Chadwick, S. (2016, April 27). Mondrian, Composition with Red, Blue, and Yellow. Smarthistory. https://smarthistory.org/mondrian-composition-ii-in-red-blue-and-yellow/

Dainese, E. (2015, August 9). Great Mosque of Djenné (Djenné peoples). Smarthistory. https://smarthistory.org/great-mosque-of-djenne/

Dalal, R. (2015, August 8). The Great Mosque (or Masjid-e Jameh) of Isfahan. Smarthistory. https://smarthistory.org/the-great-mosque-or-masjid-e-jameh-of-isfahan/

Dardashti, A. L. (2015, August 9). Master of Calamarca, Angel with Arquebus. Smarthistory. https://smarthistory.org/master-of-calamarca-angel-with-arquebus/

Demerdash, N. (2016, October 8). Great Zimbabwe. Smarthistory. https://smarthistory.org/great-zimbabwe/

Demerdash, N., Phillip, F. Ç., & Chagnon, M. C. (2020, July 3). The Court of Gayumars. Smarthistory. https://smarthistory.org/the-court-of-gayumars/

DeWitte, D. J., Larmann, R. M., & Shields, K. M. (2015). Gateways to Art: Understanding the Visual Arts (2nd Edition). Thames & Hudson.

Dosch, M. (2015, August 9). Claes Oldenburg, Lipstick (Ascending) on Caterpillar Tracks. Smarthistory. https://smarthistory.org/oldenburg-lipstick-ascending-on-caterpillar-tracks/

Egloff, B. (2008). Bones of the Ancestors: The Ambum Stone. AltaMira Press.

Engel, E. (2015, August 9). Maize cobs. Smarthistory. https://smarthistory.org/maize-cobs/

Farber, A. (2015a, August 8). Basilica of Santa Sabina, Rome. Smarthistory. https://smarthistory.org/santa-sabina/

Farber, A. (2015b, August 8). San Vitale and the Justinian Mosaic. Smarthistory. https://smarthistory.org/san-vitale/

Folland, T. (2015, December 9). Édouard Manet, Olympia. Smarthistory. https://smarthistory.org/edouard-manet-olympia/

Foster, E. (2015a, August 8). Church and Reliquary of Sainte-Foy, France. Smarthistory. https://smarthistory.org/church-and-reliquary-of-sainte%e2%80%90foy-france/

Foster, E. (2015b, August 8). The Golden Haggadah. Smarthistory. https://smarthistory.org/the-golden-haggadah/

Fox, A. (2016, January 8). Joseph Wright of Derby, A Philosopher Giving a Lecture at the Orrery. Smarthistory. https://smarthistory.org/joseph-wright-of-derby-a-philosopher-giving-a-lecture-at-the-orrery/

Fricke, S. N. (2015, August 9). Puebloan: Maria Martinez, Black-on-black ceramic vessel. Smarthistory. https://smarthistory.org/puebloan-maria-martinez-black-on-black-ceramic-vessel/

Fricke, S. N. (2018, September 7). Jaune Quick-to-See Smith, Trade (Gifts for Trading Land with White People). Smarthistory. https://smarthistory.org/jaune-quick-to-see-smith-trade-gifts-for-trading-land-with-white-people-2/

Gordon, R. E. (2015, August 9). Borobudur. Smarthistory. https://smarthistory.org/borobudur/

Graham, H. (2021, August 10). Donatello, David. Smarthistory. https://smarthistory.org/donatello-david/

Green, A. G., & Zucker, S. (2020, March 6). From quills to beads: the bandolier bag. Smarthistory. https://smarthistory.org/seeing-america-2/bandolier-bag-sa/

Hager, N. (2013). Running Horned Woman, Tassili n'Ajjer. Khan Academy. https://www.khanacademy.org/humanities/ap-art-history/global-prehistory-ap/paleolithic-mesolithic-neolithic-ap-ah/a/running-horned-woman-tassili-najjer?modal=1

Harris, B. [Smarthistory]. (2013, October 4). Charles Barry and A.W.N. Pugin, Palace of Westminster (Houses of Parliament) [Video]. YouTube. https://www.youtube.com/watch?v=7oBUIo5R5qg

Harris, B., & Klemm, P. (2015, August 9). Male Reliquary Guardian Figure (Fang peoples). Smarthistory. https://smarthistory.org/fang-reliquary-figure/

Harris, B., & Zucker, S. (2015a, July 19). Gian Lorenzo Bernini, Ecstasy of Saint Teresa. Smarthistory. https://smarthistory.org/bernini-ecstasy-of-st-teresa/

Harris, B., & Zucker, S. (2015b, August 8). Polykleitos, Doryphoros (Spear-Bearer). Smarthistory. https://smarthistory.org/polykleitos-doryphoros-spear-bearer/

Harris, B., & Zucker, S. (2015c, August 9). Constantin Brancusi, The Kiss. Smarthistory. https://smarthistory.org/constantin-brancusi-the-kiss/

Harris, B., & Zucker, S. (2015d, August 9). Fra Filippo Lippi, Madonna and Child with Two Angels. Smarthistory. https://smarthistory.org/lippi-madonna-and-child-with-two-angels/

Harris, B., & Zucker, S. (2015e, August 9). Georges Braque, The Portuguese. Smarthistory. https://smarthistory.org/braque-the-portuguese/

Harris, B., & Zucker, S. (2015f, August 9). Gustave Courbet, The Stonebreakers. Smarthistory. https://smarthistory.org/courbet-the-stonebreakers/

Harris, B., & Zucker, S. (2015g, August 9). Pablo Picasso, Les Demoiselles d'Avignon. Smarthistory. https://smarthistory.org/pablo-picasso-les-demoiselles-davignon/

Harris, B., & Zucker, S. (2015h, August 9). Vasily Kandinsky, Improvisation 28 (second version). Smarthistory. https://smarthistory.org/kandinsky-improvisation-28-second-version/

Harris, B., & Zucker, S. (2015i, November 18). Caravaggio, Calling of St. Matthew. Smarthistory. https://smarthistory.org/caravaggio-calling-of-st-matthew/

Harris, B., & Zucker, S. (2015j, November 18). Francesco Borromini, San Carlo alle Quattro Fontane, Rome. Smarthistory. https://smarthistory.org/borromini-san-carlo-alle-quattro-fontane/

Harris, B., & Zucker, S. (2015k, November 23). Diego Velázquez, Las Meninas. Smarthistory. https://smarthistory.org/diego-velazquez-las-meninas/

Harris, B., & Zucker, S. (2015l, November 25). Jan Van Eyck, The Arnolfini Portrait. Smarthistory. https://smarthistory.org/jan-van-eyck-the-arnolfini-portrait/

Harris, B., & Zucker, S. (2015m, December 5). Sandro Botticelli, The Birth of Venus. Smarthistory. https://smarthistory.org/sandro-botticelli-the-birth-of-venus/

Harris, B., & Zucker, S. (2015n, December 6). Filippo Brunelleschi, Pazzi Chapel, Florence. Smarthistory. https://smarthistory.org/filippo-brunelleschi-pazzi-chapel-florence/

Harris, B., & Zucker, S. (2015o, December 9). Marcel Duchamp, Fountain. Smarthistory. https://smarthistory.org/marcel-duchamp-fountain/

Harris, B., & Zucker, S. (2015p, December 11). The David Vases. Smarthistory. https://smarthistory.org/the-david-vases/

Harris, B., & Zucker, S. (2015q, December 15). Mohammed ibn al-Zain, Basin (Baptistère de Saint Louis). Smarthistory. https://smarthistory.org/mohammed-ibn-al-zain-basin-baptistere-de-saint-louis

Harris, B., & Zucker, S. (2015r, December 15). Rachel Ruysch, Fruit and Insects. Smarthistory. https://smarthistory.org/rachel-ruysch-fruit-and-insects/

Harris, B., & Zucker, S. (2015s, December 16). Catacomb of Priscilla, Rome. Smarthistory. https://smarthistory.org/catacomb-of-priscilla-rome/

Harris, B., & Zucker, S. (2015t, December 18). Cathedral of Notre Dame de Chartres. Smarthistory. https://smarthistory.org/cathedral-of-notre-dame-de-chartres-part-1-of-3/

Harris, B., & Zucker, S. (2015u, December 18). Workshop of Robert Campin, Annunciation Triptych (Merode Altarpiece). Smarthistory. https://smarthistory.org/robert-campin-merode-altarpiece/

Harris, B., & Zucker, S. (2015v, December 30). Giotto, Arena (Scrovegni) Chapel. Smarthistory. https://smarthistory.org/giotto-arena-scrovegni-chapel/

Harris, B., & Zucker, S. (2016, October 8). Willem de Kooning, Woman, I. Smarthistory. https://smarthistory.org/de-k-woman/

Harris, B., & Zucker, S. (2021, April 8). Il Gesù, Rome. Smarthistory. https://smarthistory.org/il-gesu-rome/

Harris, L. A. (2015, August 9). Hokusai, Under the Wave off Kanagawa (The Great Wave). Smarthistory. https://smarthistory.org/hokusai-under-the-wave-off-kanagawa-the-great-wave

Harris, S. L., & Klemm, P. (2015, August 9). Power Figure (Nkisi Nkondi), Kongo peoples. Smarthistory. https://smarthistory.org/nkisi-nkondi-kongo-people/

Harvey, B. (2015, August 9). Paul Cézanne, Mont Sainte-Victoire. Smarthistory. https://smarthistory.org/cezanne-mont-sainte-victoire/

Herman, M. (2015, August 9). Louis Sullivan, Carson, Pirie, Scott Building. Smarthistory. https://smarthistory.org/sullivan-carson-pirie-scott-building/

Hickson, S. (2015, August 9). Grünewald, Isenheim Altarpiece. Smarthistory. https://smarthistory.org/grunewald-isenheim-altarpiece/

Hill, J. (2018). Sobekneferu | Ancient Egypt Online. Ancient Egypt Online. https://ancientegyptonline.co.uk/sobekneferu/

Howard Carter and A. C. Mace, The Tomb of Tut-ankh-amen (New York City: Cooper Square Publishers. 1933), (vol. 1) pp.95–96.

Jewitt, J. R. (2020, August 20). Titian, Venus of Urbino. Smarthistory. https://smarthistory.org/titian-venus-of-urbino/

Kapadia, R. (2015, August 9). Bichitr, Jahangir Preferring a Sufi Shaikh to Kings. Smarthistory. https://smarthistory.org/bichtir-jahangir-preferring-a-sufi-shaikh-to-kings/

Kapadia, R. (2018, January 29). The Taj Mahal. Smarthistory. https://smarthistory.org/the-taj-mahal-2/

Khalid, F. (2015a, August 9). Helen Frankenthaler, The Bay. Smarthistory. https://smarthistory.org/frankenthaler-the-bay/

Khalid, F. (2015b, August 9). Mary Cassatt, The Coiffure. Smarthistory. https://smarthistory.org/cassatt-the-coiffure/

Khalid, F. (2015c, August 9). Shiva as Lord of the Dance (Nataraja). Smarthistory. https://smarthistory.org/shiva-as-lord-of-the-dance-nataraja/

Kilroy-Ewbank, L. (2015a, August 9). Cabrera, Portrait of Sor Juana Inés de la Cruz. Khan Academy. https://www.khanacademy.org/humanities/ap-art-history/later-europe-and-americas/enlightenment-revolution/a/cabrera-portrait-of-sor-juana-ins-de-la-cruz

Kilroy-Ewbank, L. (2015b, August 9). Eastern Shoshone: Hide Painting of the Sun Dance, attributed to Cotsiogo (Cadzi Cody). Smarthistory. https://smarthistory.org/eastern-shoshone-hide-painting-of-the-sun-dance-attributed-to-cotsiogo-cadzi-cody/

Kilroy-Ewbank, L. (2015c, August 9). Frontispiece of the Codex Mendoza. Smarthistory. https://smarthistory.org/frontispiece-of-the-codex-mendoza/

Kilroy-Ewbank, L. (2015d, August 9). Mesa Verde. Smarthistory. https://smarthistory.org/mesa-verde-cliff-dwellings/

Kilroy-Ewbank, L. (2015e, August 9). The Templo Mayor and the Coyolxauhqui Stone. Smarthistory. https://smarthistory.org/templo-mayor-at-tenochtitlan-the-coyolxauhqui-stone-and-an-olmec-mask/

Kilroy-Ewbank, L. (2015f, August 9). Transformation masks. Smarthistory. https://smarthistory.org/transformation-masks/

Kilroy-Ewbank, L. (2016, April 9). Yaxchilán—Lintels 24 and 25 from Structure 23 and structures 33 and 40. Smarthistory. https://smarthistory.org/yaxchilan-lintels/

Kilroy-Ewbank, L. (2017, August 22). Miguel González, The Virgin of Guadalupe. Smarthistory. https://smarthistory.org/gonzalez-guadalupe/

Kilroy-Ewbank, L. (2022, May 31). Screen with the Siege of Belgrade and Hunting Scene (or Brooklyn Biombo). Smarthistory. https://smarthistory.org/screen-with-the-siege-of-belgrade-and-hunting-scene-or-brooklyn-biombo/

Kilroy-Ewbank, L., & Harris, B. (2015, August 10). Aztec feathered headdress. Smarthistory. https://smarthistory.org/feathered-headdress-aztec/

Kilroy-Ewbank, L., & Sifford, E. F. (2015, August 9). Spaniard and Indian Produce a Mestizo, attributed to Juan Rodríguez Juárez. Smarthistory. https://smarthistory.org/spaniard-and-indian-produce-a-mestizo-attributed-to-juan-rodriguez/

Kinnecome, M. (2015, November 28). Magdalena Abakanowicz, Androgyne III. Smarthistory. https://smarthistory.org/magdalena-abakanowicz-androgyne-iii/

Klemm, P. (2016, April 1). Owie Kimou, Portrait Mask (Mblo) of Moya Yanso (Baule peoples). Smarthistory. https://smarthistory.org/owie-kimou-portrait-mask-mblo-of-moya-yanso-baule-peoples/

Klemm, P., & Harris, B. (2015a, August 9). Female (pwo) Mask. Smarthistory. https://smarthistory.org/female-pwo-mask/

Klemm, P., & Harris, B. (2015b, August 9). Golden Stool (Sika Dwa Kofi), Asante peoples. Smarthistory. https://smarthistory.org/sika-dwa-kofi-golden-stool/

Klemm, P., & Harris, B. (2015c, August 9). Mask (Buk), Torres Strait, Mabuiag Island. Smarthistory. https://smarthistory.org/mask-buk-torres-strait-mabuiag-island/

Klemm, P., & Zucker, S. (2015a, November 11). Elephant Mask (Bamileke Peoples). Smarthistory. https://smarthistory.org/elephant-mask-kuosi-society-bamileke-peoples-cameroon/

Klemm, P., Zucker, S., Clarke, C. (2015b, November 12). Bundu / Sowei Helmet Mask (Mende peoples). Smarthistory. https://smarthistory.org/bundu-sowei-helmet-mask/

Klemm, P., Zucker, S., & Sanyal, S. K. (2021, July 6). Ikenga (Igbo peoples). Smarthistory. https://smarthistory.org/ikenga/

Landay, L., & Harris, B. (2015, December 9). J. M. W. Turner, Slave Ship. Smarthistory. https://smarthistory.org/j-m-w-turner-slave-ship/

Lhote, H., & Brodrick, A. H. (1959). The search for the Tassili frescoes: The story of the prehistoric rock-paintings of the Sahara; (Translated from French ed.). Hutchinson of London. https://

archive.org/details/HenriLhote The Search For The Tassili-Frescoes The Story Of The Prehistoric Rock Painting Of The Sahara1959/

Looney, M. B. (2015, November 19). Cindy Sherman, Untitled #228. Smarthistory. https://smarthistory.org/cindy-sherman-untitled-228/

Lynch, A. R. (2016, January 7). Élisabeth Louise Vigée Le Brun, Self-Portrait. Smarthistory. https://smarthistory.org/elisabeth-louise-vigee-le-brun-self-portrait/

Lythberg, B. (2015, November 28). Gottfried Lindauer, Tamati Waka Nene. Smarthistory. https://smarthistory.org/gottfried-lindauer-tamati-waka-nene/

Lythberg, B. (2018, August 20). Nan Madol: "In the space between things." Smarthistory. https://smarthistory.org/nan-madol/

M.A., J. N. B. (2020). AP Art History: With 5 Practice Tests (Barron's Test Prep) (Fifth ed.). Barron's Educational Services. https://www.amazon.co.uk/AP-Art-History-Practice-Barrons/

Macaulay, E. (2015a, August 8). Mimar Sinan, Mosque of Selim II, Edirne. Smarthistory. https://smarthistory.org/mimar-sinan-mosque-of-selim-ii-edirne/

Macaulay, E. (2015b, August 8). Pyxis of al-Mughira. Smarthistory. https://smarthistory.org/pyxis-of-al-mughira/

Macaulay, E. (2015c, August 8). The Dome of the Rock (Qubbat al-Sakhra). Smarthistory. https://smarthistory.org/the-dome-of-the-rock-qubbat-al-sakhra/

Macaulay, E. (2015d, August 9). The Ardabil Carpet. Smarthistory. https://smarthistory.org/the-ardabil-carpet/

Macaulay, E. (2018a, June 8). Petra: The rose red city of the Naba-
taeans. Smarthistory. https://smarthistory.org/petra-the-rose-
red-city-of-the-nabataeans/

Macaulay, E. (2018b, June 30). The Kaaba. Smarthistory. https://
smarthistory.org/the-kaaba-2/

MacDonald, D. (2015, November 27). Tōdai-ji. Smarthistory.
https://smarthistory.org/todai-ji/

Manitoba Education. (2019). Origins of Judaism. Judaism: A Sup-
plemental Resource for Grade 12 World of Religions: A Cana-
dian Perspective, 15–22. https://www.edu.gov.mb.ca/k12/docs/
support/world_religions/judaism/origins.pdf

McCoy, C. B. (2016, January 7). Jacques-Louis David, Oath of the
Horatii. Smarthistory. https://smarthistory.org/jacques-louis-
david-oath-of-the-horatii/

McIntire, J. N. (2015a, August 9). Funeral banner of Lady Dai (Xin
Zhui). Smarthistory. https://smarthistory.org/funeral-banner-
of-lady-dai-xin-zhui/

McIntire, J. N. (2015b, August 9). Longmen caves, Luoyang.
Smarthistory. https://smarthistory.org/longmen-caves-luoyang/

McIntire, J. N. (2015c, August 9). Neo-Confucianism and Fan
Kuan, Travelers by Streams and Mountains. Smarthistory.
https://smarthistory.org/neo-confucianism-fan-kuan-travelers-
by-streams-and-mountains/

Mir, R. (2015, August 8). Fibulae. Smarthistory. https://smarthis-
tory.org/fibulae/

Mirmobiny, S. (2015a, August 8). The Alhambra. Smarthistory.
https://smarthistory.org/the-alhambra/

Mirmobiny, S. (2015b, August 8). The Great Mosque of Córdoba. Smarthistory. https://smarthistory.org/the-great-mosque-of-cordoba/

Mondrian, P., Holtzman, H., & James, M. S. (1986). The New Art--the New Life. Prentice Hall.

Moss, J. (2015, November 28). Lukasa (Memory Board) (Luba peoples). Smarthistory. https://smarthistory.org/lukasa-memory-board-luba-peoples/

Mui, S., & Tully, B. (2020). AP Art History Course & Exam Description, Effective Fall 2020. Advanced Placement College Board. https://apcentral.collegeboard.org/pdf/ap-art-history-course-and-exam-description-0.pdf

Museum, T. B. (2017, March 1). Feather cape. Smarthistory. https://smarthistory.org/feather-cape/

Nachescu, A. (2021, August 15). The Terracotta Warriors. Smarthistory. https://smarthistory.org/the-terracotta-warriors/

National Geographic Society. (2022, May 20). *May 28, 1830 CE: Indian Removal Act | National Geographic Society*. National Geographic. https://education.nationalgeographic.org/resource/indian-removal-act/

Newell, J., & Harris, B. (2022, June 24). Rapa Nui (Easter Island) Moai. Smarthistory. https://smarthistory.org/easter-island-moai/

Newell, J., & Zucker, S. (2017, April 1). Navigation Chart, Marshall Islands. Smarthistory. https://smarthistory.org/chart-marshall/

Noble, B. (2015a, August 9). Albrecht Dürer, Adam and Eve. Smarthistory. https://smarthistory.org/durer-adam-and-eve/

Noble, B. (2015b, August 9). Lucas Cranach the Elder, Law and Gospel (Law and Grace). Smarthistory. https://smarthistory.org/cranach-law-and-gospel-law-and-grace/

Ortega, E. (2015, August 9). José María Velasco, The Valley of Mexico from the Santa Isabel Mountain Range. Smarthistory. https://smarthistory.org/velasco-the-valley-of-mexico/

Ostergaard, T. E. (2016, February 25). Monet, The Gare Saint-Lazare. Smarthistory. https://smarthistory.org/monet-the-gare-saint-lazare/

Paulson, N. (2015a, August 9). Edvard Munch, The Scream. Smarthistory. https://smarthistory.org/munch-the-scream/

Paulson, N. (2015b, August 9). Paul Gauguin, Where do we come from? What are we? Where are we going? Smarthistory. https://smarthistory.org/gauguin-where-do-we-come-from-what-are-we-where-are-we-going/

Paulson, N. (2015c, August 9). Vincent van Gogh, The Starry Night. Smarthistory. https://smarthistory.org/van-gogh-the-starry-night/

Postal, M. A. (2015, August 9). Robert Venturi, House in New Castle County, Delaware. Smarthistory. https://smarthistory.org/venturi-house-in-new-castle-county-delaware/

Postal, M. A., & Zucker, S. (2021, March 31). Ludwig Mies van der Rohe, Seagram Building, New York City. Smarthistory. https://smarthistory.org/ludwig-mies-van-der-rohe-seagram-building-new-york-city/

Rod-Ari, M. (2015a, August 9). Angkor Wat. Smarthistory. https://smarthistory.org/angkor-wat/

Rod-Ari, M. (2015b, November 21). Bamiyan Buddhas. Smarthistory. https://smarthistory.org/bamiyan-buddhas/

Rod-Ari, M. (2016, March 29). Jowo Rinpoche, Jokhang Temple, Tibet. Smarthistory. https://smarthistory.org/jowo-rinpoche-jokhang-temple-tibet/

Roggenkamp, S. (2015a, August 9). Ernst Ludwig Kirchner, Self-Portrait As a Soldier. Smarthistory. https://smarthistory.org/kirchner-self-portrait-as-a-soldier/

Roggenkamp, S. (2015b, August 9). Käthe Kollwitz, In Memoriam Karl Liebknecht. Smarthistory. https://smarthistory.org/kathe-kollwitz-in-memoriam-karl-liebknecht/

Rose, J. R., Zucker, S., & Harris, B. (2022, April 9). Meret Oppenheim, Object (Fur-covered cup, saucer, and spoon). Smarthistory. https://smarthistory.org/meret-oppenheim-object-fur-covered-cup-saucer-and-spoon/

Ross, N. (2015, August 8). Röttgen Pietà. Smarthistory. https://smarthistory.org/roettgen-pieta/

Ross, N. (2016, January 21). Bible moralisée (moralized bibles). Smarthistory. https://smarthistory.org/bible-moralisee-moralized-bibles/

Rowney, E. (2015, August 9). Auguste Rodin, The Burghers of Calais. Smarthistory. https://smarthistory.org/rodin-the-burghers-of-calais/

Ryan, T. R. (2015, August 9). Andy Warhol, Marilyn Diptych. Smarthistory. https://smarthistory.org/warhol-marilyn-diptych/

Sarikas, C. (2022, February 9). What Is AP Art History? Should You Take It? PrepScholar. https://blog.prepscholar.com/what-is-ap-art-history

Schaller, W. (2015, August 8). Rembrandt, Self-Portrait with Saskia. Smarthistory. https://smarthistory.org/rembrandt-self-portrait-with-saskia/

Scher, S. (2015a, August 9). All-T'oqapu Tunic. Smarthistory. https://smarthistory.org/all-toqapu-tunic/

Scher, S. (2015b, August 9). Chavín de Huántar. Smarthistory. https://smarthistory.org/chavin-de-huantar/

Scher, S. (2015c, August 9). City of Cusco. Smarthistory. https://smarthistory.org/city-of-cusco/

Scher, S. (2015d, August 9). Machu Picchu. Smarthistory. https://smarthistory.org/machu-picchu/

Seo, Y. (2016, September 18). Ryōanji (Peaceful Dragon Temple). Smarthistory. https://smarthistory.org/ryoanji-peaceful-dragon-temple/

Sethi, C. M. (2016, May 15). Sacred space and symbolic form at Lakshmana Temple, Khajuraho (India). Smarthistory. https://smarthistory.org/lakshmana-temple/

Shan, J. (2018, December 6). Importance of Jade in Chinese Culture. ThoughtCo. https://www.thoughtco.com/about-jade-culture-629197

Shang, D. (2015, August 9). Yayoi Kusama, Narcissus Garden. Smarthistory. https://smarthistory.org/yayoi-kusama-narcissus-garden/

Shelby, K. (2018, December 14). The Great Stupa at Sanchi. Smarthistory. https://smarthistory.org/the-stupa-sanchi/

Sigur, H. (2016a, January 21). Ogata Kōrin, Red and White Plum Blossoms. Smarthistory. https://smarthistory.org/ogata-korin-red-and-white-plum-blossoms/

Sigur, H. (2016b, February 1). Song Su-Nam, Summer Trees. Smarthistory. https://smarthistory.org/song-su-nam-summer-trees-2/

Sigur, H. (2016c, April 1). Night Attack on the Sanjô Palace. Smarthistory. https://smarthistory.org/night-attack-on-the-san-jo-palace/

Simon, M. (2015, August 9). Le Corbusier, Villa Savoye. Smarthistory. https://smarthistory.org/le-corbusier-villa-savoye/

Smarthistory. (2014, March 14). Anavysos Kouros [Video]. YouTube. https://www.youtube.com/watch?v=v1_pCZBVWuY

Stokes, D. (2019, October 26). Olowe of Ise, Veranda Post of Enthroned King and Senior Wife. Smarthistory. https://smarthistory.org/olowe-ise-veranda-post-king-senior-wife/

Stuart, G. (2015, December 22). Benin plaque: Equestrian Oba and Attendants. Smarthistory. https://smarthistory.org/benin-plaque-equestrian-oba-and-attendants/

Tanton, K. (2015, August 8). The Bayeux Tapestry. Smarthistory. https://smarthistory.org/the-bayeux-tapestry/

Taylor, R. (2016, September 18). Robert Smithson, Spiral Jetty. Smarthistory. https://smarthistory.org/robert-smithson-spiral-jetty/

The Albert Team. (2022, March 1). AP® Art History Redesign: What You Need to Know | Albert.io. Albert Resources. https://www.albert.io/blog/ap-art-history-redesign-need-know/

The British Library, Woodville, L., & Doyle, K. (2015, August 8). The Lindisfarne Gospels. Smarthistory. https://smarthistory.org/the-lindisfarne-gospels/

The College Board. (2015). AP Art History Course and Exam Description. https://secure-media.collegeboard.org/digitalServices/pdf/ap/ap-art-history-course-and-exam-description.pdf

Veys, F. W. (2015, November 21). Wooden sculptures from Nukuoro. Smarthistory. https://smarthistory.org/wooden-sculptures-from-nukuoro/

Wagelie, J. (2017, April 15). Presentation of Fijian Mats and Tapa Cloths to Queen Elizabeth II. Smarthistory. https://smarthistory.org/presentation-of-fijian-mats-and-tapa-cloths-to-queen-elizabeth-ii-2/

Watson, J. (2015, August 9). Varvara Stepanova, The Results of the First Five-Year Plan. Smarthistory. https://smarthistory.org/stepanova-the-results-of-the-first-five-year-plan/

Wiebe, C. (2015, August 9). Frank Lloyd Wright, Fallingwater. Smarthistory. https://smarthistory.org/frank-lloyd-wright-fallingwater/

Wilkins, C. (2015, August 9). Henri Matisse, Goldfish. Smarthistory. https://smarthistory.org/matisse-goldfish/

Woodville, L. (2015, August 8). Saint Louis Bible (Moralized Bible or Bible moralisée). Smarthistory. https://smarthistory.org/saint-louis-bible-moralized-bible-or-bible-moralisee/

Yantz, J. (2017, January 20). Bahram Gur Fights the Karg (Horned Wolf). Smarthistory. https://smarthistory.org/bahram-gur-fights-the-karg/

Ying-Chen Peng. (2015, August 9). The Forbidden City. Smarthistory. https://smarthistory.org/the-forbidden-city/

Young, A. (2015, August 9). Kiki Smith, Lying with the Wolf. Smarthistory. https://smarthistory.org/kiki-smith-lying-with-the-wolf/

Young, A. (2018, September 7). Julie Mehretu, Stadia II. Smarthistory. https://smarthistory.org/julie-mehretu-stadia-ii-2/

Zappella, C. (2015a, August 9). Ceiling of the Sistine Chapel. Smarthistory. https://smarthistory.org/michelangelo-ceiling-of-the-sistine-chapel/

Zappella, C. (2015b, August 9). Francisco Goya, And there's nothing to be done from The Disasters of War. Smarthistory. https://smarthistory.org/goya-and-theres-nothing-to-be-done-from-the-disasters-of-war/

Zappella, C. (2015c, August 9). Leon Battista Alberti, Palazzo Rucellai. Smarthistory. https://smarthistory.org/alberti-palazzo-rucellai/

Zucker, S., & Harris, B. (2015a, August 9). Jacob Lawrence, The Migration Series. Smarthistory. https://smarthistory.org/jacob-lawrence-the-migration-series/

Zucker, S., & Harris, B. (2015b, August 9). Leonardo, Last Supper. Smarthistory. https://smarthistory.org/leonardo-last-supper/

Zucker, S., & Harris, B. (2015c, December 5). Gustav Klimt, The Kiss. Smarthistory. https://smarthistory.org/gustav-klimt-the-kiss/

Zucker, S., & Harris, B. (2015d, December 11). William Hogarth, Marriage A-la-Mode. Smarthistory. https://smarthistory.org/william-hogarth-marriage-a-la-mode/

Zucker, S., & Harris, B. (2015e, December 15). Raphael, School of Athens. Smarthistory. https://smarthistory.org/raphael-school-of-athens/

Zucker, S., & Harris, B. (2020, September 30). Jacopo Pontormo, Entombment (or Deposition from the Cross). Smarthistory. https://smarthistory.org/jacopo-pontormo-entombment-or-deposition-from-the-cross/

Zygmont, B. (2015a, August 9). Painting colonial culture: Ingres's La Grande Odalisque. Smarthistory. https://smarthistory.org/painting-colonial-culture-ingress-la-grande-odalisque/

Zygmont, B. (2015b, August 9). Thomas Cole, The Oxbow. Smarthistory. https://smarthistory.org/cole-the-oxbow/

Zygmont, B. (2015c, August 9). Thomas Jefferson, Monticello. Smarthistory. https://smarthistory.org/jefferson-monticello/

Zygmont, B. (2015d, November 22). Eugène Delacroix, Liberty Leading the People. Smarthistory. https://smarthistory.org/delacroix-liberty-leading-the-people/

Image References

Disclaimer: The provided list contains external links to sources and references. These links have not been activated by the publisher, and therefore, we cannot guarantee their accuracy, relevance, timeliness, or completeness beyond the date of publication. The content on these sites is subject to change over time. Though our intention in providing these external links is to offer additional references and potential sources of information, we highly encourage readers to exercise discretion and independent judgment when accessing these links, as the nature and content of the sites may change over time. We are not liable for any errors, omissions, or damages resulting from the use of or reliance on the information found on these external sites. By accessing these links, you acknowledge and accept all associated risks.

Bezanger, J. (2021, September 13). *Art of Kanak* [Photograph]. Unsplash. https://unsplash.com/photos/Z8RSCtYs62c

Chamb, J. (2019, July 30). *Taj Mahal* [Photograph]. Unsplash. https://unsplash.com/photos/iWMfiInivp4

Chilese, M. (2021, June 4). *Colosseum* [Photograph]. Unsplash. https://unsplash.com/photos/PWdWPYF0_RY

DeMers, J. (2012, October 4). *Monticello* [Photograph]. Pixabay. https://pixabay.com/photos/monticello-dome-museum-house-home-59152/

Greenwood, A. (2018, June 2). *Terracotta Warriors* [Photograph]. Unsplash. https://unsplash.com/photos/xZDWEEMS3sA

Griggs, T. (2018, April 24). *Easter Island* [Photograph]. Unsplash. https://unsplash.com/photos/2Qjk2PfaH3o

Idowu, S. (2022, May 9). *African Mask* [Photograph]. Unsplash. https://unsplash.com/photos/eiDEJgGrteo

JaneB13. (2016, January 8). *Last Supper* [Photograph]. Pixabay. https://pixabay.com/illustrations/leonardo-devinci-the-lord-s-supper-1128923/

Krum, A. (2020, February 12). *Mesa Verde* [Photograph]. Unsplash. https://unsplash.com/photos/qWdKseoimhw

Mangela, S. (2021, May 14). *Great Pyramids of Giza* [Photograph]. Unsplash. https://unsplash.com/photos/YlIy_s8mtmY

Oun, T. (2019, July 29). *Grotte de Sabart* [Photograph]. Unsplash. https://unsplash.com/photos/9VHCFWlvVzI

Prawny. (2021, February 2). *Starry night* [Photograph]. Pixabay. https://pixabay.com/illustrations/vintage-sky-night-starry-night-5971661/

Rouichi, A. (2020, January 22). *Machu Picchu* [Photograph]. Unsplash. https://unsplash.com/photos/KNJL3_l3M0k

Teo, R. (2022, April 7). *Narcissus Garden* [Photograph]. Unsplash. https://unsplash.com/photos/9MWgAEOH6E8

Van den Berg, P. (2016, April 11). *Marilyn Diptych* [Photograph]. Pixabay. https://pixabay.com/photos/marilyn-monroe-andy-warhol-art-1318440/

Vonk, M. (2021, July 4). *Stonehenge* [Photograph]. Unsplash. https://unsplash.com/photos/M9Ys5bepa-U

Wahid, A. (2019a, June 1). *Quran* [Photograph]. Unsplash. https://unsplash.com/photos/tfD5vnMMewA

Wahid, A. (2019b, September 22). *Hagia Sophia* [Photograph]. Unsplash. https://unsplash.com/photos/IavBkAdcpdQ

WikiImages. (2016, March 9). *The Great Wave* [Photograph]. Pixabay. https://pixabay.com/illustrations/picture-woodblock-printing-woodcut-1247354

Zhou, P. (2020, May 24). *Parthenon* [Photograph]. Unsplash. https://unsplash.com/photos/WLdHQepgdTU

DOWNLOAD YOUR FREE E-BOOK

As our way of thanking you for purchasing the ***Study and Exam Guide of AP® Art History: The Official Genius Exam Coaches Edition,*** you'll get the ***Three Highly Effective Test-Taking Strategies According to My Research*** for free! This e-book features three research-supported strategies combining mental, emotional, and behavioral practices for successful test performance and outcome.

To get your free e-book, kindly go to
https://thegeniusexamcoaches.com/APArtHistory
to receive the download instructions.

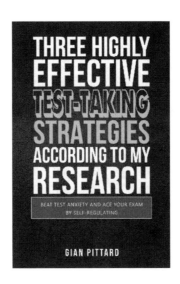

We'd Like to Hear From You

The publisher invites you to share your feedback by leaving a review on our page.

We value your thoughts and testimonies as we continue to write high-quality study and exam guides to help our readers succeed in their careers and life in general.

Made in United States
Troutdale, OR
12/04/2024

25785786R00193